Derek Jarman

MODERN NATURE
The Journals of Derek Jarman

VINTAGE

Published by Vintage 1992

10

© Derek Jarman 1991

The right of Derek Jarman to be identified as the author of this work
has been asserted by him in accordance with the Copyright, Designs
and Patents Act, 1988

First published by Century, 1991

Vintage Books
Random House, 20 Vauxhall Bridge Road, London SW1V 2SA

Random House Australia (Pty) Limited
20 Alfred Street, Milsons Point, Sydney,
New South Wales 2061, Australia

Random House New Zealand Limited
18 Poland Road, Glenfield,
Auckland 10, New Zealand

Random House South Africa (Pty) Limited
Isle of Houghton, Corner of Boundary Road & Carse O'Gowrie,
Houghton 2198, South Africa

The Random House Group Limited Reg. No. 954009
www.randomhouse.co.uk

A CIP catalogue record for this book
is available from the British Library

ISBN 9780099116318

Printed and bound in Great Britain by
CPI Antony Rowe, Chippenham, Wiltshire

CONTENTS

1989

1990

1989

JANUARY

Sunday 1

Prospect Cottage, its timbers black with pitch, stands on the shingle at Dungeness. Built eighty years ago at the sea's edge – one stormy night many years ago waves roared up to the front door threatening to swallow it . . . Now the sea has retreated leaving bands of shingle. You can see these clearly from the air; they fan out from the lighthouse at the tip of the Ness like contours on a map.

Prospect faces the rising sun across a road sparkling silver with sea mist. One small clump of dark green broom breaks through the flat ochre shingle. Beyond, at the sea's edge, are silhouetted a jumble of huts and fishing boats, and a brick kutch, long abandoned, which has sunk like a pillbox at a crazy angle; in it, many years ago, the fishermen's nets were boiled in amber preservative.

There are no walls or fences. My garden's boundaries are the horizon. In this desolate landscape the silence is only broken by the wind, and the gulls squabbling round the fishermen bringing in the afternoon catch.

There is more sunlight here than anywhere in Britain; this and the constant wind turn the shingle into a stony desert where only the toughest grasses take a hold – paving the way for sage-green sea kale, blue bugloss, red poppy, yellow sedum.

The shingle is home to larks. In the spring I've counted as many as a dozen singing high above, lost in a blue sky. Flocks of greenfinches wheel past in spirals, caught in a scurrying breeze. At low tide the sea rolls back to reveal a wide sandbank, on which seabirds vanish like quicksilver as they fly close to the ground. Gulls feed alongside fishermen digging lug. When a winter storm blows up, cormorants skim the waves that roar along the Ness – throwing stones pell-mell along the steep bank.

The view from my kitchen at the back of the house is bounded to the left by the old Dungeness lighthouse, and the iron grey bulk of the nuclear reactor – in front of which dark green broom and gorse, bright with yellow flowers, have formed little islands in the shingle, ending in a scrubby copse of sallow and ash dwarfed and blasted by the gales.

In the middle of the copse is a barren pear tree that has struggled for a century to reach ten feet; underneath this a carpet of violets. Gnarled dog roses guard this secret spot – where on a calm summer day meadow browns and blues congregate in their hundreds, floating past the spires of nettles thick with black tortoiseshell caterpillars.

High above a lone hawk hovers, while far away on the blue horizon the tall medieval tower of Lydd church, the cathedral of the marshes, comes and goes in a heat haze.

~

A sky blue borage plant in flower, one of a clump that self-seeded by the back door. It droops in the early morning frost but recovers quickly: 'I borage bring courage.'

Thursday 5
The first crocus is out in the front garden, one of the corms I planted last year in little pockets of peat in the shingle. It struggled to open all morning, finally drawing the sunlight to itself as the sun disappeared behind the house.

Monday 9
Planted roses: *Rugosa double de Coubert Harrisonii, Rosa mundi* – a selection of old roses from Rassell's in Earls Court. By the time I have finished there will be over thirty scattered in clumps through the garden, disrupting its wildness as little as possible.

I arrived at dusk in the nursery set in its little square under the plane trees – it's a romantic place. Walking around in the deepening gloom through the rows of plants you are drawn into dreams of long summer days, looking at the ageing photos above each plant. *Rosa mundi*, rose of the world, with its crimson and blush striped flowers, an old sport from the apothecary's *Rose officionalis* the rose of Provins. It was brought back by a 12th century crusader and immortalised by Guillaume de Lorris in his poem the *Roman de La Rose*. When I took my roses to pay for them I found my old friend André manning the till. He laughed at the idea of my wilderness garden.

Monday 16
The second of my small holly bushes has been devoured by a voracious rabbit that has gnawed clean through the stem to get at leaves out of reach. I trimmed back the little that remained. Last year, transplanted from its cosy inland bed, it lost all its leaves to a freezing easterly; the blackened remains slowly came back to life.

These hollies were the first plants I nurtured – in large tubs sunk into the stones. I was encouraged by the fact that they grow on the other side of the

Ness at Holmstone.

Blasted by the winds into frightful shapes, these ancient trees are first mentioned by Leland in his *Itineraries*; there he says 'they bat fowl and kill manye birds'.

Wednesday 18

Continued my rose planting: *Rosa Foetida bicolor*, another old rose, grown in the Middle East since the twelfth century, with single flowers – bright yellow and red; and *Cantabrigiensis*, pale yellow, found in the 1930s in the botanic gardens at Cambridge.

A brilliant sunny day, as the greenhouse effect takes hold, winter evaporates.

At twelve a load of manure arrived from the local stables. As I shovelled it I realised how unfit I was, I had great difficulty keeping up with the cheerful Glaswegian farmer, who must have been in his mid-sixties. Without a wheelbarrow, I had to pull heavy sacks all day to transport even a third of the load around the garden. The cost of the manure was £24, the whole enterprise – manure and roses – has cost about £200, and has filled me with happiness. By tea time I ached so much I thought it was time to give up. At 4:30 the sun sank behind the nuclear power station.

~

On either side of the front door are two neat flower beds each twelve feet long, and two feet six inches wide; they were filled with old blocks of concrete and broken bricks which I carefully extracted and used to reinforce the foundations of the drive. Cars sink easily in the shingle and have to be towed out.

At low tide I collect large oblong flints which are uncovered by a good storm and plant them upright like dragon's teeth in the beds. In front of them two small circles of twelve stones each form a primitive sundial. In spite of the dry summers these flower beds thrive. A little mulching helps.

Amongst the plants which grow in them are houseleeks and sedums, thrift, dianthus, saxifrage, campion, wallflower, purple iris, calendula, curry plant, rue, camomile, columbine, shirley poppy, santolina and nasturtium – and night scented stock to fill the evenings with its heavenly scent, attracting moths to drink its nectar.

Thursday 19

Cut a strong shoot from the base of one of the elder bushes by the Long Pits, under a chalky moon at dusk; planted it straight in front of the kitchen window next to the burnet rose.

I took a similar cutting last March and planted it right against the kitchen wall; it shot up and ended the summer over two foot high.

On the Ness, elder forms compact pyramidal bushes about nine feet high; there are four or five of them within a mile; they are easily burnt by the salt spray but apart from that seem happy; they are very advanced this year, the buds are breaking.

Elder keeps the witches at bay, and if grown near the house should never be uprooted.

Tuesday 31
My 47th birthday.
The sea mist cleared leaving a bright sunny day. As I walked round the garden a lark was singing. In front of the house the crocuses are blooming and the daffodils are in bud. The roses are already breaking into leaf. One of the rosemary bushes is in flower, and the globular seeds of the sea kale have germinated.

I spent an hour after lunch sitting in the sun with only a pullover – something I have never done on my birthday, which has always been a cold, grey day.

~

Planted a handful of sea kale seedlings about the garden, they grow rapidly, making luxurious plants within the year; large grey-green leaves catch the summer dew like pearls; their perfection untouched by predatory caterpillars. They fringe the sea, their frilly leaves dance a Can-Can amongst the flotsam. At this time of the year they are nearly invisible, but if you look closely they are already sprouting their sturdy purple leaves. By April they will have turned a glaucous green, which in turn will be submerged in June by a froth of white flowers.

FEBRUARY

Wednesday 1

Flowers spring up and entwine themselves like bindweed along the footpaths of my childhood. Most loved were the blue stars of wild forget-me-nots that shimmered in the dark Edwardian shrubberies of my grandmother's garden. Pristine snowdrops spread out in the welcoming sun – a single crocus, purple among its golden companions. Wild columbine with its flowers shaped like vertebrae, and the ominous fritillaria that crouched snakelike in corners . . .

These spring flowers are my first memory, startling discoveries; they shimmered briefly before dying, dividing the enchantment into days and months, like the gong that summoned us to lunch, breaking up my solitude.

The gong brought the pressing necessity of that other world into the garden where I was alone. In that precious time I would stand and watch the garden grow, something imperceptible to my friends. There, in my dreaming, petals would open and close, a rose suddenly fall apart scattering itself across the path, or a tulip lose a single petal, its perfection shattered for ever.

Dusty ivy, spooky with cobwebs – nettles which sprang up with the summer to sting bare knees – I learned to skirt round the deadly nightshade, to view it with grudging respect. But of all plants, dandelions, which bled white when you picked them, filled me with most fear.

But Gran's garden, in spite of its shadows, was a place of sunlight; no longer cultivated, its herbaceous borders long since softened by invading daisies and buttercups, it was slowly returning to the wild.

Thursday 2

The gorse is a blaze of golden flowers forced by the wind into an agony of weird shapes, twisted branches wrung out like washing. It's the only winter flower on the Ness; some of the bushes are six feet high, crowned with tight bunches of spines which creak in the wind. Other bushes cling to the ground, shaped in neat cones and pyramids which are clipped by the rabbits with the precision of topiary. 'Kissing is out of season when gorse is out of bloom.' No-one need worry – here it is always in flower.

Friday 3

For two months after moving here I spent hours each day picking up fragments of countless smashed bottles, china plates, pieces of rusty metal. There was a bike, cooking pots, even an old bedstead. Rubbish had been scattered over the whole landscape. Each day I thought I had got to the end of the task only to find the shingle had thrown up another crop overnight.

Sunny days were the best for clearing up, as the glass and pottery glinted. I buried the lot on the site of an old bonfire at the bottom of the garden in a large mound, which I covered with the clumps of grass I dug out when I built the shingle garden.

~

I was describing the garden to Maggi Hambling at a gallery opening. And said I intended to write a book about it.

She said: 'Oh, you've finally discovered nature, Derek.'

'I don't think it's really quite like that,' I said, thinking of Constable and Samuel Palmer's Kent.

'Ah, I understand completely. You've discovered modern nature.'

~

In July my bank bloomed with two distinct wild poppies – the long headed poppy, *P. dubium*, and the field poppy, *P. rhoeas*. I carefully gathered the seed heads and raked the mound – as poppies like to grow in newly disturbed soil. The rest of the seed is scattered far and wide ... Some of the seedlings are already two inches across, but the slugs seem particularly fond of them and continually crop them; they survive though, and are soon sprouting again.

I filmed last year's poppies with a bee hovering over them and put the shot into *War Requiem*. Poppies have sprung up in many of my films: *Imagining October, Caravaggio, The Last Of England* and *War Requiem*.

Scarlet Poppies
This is a poppy
A flower of cornfield and wasteland
Bloody red
Sepals two
Soon falling
Petals four
Stamens many
Stigma rayed
Many seeded
For sprinkling on bread

8

The staff of life
Woven in wreaths
In memory of the dead
Bringer of dreams
And sweet forgetfulness

Monday 6

A fine sunny day with a bank of cloud which advanced and retreated more than once over the Ness. By three the tide was out and I walked for an hour across the sands to Jack's store to buy cigarettes. On the way I passed two oiled guillemots, one already dead, the other quite motionless. There are dead or dying birds along the shore almost every day. I hadn't the heart to kill it; tomorrow of course it will be dead, picked to pieces by the carrion crows which strut about amongst the seagulls, waiting for the end.

Back home I lit a cigarette and wandered into the garden – where to my surprise the rosemary was now covered in flowers.

~

Last year the icy February winds cut back my plants – by April they were blackened and bedraggled; but the summer revived them and they grew into strong healthy bushes about a foot high. Rosemary – *Ros marinus*, sea dew – has proved quite hardy here. My next door neighbour has an ancient gnarled specimen – all the garden books are emphatic it hates the wind, but a more windy and exposed spot you could not find. Thomas More, who loved it, wrote, 'As for Rosemarie, I let it run all over my garden walls, not because bees love it but because it is the herb sacred to remembrance and therefore to friendship, whence a sprig of it hath a dumb language.'

The herb was part of Ophelia's bouquet: 'here's rosemary for remembrance.' Gilded and tied with ribbons it was carried at weddings; also, a sprig of it was placed in the hands of the dead.

Legend has it that originally its flowers were white until the day the Virgin Mary laid out her robe to dry on some bushes, colouring them a heavenly blue.

'Where rosemary flourishes women rule': years ago on the island of Patmos, the old woman on whose roof I was sleeping washed my clothes for me, and scented them with wild rosemary from the hillside. In ancient Greece young men wore garlands of rosemary in their hair to stimulate the mind; perhaps the gathering of the Symposium was scented with it.

Villa Zuassa 1946

In 1946 we flew to Italy, where my father after some months became Commandant of the airfield in Rome, and a witness in the Venice war trials. Villa Zuassa was requisitioned for us – a large house on Lake Maggiore, with extensive gardens on the lakeside.

Beautiful Flowers And How To Grow Them – a few months after my fourth birthday my parents gave me this large Edwardian garden book full of delightful watercolour illustrations and neat little line drawings: 'Tea roses, chimney campanulas and snapdragons' by Hugh Norris; and Francis James' 'Chinese primulas' are my favourites, they held me spellbound on many a rainy day. Where my parents found this book, or why they gave it to me, with its carefully inscribed dedication, I cannot imagine. I certainly couldn't read it; and even if I had I don't know what I would have made of the long lists of acacias, acanthus and achilleas.

Perhaps my father found it in a dusty corner of some bookshop in Milan. Or perhaps my mother discovered the book in the house and gave it to me.

Beautiful Flowers was to be my bible for many years: I pored over its exotic pages, scribbled in coloured crayon across its illustrations and made my own first drawings of flowers by copying it.

Many years later I had one of the watercolours blown up to vast proportions for the backdrop of a short *pas de deux* set to Sibelius' *Nocturne*: an enormous arch of blush pink orchids, which reduced the dancers to the size of fairies conjured so artfully in turn-of-the-century spirit photos.

~

Beautiful Flowers opens with the rose. It is lavish in its praise: there should be nothing stiff, stilted or formal about roses, whether in the growing of them, the utilisation of them, or the writing about them – beauty begets beauty. Who can look on a picture of a beautiful garden without feeling the impulse to grow flowers, and what results this can have! A garden, where poor wayward humanity is capable of being swayed by emotions which make for peace and beauty. 'Look to the rose', it commands:

> Look to the rose that blows about us,
> Laughing, she says, into the world I blow,
> At once the silken tassel of my purse
> Tear, and its treasure on the garden throw ...

So the *Rubaiyat* was the first poem I laid eyes on. Dunbar and the Bard himself followed quickly; there was no better path to poetry than this garden book.

My father filmed my mother picking the pink cabbage roses on my grandmother's wall as they fell apart in her hands; and my sister and myself in the garden of Zuassa, standing in front of a bed of scarlet geraniums – 'Zonal pelargoniums' as my old book carefully reminds us.

Zonal pelargoniums! Geraniums remain for me geraniums. *Beautiful Flowers* describes them as 'once the reigning Queen of the flower garden, the cheerful zonal has declined in favour'. But not with me: I have carefully nurtured them for years on my balcony in London, where they have bloomed continuously in the most adverse conditions.

Nowadays the plants come in the most ghastly colours and *Paul Crampnel* the true scarlet, the one and only colour of a geranium, is a rarity.

~

True scarlet is a problem even in costuming films, and was the subject of many a conversation with Christopher Hobbs, designer on *Caravaggio*. 'I cannot find a true scarlet,' he lamented, holding up a small square of antique silk. 'Where can you find that colour today?'

~

The garden at Zuassa ran for a mile along the banks of Lake Maggiore. It spilled over its stone terraces – a cornucopia of cascading blossom, abandoned avenues of mighty camellias, old roses trailing into the lake, huge golden pumpkins, stone gods overturned and covered with scurrying green lizards, dark cypresses, and woods full of hazel and sweet chestnut.

Far away in a corner of the woods was a gatehouse where an old crone who lived in another time, pottered around vast trays, one above the other, and carried bundles of mulberry leaves to feed armies of voracious silk worms. In this Eden my sister and I walked arm-in-arm, naked, along a jetty submerged in the waters of the lake.

The weather was capricious: the sun quickly disappeared and thunderstorms descended from the mountains. Once a large glass door blew shut with such violence it shattered into a thousand pieces sending us all scurrying from the supper table. But the storm would soon be over; and these days remain in my memory full of sunlight. The dawn would bring Cecilia the housekeeper bustling into my bedroom – with a long feather duster to shoo out the swallows that flitted through the windows to build their nests in the corners of the room. Then she stood me on the bed and watched me dress, always re-tying my shoelaces neatly.

After breakfast Davide, her handsome eighteen year old nephew, would place me on the handlebars of his bike and we'd be off down country lanes – or out on to the lake in an old rowing boat, where I would watch him strip in the heat as he rowed round the headland to a secret cove, laughing all the way. He was my first love.

Tuesday 7

I counted well over 50 buds on the daffodils I planted last year. None are open yet, but if this warm weather continues they should be out within the week.

These are an early variety. The King Alfreds I put in early last September are hardly breaking through the ground.

~

'Daffodowndillies' writes Thomas Hill 'is a timely flower good for shew.' Gerard in his Herbal tells us that 'Theocritus affirmeth the daffodils to grow in meadowes ... he writeth that the fair lady Europa, entering with her nymphs into the meadowes, did gather the sweet smelling daffodils, in these verses which we may English thus:

> *But when the girles here come into,*
> *The meadowes flouring all in sight,*
> *That wench with these, this wench with those,*
> *Trim floures, themselves did all delight;*
> *She with the Narcisse good in scent,*
> *And she with Hyacynths content.'*

Daffodil bulbs were used by Galen, surgeon of the school of gladiators, to glue together great wounds and gashes; the bulbs were carried for a similar purpose in the back-packs of Roman soldiers. Perhaps this is how they first came to this country. The name daffodil, d'asphodel, is a confusion with the asphodel. They were also called Lent lily.

~

Daffodils 'come before the swallows dare and take the winds of March with beauty'. When I read these words they are tinged with sadness, for the seasonal nature of daffodils has been destroyed by horticulturists who nowadays force them well before Christmas. One of the joys our technological civilisation has lost is the excitement with which seasonal flowers and fruits were welcomed; the first daffodil, strawberry or cherry are now things of the past, along with the precious moment of their arrival. Even the tangerine – now a satsuma or clementine – appears de-pipped months before Christmas. I expect one day to see daffodils for sale in Berwick Street market in August, as plentiful as strawberries at Christmas.

Even the humble apple has succumbed. Tough green waxy specimens have eradicated the varieties of my childhood, the pink-fleshed scented August pearmains, the laxtons and russets; only the cox seems to have survived the onslaught. Perhaps my nostalgia is out of place – now daffodils are plentiful; and mushrooms, once a luxury, are ladled out by the pound. Avocados and mangoes are commonplace. But the daffodil, if only the daffodil could come with spring again, I would eat strawberries with my Christmas pudding.

~

The sun came out at four casting the longest shadows. I watched the shadow of Prospect Cottage as the sun set behind the nuclear power station, until the tip of the chimney touched the sea.

> Power hums along the lines
> to keep the fish and chips a-frying.
> In the sunset
> across the shingle
> I hear a voice:
> *Will the owner of car HXJ please . . .*
> It's been a quiet day.
> I've brewed my nuclear tea,
> mended the walls to keep the storms at bay.
> At nine-thirty the sun sets behind Lydd church;
> The night stock scents the air.
> At ten I switch the lantern on;
> a bright pink moth shimmers on the pale blue wall.
> I quickly turn the pages of my book:
> Small Elephant Hawk.

Wednesday 8
The shingle heavy with dew sparkled in the dawn. A pale blue mist washes over the willows, the larks are up. Such a show of golden crocuses, a ladybird bathes in the pale blue borage – the pussy willow opens – later, in the cold of the day I walk back home across the shingle – a shimmering opalescent light. Vermeer dipped his brush in just such iridescent solitude.

Monday 13
The first rain in weeks and that rather listless, though driven by a strong breeze. It barely dampened the shingle – overnight one of the rosemary bushes has shed its leaves, the same that proved so tender last year. The crocuses blown in circles are full out, fighting an unequal battle with the gusts; beyond them the sea is running high, splashed with white horses. By noon the first of the daffodils opens, bowed almost to the ground by the inclement weather. We've prayed for a good fat rain (last night I watered the front garden), not this short change in the isobars.

MODERN NATURE

Rome 1946 – Borghese Gardens

There we lived in a flat requisitioned from Admiral Ciano, the uncle of Mussolini's foreign secretary.

'And he walked in the garden in the cool of the day,' where he planted 'every tree that is pleasant'. Each park dreams of Paradise; the word itself is Persian for garden. This particular shadow of Eden was originally the grounds of the villa that Scipione Borghese built for himself early in the seventeenth century. Here in the cool of a summer afternoon I rode the tough little donkeys through glades of acanthus, under old cedar trees to a water clock which kept time on a cascade of fern covered rocks.

~

Time itself must have started in earnest after the Fall, because the seven days in which the world was created we now know was an eternity. The ancient Egyptians, whose lives were measured by the annual rise and fall of the Nile, were amongst the first to mark its passage systematically; the Borghese garden commemorates the Egyptians with a gateway in the form of twin pylons.

~

In every corner the park mapped out Time's History: its glades were strewn with monuments to mark its passing. Not the least of which was a circle of marble worthies put up at the end of the nineteenth century to celebrate the unification of Italy: a series of pasty po-faced poets, politicians, musicians, and engineers, who had paved the way for the modern state. Idiotically solemn, these dumb statues were always in danger of the graffiti brush – some had red noses; for me these were the most interesting.

What Scipione with his grand vision would have thought of all these worthies in the ruins of his Eden I cannot imagine. He strutted about in his cardinal's scarlet and built a dynasty and his ostentatious polychrome villa: a vulgar gilded pleasure palace in the modern manner, filled with yet more antique marbles. A far cry from Adam's wooden hut in Paradise, no doubt built from the timbers of the tree of knowledge – the very first house, which generations attempted to capture in a thousand garden houses, rustic summer houses and *cottages ornées*.

One day I returned home to our flat in via Paesiello for tea, to find that the seven days of the week were now mapped out by bells – and lessons at the American School.

Years later, in 1972, I returned to the Borghese gardens with a soldier I met in the Cinema Olympia. He had thrown his arms around me in the gods; later we made love under the stars of my Eden.

Sissinghurst, September '88

Sissinghurst, that elegant sodom in the garden of England, is 'heritized' in the institutional hands of the National Trust. Its magic has fled in the vacant eyes of tourists. If two boys kissed in the silver garden now, you can be sure they'd be shown the door. The shades of the Sackville-Wests pursuing naked guardsmen through the herbaceous borders return long after the last curious coachload has departed, the tea shoppe closed, and the general public has returned home to pore over the salacious Sundays, ferreting out another middle-aged victim driven into the not so secret arms of a boy starved of attention and affection who has spilt the beans for the illusory security of cash. 'He pulled down the boy's pants and blew him for £20 in the corridor of a cinema/a public lavatory/a deserted station, they met in a seedy club/ Half Moon Street/the Dorchester.'

Two young men holding hands on the street court ridicule, kissing they court arrest, so the worthy politicians, their collaborators, the priests, and the general public push them into corners where they can betray them in the dark. Judases in the garden of Gethsemane.

Cambridge, Autumn 1948

Back home on a storm-tossed troop ship, from the marble halls of old Admiral Ciano's house in Rome to a lead-grey Nissen hut near Cambridge – filled with thick suffocating coke fumes and running with a condensation that quickly covers our clothes with mildew.

Outside, my father inflates an old yellow dinghy: a makeshift swimming pool. It smells strongly of rubber and is quickly filled with large black water beetles, which appear as from the sky – perhaps from the huge branches of the walnut tree which casts its shadow across the lawn.

Autumn days spent throwing sticks into the tree and falling over backwards, hoping to bring down the hard little nuts in their green shells; until dizzy with fatigue we lie on our backs and watch the sky and tree revolve like a Catherine wheel.

~

The garden at Cambridge consisted of the walnut tree and an uneven lawn from whose clippings I constructed grass forts, which rotted until the fermenting grass turned slippery. The garden was bounded by an old brick wall covered with caterpillars of the Large White, basking in the sunlight in various states of pupation.

~

The yellow-green and black caterpillars remain a vivid memory. Last year, as the autumn came, the nasturtiums outside the window which I carefully nurtured here, were overwhelmed by an army of them. When the first frosts came, in October, they had eaten every leaf and flower.

> to whom it may concern
> in the dead stones of a planet
> no longer remembered as earth
> may he decipher this opaque hieroglyph
> perform an archaeology of soul
> on these precious fragments
> all that remains of our vanished days
> here – at the sea's edge
> I have planted a stony garden
> dragon tooth dolmen spring up
> to defend the porch
> steadfast warriors

Tuesday 14
Indigo sky, a bright yellow half moon set amongst the stars over the shimmering lights of the nuclear plant. A keen westerly blows in a clear blue sky. I walked along the shingle and took a slip from a valerian that grows further down the road, planting it in the corner of the front bed.

Wednesday 22
Returned here after nearly a week in Berlin, where *War Requiem* was performed in the Zoo Palast. A shadow of my expectations. The silence at the end was a total . . . 30 seconds that seemed two minutes; then the audience crept out in silence, passed quietly by me as if I was a ghost come to haunt them, chill their blood.

Flew home high above sun-bright clouds. Read Pliny's description of his house in the country:

> *At the far end of the garden is a suite of rooms which are quite truly my favourites, for I had them built myself. On one side there is a sun parlour facing on to a terrace and the sea; there is also a room with folding doors opening on to the arcade with a window looking out to sea. Opposite in the partition wall is a beautifully designed alcove which can be thrown into the room by folding back its glass doors and curtains, or cut off from it if they are closed; it is large enough to hold a couch and two armchairs and has the sea at its foot and the neighbouring villas behind and the woods beyond them. All these views can be seen separately or blended together from its many windows; next to it is a bedroom for use at night, which neither the voices of my household, or the sea's murmur, nor the noise of a storm*

can penetrate, any more than the lightning's flash, and the light of day
unless the shutters are open.

~

I've grown tired of the cinema, the preserve of ambition and folly in pursuit
of illusion, or should I say delusion?

Yesterday I was subjected to a barrage of questions for nearly seven hours
without a break, my head spinning like a child's top. I fled. Back home at the
flat in Charing Cross Road another enormous pile of letters blocked the
door: Would I write? Judge? Give advice? Attend? Approve? Help? – The
phone rings till I find myself running. What happiness has this cacophony
brought? And what have I achieved when Pliny's miraculous villa can
vanish with barely a ripple?

~

Paul was ill during our stay in Berlin. HB had to carry him up the stairs. HB
bought a battery of pills which we checked through the pharmacopoeia:
aconite, belladonna, etc. Paul spent most of his time in bed and returned
home with a lung infection. My dearest Howard remains smiling and coherent after nearly a year of illness although unable to walk, read, or write.
David was snuffed out in less than a week. I never saw him as we were in the
first week shooting the *War Requiem*.

~

Back here this evening I walked along the sea shore. The tide was far out on
the horizon and the water on the sand reflected the faded rose of the sunset
like a mirror; for a brief moment the sun lit up the boats and houses around
the bay before suddenly disappearing.

Thursday 23
Brilliant sunshine, skies so clear your vision is stretched to the horizon. As
the day passed the winds gathered force, throwing up increasingly dramatic
clouds, which eventually turned to rain falling in grey veils. A rainbow
arched over the sea, and the shingle glistened in the last moments of sunlight
– a myriad cat's eyes. Then the hail came with the dark, setting up a staccato
drumming on the corrugated metal roof. My poor daffodils, which greeted
me on my return, are now beaten to the ground.

~

Narcissus is derived not from the name of the young man who met his death
vainly trying to embrace his reflection in crystal water, but from the Greek
narkao (to benumb); though of course Narcissus, benumbed by his own

17

beauty, fell to his death embracing his shadow. Pliny says '*Narce Narcissum dictum non a fabuloso puero,*' named Narcissus from *narkê,* not from the fabled boy. Socrates called the plant 'crown of the infernal gods' because the bulbs, if eaten, numbed the nervous system. Perhaps Roman soldiers carried it for this reason (rather than for its healing properties) as the American soldiers smoked marijuana in Vietnam.

This prompted me to ring Matthew Lewis, the portrait photographer, and ask him if he would take a photo of a young man holding a daffodil. Last year he took a beautiful portrait of a handsome Italian, stripped to the waist, holding a lemon, the juice of which he used to dissolve heroin to fill his syringe. Narcissus, narcotics, self-absorption: benumbed retreat into self.

Friday 24

A grey windy day, cold too. The winter we nearly forgot arrived last night and is set to circle around us for a few days. I placed driftwood in front of the house to mark a new bed – but decided to leave the digging for a warmer day.

Yesterday I made a rather optimistic expedition to our local nurseries at Greatstone, where plants can be obtained at a fraction of the regular cost, and came away with lavender and rosemary, saxifrage, montbretia, iris, and an ostentatious yucca to crown the lot. As I packed them in an old wooden crate, the garrulous owner of the place said 'Shit! That's the secret, can't put enough of it down; now look at that border, I've not watered it once since the day I built it.'

Back home I put the plants in a sheltered corner and converted an old wooden crate into a cold frame. Planted chives, and placed the pots in the south facing window, along with the geranium cuttings that are returning to life after a dark winter in the bathroom of Phoenix House.

~

As the black twister hurled the little house in Kansas through the raging clouds to Oz, I bolted through the cinema and out into the street. How often in my childhood dreams have I found myself trapped on the emerald floors, pursued by the armies of the Wicked Witch – transformed to a relentless phalanx of marching nails which pursued me as I slipped on the glistening surface?

Childhood memories have a funny habit of repeating themselves. On the now famous October night of the Great Storm about a year ago, I awoke in the early hours of morning from a fitful sleep. A sharp wind had sprung up. At first I thought little of it; Dungeness is known to be exposed and the wind blows here without ceasing. In the dark I noticed that the glass lampshade in the centre of the room was swaying back and forth, and the room was full of dust forced by the wind from every nook and cranny. I switched on the light and nothing happened. The power lines were down.

The first dull waves of panic washed over me. I dressed fumbling in the dark. Feeling cold and nauseous I groped my way by the spectral beam of the lighthouse towards the kitchen at the back of the house, which was taking the full brunt of a storm increasing its intensity by the minute. I found a candle and lit it; if anything, its guttering flame increased my feelings of insecurity and isolation.

Outside, the nuclear power station glowed in the dark. I blew out the candle. A fisherman's hut disintegrating seemed in the dark to be the house itself; every timber was stretched to breaking point. Now and again a board split from its neighbour, 80 years of tar and paint parting like a rifle shot. The house was breaking up. I sat and waited for the roof to blow away or a window to cave in.

The hurricane grew. A deep and continuous roar now underpinned the higher notes of gutter and drainpipe: the shrieks and groans and banshee whistling took on symphonic proportion. My Prospect Cottage never seemed so dear, beaten like a drum in the rushing wind that assaulted it and flew on howling after other prey. Down the coast whole roofs of tiles were lifted high in the air, to descend in a ceramic hail. A garden wall collapsed in a series of curves like a serpent, an ancient macrocarpa shredded like matchsticks. Outhouses groaned and slid off their foundations.

~

Leaning into the grey dawn I found the house had sustained no damage; around it the sea exploding along the Ness enveloped me in a shower of salt spray, which frosted the windows and burnt the gorse and broom black. Great dark waves moved in slow motion drawn in perfect lines across the sea, their crests whipped into a white pall which hung mist-like over the desolation.

Yet Prospect stood firm on its foundations, unlike the farm in Kansas. Without light or heat for the next week, I stared at the glittering power plant on the horizon and wondered if, like the Emerald City and the great Oz himself, my life and this cottage had been dreamt all those years ago in Rome.

The Wizard Of Oz reminds me of the frightening power of movies to move. I'm glad it has a happy ending.

~

I live in borrowed time, therefore I see no reason in the world why my heart grows not dark.

A cold wind blows tonight over this desolate island.

Over the hills and dales, over mountain and marsh, down the great roads and little lanes, through the villages and small towns, through the great towns and the cities.

Everywhere it blows through empty streets and desolate houses, rattling the hedgerows and broken windows, drumming on locked doors.

This wind is blowing high in the tower blocks and steeples, down along the river, invading houses and mansions, through the corridors and up the staircases, rustling the faded curtains in bedrooms, over the carpets, up the aisles and down in the crypts, in public places and private, among forgotten secrets, round the armchair, the easy chair, across the kitchen table.

So icy is this wind that it rattles the bones in the graves and sends rats shivering down the sewers.

Fragments of memory eddy past and are lost in the dark. In the gusts yellowing half-forgotten papers whirl old headlines up and over dingy suburban houses, past leaders and obituaries, the debris of inaction, into the void. Thought illuminated briefly by lightning. The rainbows are put out, the crocks of gold lie rusting – forgotten as the fallen trees which strew the fields and dead meadows.

I consider the lives of warriors, how they suddenly left their halls.

Bold and noble leaders,
I shiver and regret my time.

But the wind does not stop for my thoughts. It whips across the flooded gravel pits drumming up waves on their waters that glint hard and metallic in the night, over the shingle, rustling the dead gorse and skeletal bugloss, running in rivulets through the parched grass – while I sit here in the dark holding a candle that throws my divided shadow across the room, and gathers my thoughts to the flame like moths.

I have not moved for many hours. Years, a lifetime, eddy past: one, two, three: into the small hours, the clock chimes. The wind is singing now.

Eternity, eternity
Where will you spend eternity?
Heaven or hell, which shall it be,
Where will you spend eternity?

And then the wind is gone, chasing itself across the shingle to lose itself in the waves which brush past the Ness, throwing up plumes of salt spray which spatter across the windows. Nothing can hide from it. Certainly no man can be wise before he has lived his share of winters in the world.

The wind calls my name, Prophesy.

Long past the creator destroyed this earth, the joyful songs of the people were silent, the ancient works of giants stood desolate.

The wind whirls in the gutters, screams in the telegraph poles.

I'll huff and I'll puff,
And I'll blow your house down.

Time is scattered, the past and the future, the future past and present. Whole lives are erased from the book by the great dictator, the screech of the pen across the page, your name, Prophesy, your name! The wind circles the empty hearth casting a pall of dust, the candle fizzes. Who called this up? Did I?

Now throughout the world stand windblown halls, frost-covered ruined buildings; the wine halls crumble, kings lie dead, deprived of pleasure, all the steadfast band dead by the wall.

Saturday 25

The storm blew itself out by two – before returning at four with a sudden blast, illuminated by one brilliant lightning flash, and no thunder.

The foghorn sounded for half an hour and then all went quiet.

Buffeted in my sleep like a boat in a high sea, I never cross the night without waking. I can't quite remember when it was different. I slept quite soundly for forty years; then something changed. Perhaps I wake myself in case I die, unconscious, at the low ebb of the night. Bergman's hour of the wolf.

The next day I can't remember what passed through my mind. Nothing, perhaps, except a vague unease.

It's cold tonight; but suddenly I'm up and pissing in the dark. Back in bed the pillows have been pummelled into uncomfortable hillocks, the sheets have parted company with the mattress – I doze off.

In the morning the storm has torn up a mountain of kelp which floats back and forth in the foam at the sea's edge. The wind is up again, seagulls float ever closer as if I gave off some imperceptible warmth in the cold. I beat the tide which is racing in, and find three stones for the new flower bed. I draw the circle to plant them but retire inside as the rain blows in; settle down at my desk for a cold wet day.

~

It's a long time since I whiled away a wet winter Saturday, quite alone, knowing the sun wouldn't appear from a chink in the sky. Wet afternoons in the town are filled in by the general hubbub. I find myself reliving my childhood feeling of trapped unease – as the rain streams down the windows, muffling the sound of cars with their headlights on too early, even for a gloomy February afternoon.

~

As a child it was wonderful to be allowed to spend afternoons like this cutting out paper fish and floating them in the bath. Or to be given grandma Mimosa's Mah Jong set, to build ivory fortifications. Or create a crystal garden with my two shilling chemistry set.

~

Wet days. Stare out the window, stare out the window . . . Endless suburban afternoons spent in the colourless houses of friends – glazed cotton cabbage roses and hard shiny French polish – practising good-mannered conversation. Or at home with some enthusiasm labelled a hobby – we all had them: stamps, cactuses, butterflies. Or a trip on the bus to wander round the empty streets of Watford, till the shops closed. I found nothing there, knew I wouldn't. Before walking back in the gathering dusk, past the grey castellations of the gas works, through the arches of Bushey rail viaduct, past the solemn empty red brick church – always too big for its congregation; past the stunted cedars in the park, and the waterworks still decked out in faded wartime camouflage; back to my attic and my paints, magazines, scissors and the surprise collisions of a collage.

Pandemonium

St. Juliana's convent ran a day school for children, whither I was sent at the age of five to be roasted with threats of hellfire by a group of tough nuns armed with sticky stars and saints to plaster at the end of twelve tables successfully conjugated – each table assigned to an apostle. God's iron maidens, armed with clamps and shackles of Catholicism, invaded my innocent garden with sugary promises – icy orange juice lollipops; but for the recalcitrant, a ruler on the back of the hand.

Sweet soap-scrubbed faces peeping through wimples hid personalities as bizarre as anything later dreamt up on the closed set of *The Devils*. These intimidating automata, brides of a celibate God, hacked my paradise to pieces like the despoilers of the Amazon – carving paths of good and evil to Heaven, Hell, and Purgatory.

These serpents brought no wisdom, only a profound distrust of arithmetic that leaves me, years later, at the mercy of the VAT inspector.

~

When I was seven, at my first boarding school at Milford, a Saturday afternoon brought two ounces of rationed sweets, for which we played marbles on the polished floor of the assembly room – a pursuit with its own terminology: blockies, spirals, cat's-eyes, hairstreaks. Someone would switch off the lights and we'd start a ghostly game of touch flee in the dark, a scrimmage of bedraggled little boys in formless grey suits; there might be ballroom dancing, fights over who should lead, treading on each other's toes – until, scooped up by one of the three towering matrons, we were forced to move in quick step.

Saturday walks in the rain to the overgrown park called 'the jungle', with its monkey puzzle trees and prehistoric weeds; or to the wreck of the *Lamorna*, grounded one stormy night at the foot of the cliffs at Barton on its way to the South Seas. 'Not too near to the cliff.'

Eyes fixed on the ground, pink sea thrift at your feet. Wet Saturdays, the timeless sadness of childhood, horizons clamped down like the drizzle; standing at the window wishing for something to happen, anything, as the rain rattled across the panes. Everyone at home. Deserted streets and those lights on the cars, on much too early.

H-bombs and Sputnik, long playing records, Elvis and droning wimpish Buddy Holly, *I Love Lucy, Bilko* and other tedious American serials week after week. The rain fell, and my father's temper deteriorated.

~

A personal mythology recurs in my writing, much the same way poppy wreaths have crept into my films. For me this archeology has become obsessive, for the 'experts' my sexuality is a confusion. All received information should make us inverts sad. But before I finish I intend to celebrate our corner of Paradise, the part of the garden the Lord forgot to mention.

Sunday 26
950 millibars, the lowest pressure recorded in the last 120 years. A long walk round the Ness to the power station; then up to the coastguard cottages, which I've never explored before. They are set in the middle of a moated mound which encloses a large area – once kitchen gardens.

It's difficult to find a good vegetable garden; even in the marshes I came across only one last autumn, as I travelled round with my camera filming the countryside for *War Requiem* – the supermarkets have wiped them out. Once all these little cottages grew their own, before the road was constructed during the war. Now no-one does.

There was a brisk breeze all day, but it was warm enough.

~

Marked, set and dug the circular bed in front of the house. Before packing in took three small cuttings from the flowering rosemary; forgot that – unlike lavender – they can't be taken at this time of year. Stumbled across this in William Lawson's *Country Housewife's Garden* of 1617:

> *Rosemary, the grace of herbs here in England, in other countries*

*common. To set slyp, immediately after Lammas is the surest way ...
brought from hot countries to us in the cold north. The use is much in
meats, more in physick, most for bees. Rosemary and sweet eglantine
are seemly ornaments about a door or window.*

Monday 27
Walked along the beach to the shop, the sun a puddled vein of molten silver
in a vast amphitheatre of cloud – descending tiers in shades of grey with
dazzling creamy edges, cascading into a sea of little waves falling over themselves in their eagerness to swallow the sands, the sands reflecting all this
like a lazy antique mirror.

I retraced my steps, took a deep breath and during the course of the day
completed the circular bed, laying in manure and marking it with driftwood, flints and rounded bricks from the sea shore. My neighbour shouted
'When are the spuds going in?'

When the whole structure was finished it looked so satisfying I felt it
needed no plants to embellish it, though lavender would look fine and there
are seven spare plants. Sat back exhausted, put Tallis' *Lamentations* on the
stereo and watched the sun slowly disappear.

Tuesday 28
Woke to clear blue skies – collected stones on beach, returned and planted
the circle of lavender, and the yucca at the back to mark the boundary. Joyful morning.

~

A serpent in the form of a $
Film has twisted itself like a serpent through my life, a rampant dodder
pushing out life-sucking tentacles into every nook and cranny – a few days
here and I feel it keenly. It has destroyed the golden silence, the idyll I last
lived at my warehouse at Bankside nearly eighteen years ago. I dwell again
on *War Requiem* – it gave me no joy, left me empty to face endless chattering interviews in which the work vanished in a deluge of repetitive
questions. I steeled myself for the days in Berlin – 30 interviews in two days
and more on the horizon.

Is film dying?

Dead?

You announced last year you were dying!

I felt the interviewer's reproach.

*This evening, just alive from Berlin for RAI's cultural news, the ghost at
the banquet.*

I've spent the afternoons and evenings reading the new biography of Eric

Gill who, although eccentric, even silly, attempted to fuse his art and life, throwing his body into the struggle. Whitman, Carpenter, Gill and, nearer in time, Ian Hamilton Finlay and John Berger seem all to have set off on that old straight track, a road pioneered by Mr. and Mrs. William Blake playing Adam and Eve nude in their London garden. Blake and William Morris . . . all of them look backward over their shoulders – to a Paradise on earth. And all of them at odds with the world around them. I feel this strongly, chose a 'novelty' medium – film – in which to search. The reels turn, every foot appropriated by commerce until I am dizzy. I forget where I started . . . if, of course, I started at all, the path of film so treacherous it was easy to get the signposts mixed – led this way and that, until led by the nose.

~

My sense of confusion has come to a head, catalysed by my public announce-ment of the HIV infection. Now I no longer know where the focus is, for myself, or in the minds of my audience. Reaction to me has changed. There is an element of worship, which worries me. Perhaps I courted it.

In any case I had no choice, I've always hated secrets, the canker that des-troys; better out in the daylight and be done with it. But if only it were that easy – my whole being has changed; my wild nights on the vodka are now only an aggravating memory, an itch before turning in. Two years have passed with a few desultory nights out. Even with safer sex I've felt the life of my partner was in my hands. Hardly the cue for a night of abandonment. I've come a long way in accepting the restraint. But I dream of an unlikely old age as a hairy satyr.

This lament is not borne out by my state of mind; because apart from the nagging past – film, sex and London – I have never been happier than last week. I look up and see the deep azure sea outside my window in the February sun, and today I saw my first bumble bee. Planted lavender and clumps of red hot poker.

MARCH

Wednesday 1
March came in with a gale. The Kalendarum Hortense says:

> Stake and binde up your weakest plants and flowers against the
> windes, before they come too fiercely and in a moment prostrate a
> whole year's labour ... Now do the farewell frosts and easterly winds
> prejudice your choicest tulips and spot them; therefore cover some with
> mats or canvas to prevent freckles and sometimes destruction. The
> same care have of your most precious anemones, auriculas, brumal,
> iris, jacynths – early cyclamen. Wrap your shorn cypress tops with
> straw whisps if the eastern blasts; prove very tedious about the end.
> Uncover some plants, but with caution; for the tail of the frosts yet
> continuing and sharp winds, with the sudden darting heat of the sun,
> scorch and destroy them in a moment. And in such weather neither
> sow nor transplant, as March is the month of seed sowing.

The roses, particularly the rugosas, which have broken bud, have been
badly scorched by the continuous wind. An inventory of the garden shows
me all else survives. The sea kale struggles on and the sea peas have germinated; so have a few self-sown nasturtiums and calendula. Parsley and poppies are thriving and the irises are a good nine inches high – quite startling in
the shingle. The rabbits continually gnaw the fennel to the ground, but seem
to leave everything else alone. The wallflowers, though, have been mauled
by slugs.

Took four lavender cuttings.
Planted saxifrage.

Autumn '88 – War Requiem
When I set up the garden sequence for the beginning of *War Requiem* I
made quite certain the seed sowing was on a windy 'Dungeness' night, lit by
a hurricane lamp. The forks, rakes, watering can, and dibber had all been
collected in the months before from piles of old garden tools in junk shops.
The rake broke today, its handle riddled with woodworm. I burnt off the remains in the fire – then found a piece of rough driftwood the right length.

MARCH

~

Many of my tools are those I used as a boy. When my father died I found them rusting in a shed behind his house, and brought them back to London, where I cleaned and oiled them.

Abingdon 1948 – Sempervivums
In 1948 my father was posted as Commanding Officer to RAF Abingdon, near Oxford. The desolate married quarters were painted in khaki and black camouflage, the garden an uneven lawn bounded by a barbed wire fence, its only ornament a concrete 'rockery', made from an old air-raid shelter.

I returned from the watermill somewhere beyond the pub called the Rose Revived clutching a bunch of houseleeks that had been given to me by the man who lived there. They grew on his stone roof, scorched red by the wind and sun, with star-shaped rose-coloured flowers and perfectly formed miniature offshoots – each plant covered by a spider's web which trapped the dew. These flowers seemed alien exotics in his rich and vivid waterside garden, a maze of scarlet runners and blue-green cabbages over which white butterflies floated. I followed the man through this luxuriant jungle to the pig pens, keeping a cautious distance from his pet swan, which had a broken wing and hissed if I got too near (a swan, I was told, could break a man's arm, so its disability gave me some satisfaction).

The man was restoring the tumbledown buildings. He was carving a mantelpiece from a huge baulk of oak. The elder, and giant cow parsley, flag irises and ancient willows seemed poised to burst through the thick stone walls and broken windows to reclaim the muddy flagstones – an uneasy balance was struck. To keep rampant nature at bay the man carried a gun, firing at the crows in the elm trees, occasionally bringing one clattering down through the branches whilst its comrades flew higher and higher in the summer afternoon, protesting angrily.

The man, handsome and self-assured, wore an old corduroy jacket with a scarlet neckerchief knotted like a cowboy's. He smoked a pipe and walked slowly and deliberately with a limp from an old wound, which made him lean dangerously and upset my equilibrium as I walked beside him. He didn't say much. He hooked the sempervivums off the roof with his stick and presented them to me.

I carefully repeated the name *sempervivums* all the way home to Abingdon – where I planted my tongue-twisting prizes, proudly showing them off to my friends, who were not the least interested in the plants but studiously learnt their name like a litany: SEM PER VIV UM.

Notice
The houseleek under the sign of Jupiter, 'the Thunderer', protects whoever grows it against storms and lightning; its effect is so powerful that the Emperor Charlemagne ordered it grown on the roof of every home. To this day you will find it grown in the same way, surviving drought and frost, ever and always living.

Thursday 2

A cold grey day with continuous rain.

My father, as Commander, was the recipient of this ugly brick house, blotched with camouflage, surrounded by barbed wire. Here we entertained a series of very unsuitable 'domestics', people uprooted to do their national service, each one more demanding than the last. Looking after them left my mother exhausted.

First there was the tyrant WAAF known as Bloody Mary, who looked like a fierce bloodstained robin. Then Jonno, the delinquent 'ton-up' boy, who rode his bike round the camp, with me on the back clutching his pubic hairs for dear life through his nonexistent pockets – a game known as 'pocket billiards'. And a wayward girl, who in her madness dreamt up an imaginary sheepshearing millionaire uncle Down Under. When we moved from Cambridge to Abingdon she hitched across the country and took up refuge secretly in the garage, until surprised early one morning by my father with a torch. She was brought shivering, naked, into the living room, where she broke down in tears.

An arrangement was made, and she stayed on for a week or two, taking my sister and I into town to shower us with expensive, 'unsuitable' presents. Her last gift to me was a bunch of arum lilies, which I brought home – to my father's visible embarrassment. I worshipped these arums, a symbol of my obsession with flowers: glossy, exotic, *fin de siècle*. Dad, I know, would have preferred a brace of pistols.

~

A short bike ride with my hands deep in Jonno's pockets brought us to the bombed-out house at the end of the road. Its garden had become a wilderness and the ruins were covered with a riot of red and white valerian; it was an ideal place to find the bees and butterflies which were absent from the bleak mown gardens of The Patch.

A further walk across the fields brought us to a group of ancient chestnuts along the bank of a stream, which early in the year was bright with celandine and the snakelike heads of cuckoo's pint. The celandine and snowdrops marked the beginning of the end of winter. Messenger of the swallow, celandine is the subject of one of the most complicated herbal remedies:

Take gallingall, cloves, cubibs, ginger, mellilote, cardamonia, maces, nutmegs, one dram. Of the juice of salandine, 8 drams. Mingle all these made in powder with the said juice and a pint of acquavit, and three pints of white wine. Put it into a stillitory of glass and the next day still it with an easy fire. This water is an excellent virtue against consumption or any other disease that proceeds from rheume, choler or fleagme.

If that seems complex, the lore of the arum is more so – Gerard informs us that:

Beares after they have lien in their dens forty days without any manner of sustenance, but what they get from licking and sucking their own feet, doe as soone as they come forth eat the herb cuckoo pint. Through the windie nature thereof the hungry gut is opened.

But the plant has more practical uses than causing bears to fart. It was used to starch the ruffs that Titian's dark young men wear – a beauty bought at the expense of the laundresses' hands, which *this most pure white starch chappeth, blistereth and maketh rough and rugged and withal smarting.*

~

That winter my parents spent two weeks skiing in St. Moritz, leaving us in the tender hands of Bloody Mary. On their return they crept into my room in the dead of night and silently fixed a Swiss clock on the wall at the foot of my bed – a gruff little owl whose eyes moved in time to the tick.

Waking, I was certain my room was host to a demon; terrified, I watched the remorseless eyes in the half light, till dawn gave me the courage to bolt shivering with fear to my parents' bed. My father laughed: 'Don't be such a pansy, Derek.'

The Pansy

Viola tricolor, heartsease, tickle-my-fancy, love-in-idleness, or herb trinity. The juice of it on sleeping eyelids will make a man or woman dote upon the next live creature they see, if you would have midsummer's dreams. A strong tea made of the leaves will cure a broken heart; for our pansy is strongly aphrodisiac, its name, pensée, *I think of you*. If it leads you astray, don't worry: the herbal says it cures the clap; for 'it is a Saturnine plant of a cold slimy viscous nature ... an excellent cure for venereal disorder'.

In the old days pansies were virgin white, until Cupid fired his arrow and turned them the colours of the rainbow.

Of one thing you must beware: picking a pansy in the first light of dawn, particularly if it is spotted with dew, will surely bring the death of a loved one.

Was the pansy pinned to us, its velvety nineteenth century showiness the texture of Oscar's flamboyant and floppy clothes? As Ficino says, the gardens of Adonis are cultivated for the sake of flowers not fruits – now what about those fruits? Pansies, before you smile, are also the flower of the Trinity. *Don't be such a lemon.*

Monday 6

A very warm day – in the garden without a jacket. The sun was bright but slightly hazy – and stayed that way. No wind. By lunch the temperature was in the mid-sixties.

The tide went out further than I can remember. I walked along the beach almost to the end of the Ness gathering flints – marked out the second circular bed in front of the cottage, drove to Hamstreet and returned with a wheelbarrow. Now I can shift the gravel without using sacks.

Weeded the back garden, wired over the fennel the rabbits keep cutting back, planted two new irises and montbretsia. At 5:30 I sat on the old wicker chair facing the setting sun and read the newspapers. A slight chill descended; a choir of gnats floated by, golden sparks catching the last rays of the sun. The wind got up, bringing the smell of the sea; a russet kestrel flew by.

Extraordinary peacefulness.

Tuesday 7

The gardener digs in another time, without past or future, beginning or end. A time that does not cleave the day with rush hours, lunch breaks, the last bus home. As you walk in the garden you pass into this time – the moment of entering can never be remembered. Around you the landscape lies transfigured. Here is the Amen beyond the prayer.

Dante, at the beginning of his journey back along the great antique spiral, entered this realm in a dark wood.

Nel mezzo del cammin di nostra vita
Mi ritrovai per una selva oscura
Che la dir itta via era smarrita

I'm brought suddenly back to the here and now by the shrill argumentative voice of the phone. My Person from Porlock is on the line, talking of time with beginning and end, literal time, monotheist time, for which you are unfailingly charged.

~

Rain streaking the windows throws the landscape out of focus, brings sparkling colour to my standing stones. The crocuses close as tight as umbrellas; the borage is spangled with raindrops and blue stars. Grape hyacinths nestle in the flints, and the first golden wallflower breaks into bloom.

This year the old name for the wallflower, 'Winter July flower', could not be more timely. Of all the spring flowers the clove-scented gilly flower has a special place in my heart. It grows wild here on the cliffs of Folkestone. And in Somerset, where I spent much of my childhood, it covered the stone walls between the cottages; it was usually a bright yellow, shedding its 'tints of golden dye on which the morning sunbeams love to rest'.

The troubadours stuck the gilly flower into their caps for good luck; it had the sweetest scent of spring. Geoffrey Rudel wandered the length and breadth of the Holy Roman Empire wearing a wallflower, singing outside the mottes and keeps, till his sweet song fell on the ears of Richard Lionheart, deep in a dungeon. For this the flower is known as 'True-love-in-adversity'.

~

The rain and fine warm weather have quickened the landscape – brought the saturated spring colours early. The dead of winter is passed. Today Dungeness glowed under a pewter sky – shimmering emeralds, arsenic, sap, sage and verdigris greens washed bright, moss in little islands set off against pink pebbles, glowing yellow banks of gorse, the deep russet of dead bracken, and pale ochre of reeds in clumps set against the willow spinney – a deep burgundy, with silvery catkins and fans of ochre yellow stamens fringed with the slightest hint of lime green of newly burst leaves.

This symphony of colour I have seen in no other landscape. Dungeness is a premonition of the far North, a landscape Southerners might think drear and monotonous, which sings like the birch woods in Sibelius' music.

From my home I can see the sun clamber out of a misty sea. It wakes me through the bedroom window and then stays with me all day. There are no trees or hills to hide it. When it sets over the flatlands in the west I sit and watch it on a throne-like chair that I rescued from a rubbish dump. I never miss the setting sun, however cold the weather.

Tonight it hangs huge and scarlet after a day of dark clouds. It appears for a few brief minutes, a perfect circle before disappearing – then the darkness comes rushing across the sky to embrace the inky timbers of Prospect Cottage; but before the light is extinguished the house reflects gold, or, as this evening, blazes ruby, its panes of glass a dazzling scarlet. At this moment so red is the light all the greens turn black as pitch, the gorse and broom like jet-black sea anemones, a vast and sombre silhouette.

Wednesday 8

From Bachelard's *Poetics of Space*:

What special depth there is in a child's daydream! And how happy the child who really possesses his moments of solitude ... there are children who will leave a game to go and be bored in the corner of a garret. How often I have wished for the attic of my boredom, when the complications of life made me lose the very germ of freedom! And so beyond all positive values of protection the house we are born in becomes imbued with dream values which remain after the house is gone.

~

I have re-discovered my boredom here. The train could carry me to London – the bookshops, tea at Bertaux', a night in a bar; but I resist.

Film had me by the tail. Once it was naïvely adventurous – it seemed then there were mountains to climb. So I slogged onwards and upwards, often against a gale, only to arrive exhausted, and find I had climbed a molehill from where I had a view of a few yards, not endless mountain vistas. All around the traps were set. Traps of notoriety and expectation, of collaboration and commerce, of fame and fortune.

But the films unwinding themselves in the dark seemed to bring protection. Then came the media and the intrusion. At first a welcome trickle, something new. Then a raging flood of repetition, endless questions that eroded and submerged my work, and life itself. But now I have re-discovered boredom, where I can fight 'what next' with nothing.

You can't do *nothing*: accusations of betrayal, no articles or airtime to fill. I had foolishly wished my film to be home, to contain all the intimacies. But in order to do this I had to open to the public. At first a few genuine enthusiasts took up the offer, then coachloads arrived.

~

Prospect Cottage has four rooms. I call this room the Spring room; it is my writing room and bedroom, 12ft by 10 of polished tongue and groove with a single window facing the sea. In front of the window is my desk: a simple 18th century elm table. On it is a reading lamp of tarnished copper, two pewter mugs full of stamps, loose change, paperclips, several bottles of ink, and pens, envelopes, scraps of paper on which to make notes for this diary, an iron spittoon used as an ashtray; in the centre a lead tobacco box in the shape of a little Victorian cottage, in which I keep my chequebook and money.

To the left and right against the wall are two Red Cross medicine chests from an army surplus store; here I keep my clothes. A large oak chest dominates the room: it has 15th century panels carved with decorative ogee arches, perhaps once part of a rood screen. I keep my bedding in it. Next to it is a teak and khaki canvas campaign chair. By the desk is a small chair with a rush seat carved with two Maltese crosses.

On three walls are three paintings:

Night Life
The scarlet and black painting of fire, done in 1980.
Sleep has the House
A driftwood and glass construction with a carved figure, 21 December 1987.
Glittering Astronaut
By John Maybury.

In the four corners of the room are driftwood staffs crowned with garlands of stone and polished bone; on one of these sits my pixie Twinkle-in-the-eye. Purple velvet curtains shut out the winter stars.

~

Curry Malet, Somerset 1952
Late one winter's afternoon the stone gable of the old farm collapsed without warning into the yard on a tidal wave of honey, leaving the apple-scented attic in which my sister and I secretly whiled away rainy days open to the wind and rain. For years playing in the attic had been accompanied by the buzzing of wild bees hidden deep in the old stones; they had nested there as long as anyone could remember, building an enormous comb.

That afternoon the house shuddered: and with a great rumble the ripe wall burst, scattering its contents. The gnarled magnolia dripped honey.

No bonnets or silky top hats, fragile crinolines or rusty swords that day. The sleeping butterflies flapped their wings in the cold draught and crept, uncertainly, deeper into the crevices between the bleached beams. Spiders scuttled into the dark as their ancient cobwebs disintegrated; and the wind blew the lavender-scented dust and desiccated corpses of flies in little spirals. The door of a broken-backed cabinet rocked sending little jets of sawdust from the boreholes of woodworm. While outside, the owl who lived high up near the chimney flew disorientated in the dusk, attacking a farm-hand who disturbed it in the old cherry tree.

Like Noah's flood the great deluge of sweetness swept away the past, leaving the ghostly inhabitants of the attic shivering.

~

In this attic of honeyed memory I would take out my HMSO notebook and

spend an afternoon drawing. To this day I remember every page of the
thick-lined book with clarity, the first of many similar books. It fell into sections or enthusiasms: neatly copied handwriting exercises, dinosaurs – Ste-
gosaurus, Triceratops, Diplodocus – carefully copied from a King Penguin
'inspired' by Conan Doyle's *Lost World*. My childhood books can only be
described as Edwardian adventures: *King Solomon's Mines, Prester John,
The 39 Steps*.

~

Another enthusiasm was the caricature – there was a good one of the
American politician Dewey. Then there were the inventions: great medieval
cities of wattle and daub carefully delineated in black and white, over which
grim aerial battles were fought.

There were the poems and plays which were dramatised late at night on
the washbasin stand in the school dormitory. We dressed in sheets with
elaborate hats made of crêpe paper and toilet rolls, complete with carefully
chosen props filched from the garden, the kitchen or the matron's dressing
table.

~

*Dear Aunt, I write to break the news
That Archibald is dead.
He died at twelve o'clock today
With Gertrude at his bed.
Dear Gertrude's in a dreadful state
And can't refrain from crying.
And Ron is off his head, you know,
With little sobs and sighing.
I really don't know what to do
With Archie dead in bed,
And little Jane with mumps, you know,
And Ronnie off his head.*

~

Another enthusiasm was cacti: these were very carefully coloured in with
watercolour, and the most successful of these drawings was of an *Aloe
variegata*.

~

Miss Pilkington was born in the cottage next to the old manor house in
Curry Malet in the 1860s. By 1952, well into her eighties, she resembled the
Good Queen herself, small and dumpy with the gruff manners of Popeye.

Like Popeye, her secret was spinach, which she cultivated in her garden. Miss P. was the terror of all creeping annoyances: chasing slugs with a packet of salt she swiftly dealt out a fizzy saline death, which I watched with horrified fascination.

Her green-fingered war on the enemies of husbandry was remorseless: a boiling kettle dispatched a conurbation of ants; a pierced jam-jar imprisoned a multitude of struggling wasps, who drowned with their faces tucked into their legs. Twitchybells were ferreted out in the heart of dahlias, to be cracked alive in her gnarled fingers. As her shadow passed along the neat rows of vegetables, caterpillars dived for cover.

Miss P.'s scarecrow resembled Giles the cartoonist's famous granny, and sported a large black crow for a hat. I was just ten years old. She would sit me in her parlour and brew a cup of tea on the stove and talk of gardens. Out of the room we carried on talking, but as she was stone deaf the conversation became a monologue.

I listened spellbound, staring at her cactus: an *Aloe variegata*, with a host of babies, under a silver witch's ball in the window. This huge plant only flowered, she told me, once in seven years. Bitter aloes gave you the runs, she said, if you were constipated; no less a person than the Sultan of Jerusalem had recommended it to King Alfred, when he was stopped short by the effect of eating those burnt cakes.

Miss Pilkington herself had never been further than Taunton, 11 miles down the road; and that infrequently. When my parents were out late she would baby-sit. As the Manor House was haunted she would insist we stayed up with her in the kitchen. No other villager visited the place after dark. So we would sit with our spooky old visitor, listening to *Dick Barton Special Agent* on the wireless, solving some ominous mystery, with it's helter-skelter theme tune; and shiver with fear as Miss P.'s knitting needles clicked like those of some grotesque tricoteuse at the foot of the guillotine.

Thursday 9

Built a table out of wood I discovered in the fishing loft and the two huge planks that were lying in the garden. It took most of the day, though the construction was simple – the whole thing pegged together and glued. The legs are buried a foot or so into the shingle: it is narrow and has surprisingly elegant proportions. A circle cut in the planks acted as the perfect container for a flower pot which I filled with sempervivums: here, on the rare days when the wind does not blow, I will be able to give alfresco suppers with the nuclear power station as a backdrop.

Friday 10

Walked to the sea and brought back several large flints in the old plumber's bag. Then sat for nearly an hour in a daze wishing to write but . . . unable – Some words of Huxley's remembered. To my surprise I found them in *The Doors Of Perception*:

> *We live together, head on, and react to one another, but always and in all circumstances, we are by ourselves . . . by its very nature every embodied spirit is doomed to suffer and enjoy in solitude sensations, feelings, insights, fancies; all these are private and, except through symbols and at second-hand, incommunicable . . .*

~

It crossed my mind that all my childhood gardeners were women.

There were roses, but no lilies in Miss Pilkington's garden. I wonder what has become of the little cottage, where she was born over 120 years ago? In this page she lives on, the ghost of a garden, like the spirits who never frightened her in the old manor: 'The starres have us to bed, night draws the curtain.'

Saturday 11

Worked in the garden from sunrise. A warm overcast day. It took the morning to complete the second circular bed in front of the house – mulched the santolinas and started on the lavenders in the back garden. Cut back the artemesias and the curry plants, and potted the off-cuts, planted seed of pennyroyal and Californian poppy in flower pots (the chives have germinated). Saw the first migrant wheatear, and, about lunch time, a rather faded tortoiseshell butterfly on the ivy.

Sunday 12

Warm overcast day with a sea mist that triggered the foghorn at the lighthouse. Worked on the front garden, weeding; planted carnations and more sea kale seedlings. Spent the evening assembling objects from the flotsam and jetsam gathered on the beach.

Tuesday 21

The heavy rain has left sheets of water reflecting the grey sky lying on the sharp green of the spring fields. All along the rail embankment to Ashford the buds are breaking on the hawthorn bushes. There are drifts of primroses everywhere.

It's a cold windy day; a drizzle blankets the view, stinging the eyes. Nevertheless a week's absence has brought the garden on. A quick look showed the irises have grown inches and a second helping of daffodils are unfolding in the broom. The roses are all in bud and are coping with the cold winds.

At the end of the garden the dwarf sloe bushes have blossomed; and the woods along the Long Pits shimmer with silver pussy willow. The Pits are two flooded gravel quarries – there is a pumping station in case anything goes wrong with the nuclear power station's cooling system.

Deep in the middle of the woods, in the most secret glade, primroses are blooming, the only ones I have found; but there are carpets of violets almost hidden by their bright green leaves.

The unobservant could walk by them without noticing as the leaves and flowers create an almost perfect camouflage, the elusive purple vanishing in the green.

~

At midnight I wandered into the night under a bright full moon, which lit the shingle. The moonlight here is different: sandy beaches can't reflect the light like the myriad pebbles of Dungeness.

Wednesday 22
Gerard says of violets – that they:

> *Stirre up a man to that which is comely and honest; for flowres through their beauty, variety of colour, and exquisite forme, do bring to a liberal and gentle manly minde, the remembrance of honesty, comlinesse and all kinds of virtues, because it would be an unseemly and filthy thing (as a certain wise man sayeth) for him that look upon and handle faire and beautiful things to have his mind not faire, but filthy and deformed.*

Culpeper adds, 'They are a fine pleasing plant of Venus, of a mild nature, no way harmful.' Pindar called Athens 'violet crowned'; garlands of violets were worn on all festive occasions, particularly on the feast of Demeter, when young men were crowned with them. In German it is still known as 'boy's herb'. Goethe always carried violet seeds on his country walks and scattered them.

~

The violet held a secret. Along the hedgerow that ran down to the cliffs at Hordle deep purple violets grew – perhaps no more than a dozen plants. I stumbled across them late one sunny March afternoon as I came up the cliff path from the sea. They were hidden in a small recess. I stood for some moments dazzled by them.

Day after day I returned from the dull regimental existence of an English boarding school to my secret garden – the first of many that blossomed in my dreams. It was here that I brought him, sworn to secrecy, and then watched him slip out of his grey flannel suit and lie naked in the spring sunlight. Here our hands first touched; then I pulled down my trousers and lay beside him. Bliss that he turned and lay naked on his stomach, laughing as my hand ran down his back and disappeared into the warm darkness between his thighs. He called it 'the lovely feeling' and returned the next day, inviting me into his bed that night.

Obsessive violets drawing the evening shadows to themselves, our fingers touching in the purple.

Term ended. I bought myself violets from the florist's and put them by my bedside. My grandmother disapproved of flowers in the bedroom, said they corrupted the air. Violets, she said, were the flower of death.

But the violet, I discovered, was third in the trinity of symbolic flowers, flower of purity,

> *Whose virtue neither the heat of the sun melted away,*
> *Neither the rain has washed and driven away.*

The violet, *Nothing behind the best for smelling sweetly, a thousand more will provoke your content.*

A new orchard and garden was mine.

That summer, when the wheat had grown waist high, we carved a secret path from the violet grove into the centre of the field, and lay there chewing the unformed seeds, rubbing ourselves all over each other's bronzed and salty bodies, such was our happy garden state.

~

During the long Saturday afternoons we formed a plan to dig to the other side of the world, far away from the bullying sports masters and the bells that marked out our lessons. At least we would carve out a cavern. So when no-one was looking we smuggled the small trowel (the one I used for my prizewinning garden that lay between the kitchens and the chapel) into the fields and slowly dug down into the sandy subsoil. Until, exhausted and waist-deep in the sweet-smelling earth, we gave up and licked each other's muddy feet.

~

Napoleon loved the violet, Disraeli the primrose – April 11, his birthday, is primrose day in his honour. My grandmother's flower was mimosa, which became her nickname. My mother adored lily of the valley. Miss Nichols, my school teacher at 8, surrounded herself with primroses like Dizzy.

MARCH

~

Miss Nichols lived at the top of a winding staircase in the old school house, in a small bed-sitting room where a one bar electric fire burned perpetually, winter and summer, like a votive candle at the shrine of a saint.

Miss Nichols bustled backwards and forwards – a formidable grey rodent trapped in a hutch, declining and conjugating. She chased small schoolboys along the wheels of fortune, ruler clenched in her strong right arm.

Miss Nichols was feared by all. Other teachers deferred to her. Little boys took wrong turnings to avoid her. Her raids on the dormitory, to catch the unwary who gabbed after Lights Out, were as legendary as those of Boadicea on the Romans.

Miss Nichols had her favourites, who dined with her on toast, and operated a sinister system of information. If you so much as stirred in your sheets, blinding lights would flash in your face; and somewhere, invisible behind them, she would subject you to a ruthless interrogation.

Miss Nichols moved in a perpetual fug, a great grey bulk of musty pullovers and thick woolly stockings and steel-capped walking-shoes that clicked like the deathwatch. Her face loomed out of the dark, wrinkles dusted with white powder that wedged itself in granules between the furrows, a ghostly mask capped by a cast iron hairstyle with steely ringlets that had not changed since the old Queen died.

Mensa mensa mensam.

Miss Nichols took all the junior classes, including art, where we were bound over to paint and study her favourite primroses, both thrum and prim, long after other classes had escaped and were streaming past our windows shouting and laughing.

Miss Nichols on summer Sundays would lead the crocodile to evensong through the walled garden, wearing a faded cotton dress covered in imaginary flowers. She would strike a path under rose pergolas between the abandoned herbaceous borders; blousy pink cabbage roses shed their petals like confetti into her hair. Oblivious of her informal chaplet, she would sit straight-backed at the harmonium and play her favourite hymn, leading the singing in a watery soprano.

Abide with me, fast falls the eventide.
The darkness deepens, Lord, with me abide.

A rose petal would fall to the floor, sending our thin wavering voices still further out of tune. Tears would form in Miss Nichols' eyes and spot her cheeks like raindrops, to reveal a faded pink under the chalky powder.

We walked back in the twilight through the garden, dewy peonies bent double as if in supplication, and sprinkled with thundery teardrops, gathering carmine shadows. Irises, purple as the sky; and scarlet poppies with blue-black interiors burst from pods as rumpled as butterflies. Heavily scented pinks lay in abandoned clusters and lupin spires bent under the weight of the day. A scarlet comma stretched its wings in the last patch of sunlight before darting off, up and over the brick wall.

Miss Nichols far up ahead. I walked entranced, scheming. Her night raids forgotten.

~

A cold winter day, overcast until the sun appeared at 5:00. At 6:30, standing on the shingle bank by the sea's edge, I watched the fishermen peg out their nets in the sands. The tide was low, the sands a pale blue, the sea ochre yellow with little white breakers blown back; above them, mauve clouds. Behind Prospect Cottage the sun was setting huge.

Later a full moon was up in a cloudless sky – very clear. At midnight your shadow had gradation. The sea swelled right up, almost to the top of the shingle, moving slowly and relentlessly; the wind had dropped. Shimmering path of the moon across the sea. Ships etched against the sky far out in the channel. Very cold.

Thursday 23

A bright sun dawned but cold winds soon blew in a very grey day. I planted the rest of the lavender in the circular bed in front of the cottage then raked the shingle, before retiring indoors to repot the geraniums which have started to recover from a dark winter spent in Phoenix House. The weather has left me quite disoriented, spring has been round the corner since November, but the icy gales of the last ten days have put the garden in suspense. The seedlings of the sea kale which germinated weeks ago have hardly moved and several have rotted away.

Good Friday

The wind roared through the night with but brief moments of calm – early this morning the whole landscape, sea and sky blended into a glowering ochre – even the lark's song was blown away. My roses are now sadly scorched and the fennel quite dead.

In the house the seeds sprout: Californian poppy, pennyroyal and chives have germinated. This afternoon a misty sun gave some respite but was quickly drawn behind a grey gloom that loomed out of the west.

At tea I walked a mile along the shore, skirting heavy leaden waves. Returned home tired, breathless and drenched with salt. Tracking back I noticed dandelions and dead-nettles growing in the shadow of a broken-backed fisherman's hut. The pitch-black timbers of Prospect Cottage, with its bright yellow windows, are silhouetted against banks of gorse ablaze with golden flowers.

Saturday 25

The sun rose and remained for the rest of the day, warm with a light breeze. At ten I walked down to the sea to pick up flints. The sand flats were quite deserted, except for a small boy sobbing as he dug for bait. I heard him clearly on the wind, he was far out near the breakers. My own sadness, which set in last night with the television screening of *War Requiem*, swept away. There are so many strangers crying in England these days.

All along the Ness they are putting up fences – more people are travelling out to the lighthouse. The local, the Britannia, has changed its name to the Smugglers' to cash in. Even this remote spot changes.

My neighbours brought me a purple sage – the first gift the garden has received. It grows apace.

~

Salvia salvatrix, sage the saviour. 'He that would live for aye must eat sage in May.' A man's business thrives or falls like the herb in his garden. Pepys writes in his diary that he saw a churchyard in which sage was grown on every grave. Gerard says:

> *Sage is singularly good for the head and brain, it quickeneth the senses and memory, strengtheneth the sinews, restoreth health to those that have the palsy and taketh away shakey trembling of the members.*

Sage attracts toads. Boccaccio's toad that lived under the sage bush was one of a long line.

Thomas Hill writes:

> *Serpents greatly hate the fire, not for the same cause, that this dulleth their sight, but because the nature of fire is to resist poison, they also hate the strong savour far flying the garlike and red onions procure. They love the savin tree, the ivy and fennel as toads do sage, and snakes the herb rocket, but they are mightily displeased and sorest hate the ash tree, in so much as the serpents neither to the morning nor the longest evening shadows of it will draw near, but rather shun the same and fly far off.*

In the evening I walked to the Long Pits, the violets under the ash tree glimmering in the dusk. No serpents about, just the hum of the power plant. In the foundations of the ruined school house periwinkle had run riot, covering an area of several hundred square feet. Brought back a small piece to plant in the garden.

Easter Sunday

> *Periwynke is an erbe of grene colour;*
> *In tyme of May he bereth blo flour.*
> *His stakys ain so feynt and feye*
> *Yet never more growyth he hey.*

~

Periwinkle, the 'sorcerer's violet' – source of potent sky-blue love philtres and charms against wyked spiritys – was often woven into garlands for the dead and crowns for the condemned.

Apulius' Herbarum says:

> *This wort is of good advantage for many purposes, that is to saye, first against devil sickness and demoniackall possessions and against shakes and wild beasts and against poisons and for various wishes and for envy and for terror and that thou mayst have grace. And if thou hast the wort with thee thou shalt be prosperous and ever acceptable. This wort thou shalt pluck thus saying* I pray the vinca pervinca, thou that art to be had for many useful qualities, that thou come to me glad blossoming with thy mainfullness, that outfit me so that I shall be shielded and ever prosperous and undamaged by poisons. *And by water when thou shalt pluck this wort thou shalt be clean of every uncleanliness, and thou shalt pick it when the moon is nine nights old, and eleven nights, and thirteen nights, and when it is one night old.*

The Virtues of Herbes:

> *Periwyke, when it is beate unto powder with worms of the earth wrapped about it and with an hearbe called houslyck, it induceth love between man and wife if it be used in their meales.*

~

It is with joy, but also regret that I recall my very first garden at Hordle. It was one of a number of small plots about 12ft by 8 marked out around the southern perimeter of the old kitchen garden, given to us like allotments. They were judged each summer at Speech Day.

My garden was a simple affair in which annuals were sown in straight rows, to be brought to showy perfection: alyssum, ageratum, cornflowers, candy tuft, lobelia, love-in-the-mist and nemesia . . . The garden formed a foil for my drawing book, and if fate had turned out different I am sure I would be a professional gardener, rather than an enthusiastic amateur.

~

It is midday on Easter Sunday. The clocks have gone forward an hour. A sea mist that set in in the early morning has not cleared; if anything it is denser. The foghorn sounds its mournful note every few minutes. I sit with my eyes shut, trying to dispel the mists of nearly forty years, to recall my little garden, a garden that each summer won me a prize of five shillings. But try as I may it is only a dim memory.

Perhaps its very tranquillity allowed it to slip away – and its simplicity. I remember the heavy somnolent scent of limes in high summer, and the pungent privet bushes beneath them; the cowparsley peashooters and ivy ammunition. Once an enormous oak eggar caterpillar escaped from its jamjar into the dormitory, frightening the boy who believed that the sticky come on his fingers was his brain leaking.

The strange masters: Captain Eriks, the Dutchman with his creaky metal leg; Mr. Howard, an elegant grey Edwardian with a rose in his buttonhole. I remember the nicknames for the nameless: Geek, Plank and One Round. I remember an aerial pathway carved through the stunted trees at the cliff top, and the continuous hunt for butterflies and moths – the mysterious drinkers that magically attracted their mates, the dizzy flight of the comma along the sun-drenched paths, pale green emeralds and white ermines fluttering into midnight lamps. All these and the enormous hawk, puss moth and waxy goat moth caterpillars pass through my memory.

But the garden itself remains only a silent iridescent patchwork of colour.

Monday 27

Bright and sunny, slightly overcast and very warm. Everyone out in their gardens. Walked with HB to the Long Pits – on the way, found a clump of alexanders. The plants were in bud, but there were a few seeds from last year on the dried flower heads, which I carefully collected and sowed back home. The alexander looks like a giant cow parsley, with large shiny leaves. Having known someone who ate hemlock (which it somewhat resembles) with fatal results, I decided not to make a meal of it.

The gorse bushes in the sallow woods were alive with bees and have already set seed. Further along the gravel pits the large sloe bushes were breaking into flower and the sunny banks of the lake were carpeted with yellow coltsfoot, once known as *filius ante patrem*, as the flowers appear from the ground before the leaves.

~

Coughwort was recommended for all lung complaints and is the main ingredient of herbal tobacco. It was recommended by Pliny, who suggested it should be smoked through a hollow reed whilst taking little sips of wine.

~

On the way back we passed two fishermen, one of whom said he had taken a 30 lb pike from the Pits.

Spent the afternoon planting seeds – nasturtium, wild cornflower – and preparing a bed for marrows. The sun continued to beat down; by five I could feel it burning my face.

On colder days as a boy I would spend hours in the nursery daydreaming among the seed packets piled on top of each other, like an old-fashioned hanging at the Academy. Here the artists had painted the promise of a flaming June with a palette of scarlets and blues. I would pick up the packets and shake them; the seeds of the poppy produced barely a whisper, while the broad bean rattled like a maraca.

Amongst the gaudy packets there were some conspicuous by their plainness; they had no pictures to seduce and I knew they were for the serious who knew their Latin. The backs of the packets had descriptions of soil (deep or light), sunlight and shade, together with the times and depths of sowing, and warnings:

Watch out for snails – they like this plant.
A hardy perennial can be sown straight in the garden for flowers the following year, and years following.
Prefers full sun, but is not fussy.
Very free-flowering in subtle shades.

I never planted all the seeds, so as years passed I would find I had generations of half-used packets. Would these old seeds remain quick and sprout like the wheat in King Tut's tomb?

Seed planting has many ceremonies – Hill's *Gardener's Labyrinth* has chapters devoted to it. I wonder if anyone took this advice of Pliny and the Neapolitan, Palladus Rutilus, that

Seeds may be preserved in safety, from all evil and garden monsters, if the bare head without flesh of either mare or she asse (having been covered by the male) be buried in the garden, or in the middest of the same fixed on a stake set with earth be erected.

Tuesday 28

A second day of bright sunshine. Spent the morning outside writing at my new garden table. Then walked along the shingle. Discovered a clump of ivy-leaved toadflax covered with bright blue flowers growing on a mound of asphalt alongside the lifeboat station.

Toadflax was brought originally from Italy to the Chelsea Physic Garden and escaped to naturalise itself all over the country on stone walls. It's another 'Madonna' flower because of its clear blue. Alongside it the speed-well was in flower, a pale blue echo of its little neighbour. At the end of the road the valerian is already flowering. The warm winter has scrambled the calendar – last year I filmed it in full bloom early in July.

Thursday 30

March 30 is my parent's wedding anniversary, neither of whom were parti-cularly interested in gardening. Though in our family film it might seem otherwise: my mother picking the roses, and dad pushing a large wheelbar-row jauntily along blooming herbaceous borders.

On this day nearly 50 years ago my parents posed for their wedding photo under a daffodil bell hanging in the lych gate of Holy Trinity, North-wood. The photo, with my father in his RAF uniform and my mother hold-ing a bouquet of carnations, her veil caught in the March breeze – captured the imagination of the press. It appeared in the national papers – *hope at a time of encroaching darkness*. Later that day my mother posed alone in an elegant formal photo holding a bouquet of lily of the valley.

~

Lily of the valley was often carried in bouquets: something old, something new, something borrowed, something blue – the lily of constancy, Mary's tears, a sign of the second coming, often called 'ladder-to-heaven'. When Mary wept at the foot of the cross her tears turned into this pure white flower of humility.

The medicinal property of the Virgin's tears was considered so strong in the Middle Ages that infusions made from them were kept in gold and silver vessels, like the jewelled reliquaries that held fragments of the True Cross. Distilled in wine and ministered to the dumb it would restore speech and re-store memory, clear as the bells of the flower.

~

I hardly remember a spring when my mother did not return with a small bunch of the flowers and put them carefully on the mantelpiece in a little white vase. Much later she fell in love with pennyroyal – I think because of the name, and was thrilled when I bought some seed and planted it in odd corners of the garden of her house at Merryfield.

~

I don't remember my father having any use for the garden except in a purely utilitarian way. For him it constantly wasted time – particularly mowing the lawn. And any tree or shrub that hindered the clean straight lines he drew across the grass was doomed. On the whole he was happiest with the axe, saw and secateurs – attacking anything that became too luxuriant, hatching plots against a willow that a neighbour had planted up against the kitchen window and which blocked out the light. At dusk he would creep out and give it a strong dose of weedkiller.

My mother would be intensely upset by these attacks on nature. The willow valiantly resisted all attempts at sabotage.

My mother liked to sit out in the garden under the apple trees, which would be subjected occasionally to a similar assault. The orchard was an old one planted in the twenties with about forty trees: there were laxtons, pearmains, pippins, russets and a large bramley, all wild and overgrown. This orchard my father set about taming with an axe, but stopped short of scorched earth through an inordinate love of apple pie.

As he ate it every night I would think of the various kings and princes who had died of an overdose of lampreys and apricots. My mother cooked an apple pie every day of the year and became the world's greatest expert in this area. With 365 days at her disposal she tuned herself to the finest variations as she peeled Eve's wretched fruit and kneaded the pastry, singing the *William Tell* overture.

My father created a tyranny through the apple pie. Predictably I hated them, and my mother would contrive to give me the smallest portion. I would have been quite happy to have received a single clove on my plate.

~

My mother was certain my interest in the garden was inherited from her father Harry Lytten, who grew prize sweet peas in Bexhill when on leave from his job at the tea and timber merchants, Harrison and Crosfield, in Calcutta. I have film of him admiring his efforts in 1930.

Also of his jazz-mad son Edward, my Uncle Teddy, who spent his youth in a Japanese POW camp in Burma and returned invalided to the country. There he dreamt up projects, one of which included growing mushrooms in the airing cupboard amongst my aunt's neatly laundered sheets.

~

Teddy's interest in the garden was perhaps the most 'advanced': he would castigate my mother's cooking, including the apple pie, and would potter around the garden making himself wild salads out of nasturtium leaves and dandelions, completely disrupting any meal he attended.

Of his many doomed projects the most successful was forcing pink tulips for the Christmas market in a series of dilapidated greenhouses, where I would work for him each Christmas holiday picking and packing. Long before the avocado made its appearance at the greengrocer's Teddy was optimistically growing bushes from pips. Mangoes, pineapples, even aubergines were cultivated on windowsills, under sinks, in the attic. Teddy pushed horticulture to a tropical extreme.

Friday 31

Sun a pure white globe in a chalky sky, mist blowing across the Ness in milky veils, silent pussy willow woods the palest pastel yellow luminous in the silvery light.

APRIL

Tuesday 4

April was brought in by a cruel cold that turned into a bitter easterly during the night. This tempest battered Prospect fearfully. I sat in a sleepless daze all the hours of darkness, fearing for every creaking timber, expecting the shrieking power lines to part. Each gust more violent than the last tightened the stomach. At 5:30 a pale premonition of dawn silhouetted the black clouds rushing up out of a boiling sea.

Throughout the night the fishermen worked to secure their boats by the spectral headlights of their cars, which now and then turned landwards to light up this room. As the hours passed the wind grew and entered the house, bringing great chill. Doors opened, slammed themselves shut.

In the exhausted dawn I brewed a cup of coffee, which turned cold in my hands, and watched the flotsam and jetsam of paper and plastic flying off the waves to disappear across the Ness.

The icy wind, as strong as last year's hurricane, has devastated my garden in a few brief hours, and is growing in intensity by the minute. I walked towards the sea's edge, but stopped a good distance away as the salt spray drenched me – blowing across the shingle it frosted the windows. White plumes whipped from the breakers stung my eyes and salty lips.

~

In the old days, when the land behind the Ness was still flooded, marsh fever was common. A charm, hung about the neck, bore these words:

Ague I thee defy
Three days shiver
Three days shake
Make me well for Jesus' sake

~

The seagulls hug the ground in the gale, stand facing the wind like soldiers on parade watching waves topple over the shingle's edge, defying them to break rank. The groaning of the shingle is swallowed in the furious wind.

Mrs. Oiller is 94 this year. She came here in 1915 and brought up nine children in the next cottage. She used to carry fresh water from the well in two buckets with a yoke, and picked heavy ballast stone for a few pence where the reactor now stands.

She tells me one sunny afternoon she saw two men fall out of a plane in a still blue sky, remain suspended in the azure while she held her breath, before they plummeted out of sight behind the holly bushes at Holmstone.

~

Holly sprang up in the footsteps of Christ when he walked this earth, blood-red scarlet berries. I was told on good authority that the flowers of holly caused water to freeze.

~

A dragon in the wilderness, forty days and forty nights.

Will the roof hold the storm's gathering strength? Look at the sea gobbling at the boats at their moorings – no fishermen out today. The ghost of Aggie-One-Tooth is running in the breakers, her domesday bell ringing in the storm. The wrecks are shifting in their sandy graves.

Mrs. Oiller's 'third' fell into the vat of molten amber in the far kutch, and just stood there like an oiled bird, weeping. She'd cut up her dressing gown, the splendid one from the London store, the only one she'd ever had, to clothe him.

~

Oh wind please chase yourself away.

Hyeme malus, aestate molestus, numquam bonus – evil in winter, generous in summer, never good.

Wednesday 5

My purple iris has died. Its mass of buds have been bruised and scorched by the salt spray – I've waited three years for these flowers, nurtured the plant from a rhizome pulled from the wild in the ruins of Victoria Dock. Only one late flower is safe amongst the wilted leaves. My consolation is Ovid's beautiful description of the goddess arriving with a message from Juno at the house of sleep:

> *Before the doors of the house poppies bloom in abundance and*
> *countless herbs, from whose juices dewy night gathers drowsiness and*
> *sprinkles it over the dark earth.*
> *There is not a door in the whole house lest some turning hinge*
> *should creak, nor is there any watchman at the threshold. In the midst*
> *of the cavern stands a lofty couch of ebon wood, dark in colour*

*covered with black draperies, feather soft, where the god himself lies,
his limbs relaxed in luxurious weariness – around him, the empty
dreams made to resemble different shapes, as many as the corn ears in
the harvest, as leaves on woodland trees, or sands scattered in the
shore. The goddess entered and brushed aside with her hands the
dreams that stood in her way. Immediately the god's dwelling was
filled with the shimmering gleam of her bright raiment, and sleep
himself struggled to raise his eyes, languid and heavy with slumber. At
length, however, he roused himself, and leaning on his elbow
recognised Iris and asked her why she had come.*

~

The rain wept through the night, quietened the grumbling shingle, stilled me
into sleep. In the distance the sea roared, churning the ochrous sandbanks.
The shoreline had changed, as if a giant hand had raked the shingle,
smoothing out the small coves, grading the dips and hollows into a perfect
straight line. At the base of the bank a fast-moving river had formed. No
stones were left to build the mazes and labyrinths of my garden.

The rain fell through the small hours. Dreamt of soldiers: I was reluctant
to wear the smart uniform. The handsomest I glimpsed high above me on
the scaffolding around some marble ruin. Stopped, held my breath for his
beauty. He slipped out of his uniform and, carefully folding it, placed it at
the foot of my bed. A rush of cool air as he slid beneath the sheets. He dared
not wake me as he knew I would disappear – I was his dream.

My elder tree died in the night, burnt black by the salt spray . . .

*Bour tree, bour tree, crooked rong
Never straight and never strong
Ever bush and never tree
Since our Lord was nailed on thee*

A great pool of water formed on the path, so that as he left the traveller saw
his face reflected. He smiled and called back.

~

In the early hours Johnny and I shared our secrets, clambering onto each
other's beds like the heroes of Edwardian picture books. Skinny nine year
olds, we explored the contours of forgotten landscapes. The imaginary
worlds of Prester John – and of Big Foot, Tight Arse, Stiff Cock. An orgy of
little devils swarming across the tympani, in the shadow of hell fire. We dug
deep in King Solomon's mines, flirted with strange tribal initiations.
Warmth and giggles before reveille.

The idiot who betrayed us was the one who thought that if he masturbated his brains would spurt out. They prized his hands from my tight cock and left us to shiver naked in the cold at the foot of the bed. We here hauled out of our element and left to asphyxiate by the Noes.

'Christ! What are you doing?' 'You'll go blind!'

Then the blows rained down, millennia of frustrated Christian hatred behind the cane. What a terrible God to take on the hurt and then hurt us all! That day a childhood idyll died in the bells and sermons, the threats to tell our parents and derision; and we were shoved into the wilderness they had created, and commanded to punish ourselves for all time. So that at last we would be able to enter their heaven truly dead in spirit.

But I knew the joy of heaven was there, the splendour and nobility of warriors, and I vowed to revenge my generations, to shred the false white veil of holy matrimony and fuck the haughty Groom, and to wipe up his come with the Saviour's shroud. Then our task completed on earth we would enter the Kingdom, a band of warriors and gang-bang the Trinity on its throne of gold before a multitude of saints, until this Christ repented and confessed his true love of Saint John. Now and forever Amen.

~

By evening the rain had stopped, leaving us damp and chill. The winds had died away. I could feel the garden sigh with relief. Spring sunlight will be that much more welcome, the plants more vigorous after this cold bath.

Thursday 6
The cold continues, the frozen larks creep about. I catch my breath. As the light fades, death comes – even for stones.

Friday 7
The day started with two brief showers. A cold breeze, but the sun came back, and stayed. Driving to Rye we noticed banks of alexanders, bright green with creamy yellow flowers, at the kerbside. At the gravel pits we counted a flock of over thirty swans grazing amongst the sheep.

All the way the gardens were bright with spring flowers, particularly marigolds, which run riot.

At the bookshop I bought Kilvert's *Journal* – the proprietor recognised me, called me by name, which startled me. We talked for a while.

Back home I walked along the deserted beach past the power station. The west side of the Ness has a different vegetation. It's flat. There are patches of moss, islands of dead broom, thrift and an abundance of foxgloves. At the sea's edge there is horned poppy, but little if any sea kale.

Further past the pylons there is a golden island of gorse. Here, even in the cold wind, the air is scented. Gorse has a delicate herbal perfume not unlike rue. In the right weather conditions the whole Ness smells of it.

There is a passage into the largest clump, a huge area a hundred yards or more in diameter; deep inside, a golden light and a heady perfume. The bushes seem ancient – serpentine gnarled trunks, as if wrung ferociously in an easterly gale. Many of them, long dead, form a carpet like a writhing snake pit.

The great bushes are about ten feet high, very luxuriant, and the warm winter has produced the most beautiful blossom.

This evening the silence in this grove was truly golden. It is a beautiful thought that Pliny says gorse was used to catch the specks of gold from the gravel that prospectors panned.

Saturday 8

Sat in the sunlight and dreamt up a 'tower of the winds' and conservatory.

There are five new paintings on the walls – *The lady who hung herself in the Garden of Eden, The boy who drowned in holy water, A day-return to the Isle of the Dead, Hushed footsteps* and *The ebbing tide* – all collages of found objects on gold backgrounds.

~

A hallucinatory dusk, washed with colours to drive Monet to suicide. At sunset the brightest sickle moon appeared in a gentle blue sky; minute by minute gathering in intensity it stayed until just before midnight.

Night clear as a bell – the blue passed through violet with strands of rose and old gold to become a deep indigo. So etched were the moon and stars they seemed to have been cut out by a child to decorate a crib.

The night sky here is a riot that outshines the brightest lights of Piccadilly; the stars have the intensity of jewels. So flat is the Ness that those stars that lie at the horizon touch your very feet and the moon tips the waves with silver.

The nuclear power station is a great ocean liner moored in the firmament, ablaze with light: white, yellow, ruby. Whilst round the bay the lights stretch from Folkestone to Dover. High above, jet liners from the south flash silent in the stars. On these awesome nights, reduced to silence, I walk across the Ness.

Never in my many sleepless nights have I witnessed a spectacle like this. Not the antique bells of the flocks moving up a Sardinian hillside, the barking of the dogs and the sharp cries of the shepherd boys, nor moonlit nights sailing the Aegean, nor the scented nights and fireflies of Fire Island, smashed glass star-strewn through the piers along the Hudson – nothing can quite equal this.

The orchestra has struck up the music of the spheres, the spectral dancers on the fated liner whirl you off your feet till you feel the great globe move. Light-hearted laughter. Here man has invaded the heavens; but the moon, not to be usurped, shines sickle bright, gathering in our souls.

Sunday 9

'Keep spending' is the cheerful cry of the proprietor of the Greatstone nursery, a bright bungalow at the sea's edge hugged by herbaceous borders, with a sign at the entrance 'say it with flowers, Valentine's day February 14'. He stands smiling at the doorstep, dark blue fisherman's jersey and yachting hat with a fine gold earring. He retired here years ago from the film studios, said he preferred the light here as he didn't have to shift it about.

He runs his nursery – which is the best value for money – like a London market barrow throwing in a santolina, or a lavender like an extra potato or cabbage, adding 'You don't need the change do you?' and 'How's the wife?' Looking at the smallest sedum he announced 'Now that'll cost you!' The sales take place in front of the house between ranks of gnomes, woodpeckers, blushing maidens and frogs, behind them in the porch are shelves of Chinese porcelain, painted with dragons and chrysanthemums, teapots in the shape of elephants, vases and caddies jostle for space. Through the net curtains elaborate gilded temple guardians and incense burners, trees of semi-precious stones, mysterious gods and goddesses dimly glimpsed.

Today I left this Shangri-La with half a dozen lavender and a large sack of potting compost with plenty of change from a £10 note.

Thursday 13

A gang of pretty model boys near-naked romping in the shingle with a large inflatable dinosaur. A glitzy invasion of bronzed work-out bodies spilling out of a silver Cadillac parked at a crazy angle in the stones. Bruce Weber collegiate haircuts, wide knowing smiles; I wanted to ask them to pose in my garden. They looked so out of place, even more so than the lads with the Apollonian lyre who romped through the Côte d'Azur garden of Cocteau's *Testament*. If he had materialised amongst them in a baggy summer suit, hair blown awry, it would have been no more surprising.

I walked past this candy store a couple of times with Tony; the make-up lady glowered at us for distracting her charges. The boys ran their fingers through their greasy hair, the dinosaur toppled over in the wind. The second time past one of the lads flipped over slowly and deliberately slid his hand down his tight, black swimming pants stroking his arse. Then they were gone as quickly as they materialised leaving a tingling in the groin.

~

Surely we were the angels denied hospitality by the Sodomites. Was not

Sodom a tight little suburban dormitory mortgaged out to the hardhearted, somewhere beyond Epsom?

~

April is much crueller than even Eliot imagined – it leaves me unhappy, gloomier than ever.

HB out on an ACTUP demo against the starvation diet for those with HIV dependent on the Department of Health? and Social Security? Deepening criminality of those who rule over us. Dear mad old Lord Hailsham telling them to get some sense into their tiny noddles on the TV. Some idiot trying to extend the blasphemy laws.

~

On the phone to dearest Howard Brookner, so far away in New York. He can only groan now, his bright mind slowly invaded by a terrible infection that is depriving him gradually of his faculties. Howard and I walked in a storm along the Ness last March, he had a sudden nose bleed, but wouldn't admit it, at last he had a chance to direct a big feature starring Matt Dillon and Madonna. All through last summer he kept on smiling.

I spoke to him for twenty minutes last night. I didn't know if he understood a word – long silences and the low wounded moaning. No words now. The echoing emptiness of those groans encircling the world by satellite. It left me confused, fearful, and terribly sad.

Emotions frozen for fear of filling the world with tears.

~

A year ago Howard arrived suddenly and rather mysteriously from New York. We drove to Rye where he was staying in Henry James' dark, rather cheerless house. We found him in the living room stoking up a large log fire from which the sparks flew as he told us a story.

Earlier in the year his grandmother had given him his grandfather's signet ring – a heavy gold band engraved with Masonic emblems. As she slipped it on his finger she made him swear he would never lose it. If he did, she said, it would bring him death.

Weeks later, in a break from filming, he was water-skiing in a deep lagoon when he lost his grip and fell into the water. The ring was torn from his finger and sank in slow-motion, glinting in the sun until swallowed in the dark deeps.

He felt an intense relief as the ring was heavy and ugly and had weighed him down during the weeks he had worn it. Now as it was disappearing for ever, a weight dropped from his shoulders.

That weekend the weather was glorious and a friend suggested they take up a microlight – something he had never done. High above the Pacific coast his friend switched off the engine so they could watch the setting sun in silence.

Imagine the thrill, he said, sitting there with the air rushing through the sails, the ocean surf far below and the sun a volcanic scarlet descending through purple clouds – the sense of weightlessness, floating, the fragility of the craft and their hushed voices. It was, he said, the most awesome thing that had ever happened to him.

As the shadows gathered his friend attempted to restart the engine, but nothing happened. For twenty minutes they drifted further out over the ocean, but the engine still would not fire. Then for another twenty minutes they struggled with the craft to bring it down beyond the surf, which would have drowned them. After an exhausting struggle they landed in the lagoon beyond the sand bar, and were able to wade to safety.

Friday 14
A cold hazy day with barely a glimmer of sunlight. I wrapped myself up against the wind and set to work in the back garden, planting a circle of santolina and several lavender bushes.

Heard the first cuckoo over in the willows and noticed masses of ladybirds congregating on favourite plants. The sloe bushes are covered in snowy blossom and there were several sand lizards basking in the sun amongst the flowers.

In the afternoon I worked in the front garden, dug beds around the two dials, planting them with a circle of marigolds. The wallflowers are now full out and since last week the saxifrage has been covered with a mass of golden bloom.

Saturday 15
My garden is a memorial, each circular bed and dial a true lover's knot – planted with lavender, helichryssum and santolina.

Santolina, under the dominion of Mercury resisteth poison, putrefaction, and heals the bites of venomous beasts. Whilst a sprig of lavender held in the hand or placed under the pillow enables you to see ghosts, travel to the land of the dead.

~

Wild dreamings through the night: some last film full of vanishing incoherent sequences, the images crystal clear but so strange I cannot decipher them. They fall off the screen into the audience, who are frozen in their seats. A table of cinephiles mutter angrily as Falmouth boys, subjects of the Victorian painter Henry Tuke, splash them.

I watch Johnny Jacket, the Cornish football hero, slip out of his clothes and time. It must be a sunny day. A sadness as deep as the continental shelf washes over me.

Johnny Jacket's unbuttoning his breeches: out slips a tumescent cock. He pours the warm linseed oil I use to paint into the palm of his hand – it smells of cricket bats and childhood. He moves his hand gently along the shaft without taking his eyes off me, and slowly jacks off. As the creamy come spatters all over his sunburnt torso he closes his eyes, smiles, pours the rest of the golden oil down his chest and over himself so he glistens.

I'm awake – the sun has not risen. The view from my window is bathed in a ghostly grey light, the sea white as milk. I try to get back to sleep, but questions, like the dreams that guard sleep, crowd into my mind. I wake again at seven in the most glorious sunny day.

As the sun rose, thoughts jostling each other like demons, invaded my garden of earthly delight. What purpose had my book? Was I a fugitive from my past? Had I condemned myself to prison here? How could I celebrate my sexuality filled with so much sadness, and frustration for what has been lost? How had my films been damaged? Look at the cash sloshing around my contemporaries. Was it not the ultimate revenge that I have not been paid for directing *War Requiem*. Had I not raised a hopeless banner against the admen of the Cinema Renaissance, entered a battle I knew I would never win – not even posthumously as they held all the aces.

Could I face the dawn cheerfully, paralysed by the virus that circles like a deadly cobra? So many friends dead or dying – since autumn: Terry, Robert, David, Ken, Paul, Howard. All the brightest and the best trampled to death – surely even the Great War brought no more loss into one life in just twelve months, and all this as we made love not war. The terrible dearth of information, the fictionalisation of our experience, there is hardly any gay autobiography, just novels, but why novelise it when the best of it is in our lives?

~

At five o'clock swallows swooped low over the roof top. A warm sunny day, the sea a deep azure.

Sunday 16

The cold easterly that has blown throughout April set in again last night. It brings with it more depression and inertia. The salt spray from a high sea stings the eyes – voices on the telephone are almost indecipherable through the noise on the line, as if frying in a distant hell.

~

At the age of twelve I was sent to another boarding school, Canford, where there were no gardens, just a magnificent park planted by ironmasters early in the nineteenth century. By the 1950s it was at its zenith.

The school lay at the very heart of the park and idyllic acres so carefully constructed to conceal the origins of wealth, to cloak with gentility the dark satanic furnaces of South Wales.

This 'gentility' had left Charlotte Guest free to ramble through the magical past of the Welsh Sagas, and entertain the likes of Austen Layard – back from a dig at Assyrian Nineveh – before turning home at dusk to the great halls, cloisters and towers of the 'palace gothick' Barry had raised on the banks of the Stour, which enclosed the old manor house that Henry VII had given to his mother Margaret Beaufort.

Beauforts, Mountjoys, Montagues, Fitzroys – all celebrated now in heraldic stained glass and mosaic in the great pile crowned by its huge tower dedicated to the imperial Victoria: a mad jumble of ambition and folly, with ornate ceremonial staircases, smoking rooms, billiard rooms, panelled and painted in the Assyrian, Roman, Tudorbethan, Gothic and Modern styles.

And the heart of the building, deep in the kitchen: rows and rows of bells, still numbered and named.

~

There was a silly myth that the survival of this House hung on the life of a venerable oak known as 'the mungy', which two lads in desperation set fire to one winter night. The oak, and the system, unfortunately survived. The boys, however, were never seen again.

A 'system' of outward calm and apparent inner rectitude covered a cauldron of fear and resentment. Its weapon, the bells, by then electrically operated, summoned us to grace, were shrill and effective in penetrating the maze of corridors and attics.

Laus Domine.

There were bells for lessons.

Bells for inspections – of shoe polish, trouser crease, clean collar, combed hair.

Punishment and beatings.

For what we are about to receive may the Lord make us truly thankful.

Bells for PT, the cadet corps marching on the spot, field days, cross country running, rugby. There were character-building bells, bells for exeat, bells for fagging.

Above all, there was the chapel bell.

~

Could all this conceivably be thought 'a normal upbringing'?

Everyone seemed to think so. And my parents, bless them, paid for it. So much that my father proudly presented me with a complete set of receipts on my twenty-first.

~

Paradise Perverted was intended to set us up for life – dimly perceived as starting some time after our eighteenth. Meanwhile we got on with our business, walled in from the pressures and temptations of the land of *oiks* – full of desperate Eves struggling to munch our apple-cheeked virginity to the sounds of loose-lipped Elvis.

To divert us from the temptations of the flesh a muddy, muscular 'christianity' was employed – 'healthy body, healthy mind'.

Wanking, however, let the side down. Let in own-goals.

The oiks, hapless victims of their own inadequacy and misfortune, were to be ruled by us benevolently. In the meantime their dreadful language and manners to be shunned like the plague. With God's help the Empire would continue to be ruled selflessly, and we would continue to bring civilisation to the strange races with their odd physiognomies and customs. The headmaster lectured us on the university that the good Shah of Iran was building to bring our democratic beliefs to his illiterate subjects, and to which he was shortly to be translated as its first Chancellor. A little sacrifice and the terrible wog Gamal Abdel-Nasser would be drowned in the Nile; P&O would sail again unimpeded through the Bitter Lakes.

We too might of course be sacrificed – like the sublieutenant of boundless mountaineering spirit crucified by the Mau Mau on the slopes of Kilimanjaro. Then we might become the glamorous subject of a sermon, midday prayers, a school holiday.

Smarting under this tortured system, the boys tortured each other, imposed valueless rules and codes of conduct, obeyed imaginary hierarchies where accidents of origin and defects of nature were magnified.

Anguish behind, ahead, and on every horizon. Have I come full circle?

Since my time there the gardens surrounding the school have gradually fallen into dereliction, many of the great trees destroyed by gales, the magnificent magnolia avenue cleared for building, the dying beeches felled, and the fine evergreen planting round the Saxon chapel grubbed up. Ilex and oak are gone. Even the ancient chestnut – old when John of Gaunt was lord of the manor – has finally rotted away; and the scarlet horsechestnuts that dotted the lawn have been senselessly hacked back to forlorn stumps.

All this happened without those who worked in their shade realising it – or if they did regret the loss, saw it as the necessary price of progress, as the school acquired a series of mismatched outbuildings.

~

Rain blew in early in the afternoon. Everything turned a sad listless grey. The sea was so blue yesterday; now the boats lie abandoned in the grey.

Dungeness is quite deserted. No washing on the lines, and nobody in their gardens. I waited, hoping for a surprise visitor, like last weekend. Even the phone went dead.

Tuesday 18
Two days shuttered against the creeping cold – numbing headache.

More restless than ever at night. Unable to concentrate I tidy the studio, re-hang paintings, gild a background and walk ceaselessly back and forth between half-finished jobs. Turn the TV on and off. Wait for the phone to ring. Put off making any calls.

I've not seen anyone for five days now, find my own company heavy-going, the sound of a car stopping makes my heart miss a beat.

The headache might be a messenger from the virus, though I'm perfectly healthy otherwise. Perhaps the restlessness, the amnesia is the first sign of dementia.

~

Programme on TV about Wittgenstein which told us absolutely nothing. All I gathered was that he spent a lifetime 'debunking tradition' – which, or what, we never quite discovered. He lived the life of a neurotic recluse in a log cabin. A fellow traveller?

Always becoming, never arriving. Life is at a standstill – only ideas flash past. In such confusion I find myself running after them: Hey! Stop! Stop! But they escape, leaving me staring at a grey English spring.

~

I rise at seven and am asleep by ten. The hours between are filled with inde-cision. There are walls to paint, floors to scrub, washing and cooking. I hate cooking for myself, would sooner starve. The headache takes over and has me imagining.

Donny phones from NYC. They are waiting for Howard to die, hoping it will be soon. It's unimaginable, rushing him into the dark.

Only a year ago he was laughing on this settee as we took photos. A whole year now he has been dumbly caged in a New York apartment watch-ing the video in which he rehearsed Matt Dillon in a love scene for his film. Then it was all fun and games – in Bob Wilson's airy riverside loft, with the two of them falling over each other, and Matt accidentally burning a hole in his white T-shirt with a cigarette.

~

Outside, the wallflowers are battling it out with the cold wind.

Another circle of stones takes shape. My back aches terribly as I haul them up from the sea shore; perhaps that's why I have this headache.

Morbidly self-absorbed, I worry that I'm forgetting something important. But what was so important it needed remembering?

Now it was at this time Oedipus tore out his guilty eyes with his vengeful hand, drowning the sin of his shame in eternal night. Chaining his living soul in a slow death, he gives himself to the shadows, to the innermost recesses of his dwelling, shrines unseen of stars or sunlight; and yet with tireless wings the savage daylight of the mind hovers over him, and the crime-avenging Furies writhe in his breast.

~

At midday the sun returned and the breeze veered to the west. It was too cold to sit outside so I walked to the Long Pits. The woods are in leaf: the pear tree is blossoming; the ash also has purple flowers, and the silver birch, catkins and bright green leaves. I saw a peacock butterfly feeding on the gorse and everywhere the dwarf forget-me-not, which, if you blinked, you might not notice.

~

Egyptian seers placed the flowers of forget-me-not on the eyes of initiates to bring dreams; the flower was sacred to Thoth, god of wisdom.

There are many stories about the name. As a child I often wondered why 'forget-me-not'? Surely it is because this beautiful blue flower is so retiring you could easily miss it.

~

In any free moment I rushed to the Art School, beyond the sound of the bells. Bells masked the disorderly conduct of the day's affairs, the fatuous rules and dead principles which yet demanded the blind obedience characteristic of a totalitarian regime.

At the art school I established my own totalitarian state – art was frankly admitted to be incomprehensible, or risible, a thin-air fantasy of mad adventurers who'd sooner cut off an ear or sail for the South Seas than enter useful society, score goals or box their mates into bloody submission.

~

Van Gogh for a vase of flowers. Monet for the garden to grow them in.

Braque for fruit and vegetables and all the paraphernalia of the still life. Scott for his practical pots and pans to cook them in. And Elizabeth Frink for folly: a giant plaster Golem guarding the portal.

These were the eyes that informed my work at fourteen.

~

Sitting in a shaft of sunlight during English lessons I would watch the deep red flowers of the chestnut tree glowing in a sea of green. Red and Green preoccupied me more than the problems of Antony and Cleopatra: *The barge she sat in like a burnished throne / Moved on the water.* I floated out, up and away into the sunlight.

~

The art school became a fortress against another reality, a defence against an everyday existence that was awry. I filled the moat with flowers – painted flowers, as I no longer had anywhere to grow them. My work set itself up against the regime of tight little boys in grey with stiff upper lips.

Wednesday 19
Long walk to the west of the nuclear power plant, lit by shafts of sunlight under an angry slate sky. A few drops of rain.

This area is very bleak: flat shingle, a few patches of dead gorse in mine craters exploded at the end of the war. A row of pylons that stretch to the horizon crackle with electricity: under them, to the east of the power station, a road constructed of railway sleepers is slowly rotting.

The northern boundary is formed by the Hoppen Pits: an area of flooded gravel pits which are still being worked by one solitary rusting crane on a barge.

In the middle of the lake is an island covered with screaming gulls. On the horizon there is a drainage canal which runs into the sea.

Several ruined buildings, not much more than their foundations visible, have been colonised by elder. But most surprising are clumps of luxuriant bluebells and periwinkle, and a few purple irises – the plants must have been brought here and have naturalised.

~

The bluebell, *Hyacinthus nonscriptus*, is the hyacinth of the ancients, the flower of grief and mourning. Hyacinth, son of the king of Sparta, whose sparkling blue eyes and jet black hair enflamed Phoebus Apollo, whipped Zephyrus into a frenzy of desire; but the boy loved the sun god best, causing the wild west wind to seek a terrible revenge. One day as Hyacinth and Apollo were playing quoits Zephyrus caught a quoit in a whirlwind and smashed the boy's beautiful face, killing him. Grief-stricken, Apollo raised the purple flower from the drops of blood on which he traced the letters *ai ai*, so his anguish would forever echo through the spring.

Whenever you walk in a sunny bluebell wood, remember it is the heart of a passionate love. It is dangerous to kiss there, as the wind sighing in the branches will want to blow you and the boy apart. Your love may wilt and die as quickly as the flowers you pick, your hands will be stained with blood.

So leave the wood in peace, empty-handed. For the blue-eyed flower with its heavy fragrance only belongs to the sun.

And remember that Ovid said that Sparta was not ashamed of having produced Hyacinth, *for he is honoured there to this very day, and every year the Hyacinthian games are celebrated with festive displays, in accordance with ancient usage.*

Saturday 22
Still very cold, with the sky overcast.

I dug and built new circular flower beds to the side of the house; then I spent the evening gathering grey pebbles on the shore to fill the circular bed in the centre front.

In spite of the cold weather the garden is flourishing. The sea kale planted last year is in bud; and a very beautiful bearded iris, pale yellow and brown, is flowering. The elder, cut back by the easterly, is beginning to recover, and the new cuttings have all taken. The lavender cuttings are also doing well. Dill, cornflower, pennyroyal have all germinated, and this evening I planted seeds of fennel and horehound.

One of the fennel plants I put in last autumn has survived, and is thriving. And the self-seeded marigolds are popping up everywhere – one is already in bloom. Grape hyacinth and nasturtium have also seeded themselves.

But the prize goes to the borage: the clump that survived the winter is still in bloom, and new seedlings are coming up all the time.

Sunday 23
Forgetting his old habits, Apollo happily carried hunting nets, or directed a pack of hounds as he accompanied Hyacinth over the rough mountain ridges, and by constant companionship, added fuel to the fire of his love. One day, when the sun was halfway between the night that was over and the night that was to come, equally far from both, the god and the boy stripped off their garments, rubbed their bodies till they gleamed with rich olive oil and began to compete with each other throwing the broad discus.

~

We learnt nothing of the love myth of these heroes in a Dorset school in the 1950s – Ovid was off-limits. Instead we marched to the beat of Caesar's interminable *Gallic Wars*. The Latin teacher Mr. Gay (long before this word had any connotations except joyful abandon) confined himself to '*we undertook a forced march of 80 miles and set up camp.*' – Are you listening Jarman?

The Outward Bound Caesar dominated. We never heard of Caesar in make up and drag, the soldier's moll, or for that matter Alexander, the greatest general of all screwing Hyphaestus. If we had known that marriage between men was totally acceptable and on an equal footing in ancient Rome, or that the Olympic games were conducted in the nude, that the emperor Heliogabalus was a temple prostitute, or that Hadrian went mad with grief when his beautiful boyfriend Antinuous drowned in the Nile, or furthermore that the crack troops in the ancient world, the Theban band, were all fags, it would have thrown quite a different light on the first Latin word we had to decline

bellum, bellum, bellum.

Ancient history was an interminable war. All violence and no sex.

bellum, bellum – No *amo, amas.*

War underpinned an English education. After all, we were also an Empire – the sun shone out of the arses of the Royal Guards. But we never knew they were selling them when the Knightsbridge pubs closed; or that the detachment who guarded the Bank of England, where all the gilt of empire was deposited, were called 'the bum boys', on service to service the Officer-in-Charge; or that the proud sailors were missing the last train from Waterloo for ten bob and a blow job, clambering onto the four o'clock milk train still buttoning up.

In the dorm sex was smutty innuendo, surreptitious jerk-offs before the breakfast bell, sizing the length of each other's cocks in the showers – a well-thumbed expurgated copy of *Lady Chatterley* falling to pieces in our grubby hands – uncomfortable as we adolescents were with our bodies, with no-one to teach us, or love us – our cocks and bums a forbidden world; and the unknown female body the terrain of the Curse.

The bell would ring three times to summon us to assembly, where a certain Dr. Matthews, sex educator, would demonstrate to us scientifically, and with the help of an ancient epidiascope, the birds and the bees of Paradise, Adam and Eve and the old serpent VD. Here were diagrams and another terminology in Latin. We learnt the lexicography of desire only permitted after Holy Matrimony: fellatio, cunnilingus, coitus interruptus, penis and anus.

Dr. Matthews rummaged in his battered Gladstone bag, pulling out ancient slides as if from a lucky dip at a gymkhana. Silver hair awry, eyes glistening, the dirty old sex educator to the crowned heads of Europe eyed up his blushing audience who squirmed with embarrassment as their innermost secrets were revealed to them – huge images of private parts, 20ft pubescent and pre-pubescent cocks, balls dropping, huge lost sperms wandering into a slide rather than the fallopian.

Sections, diagrams. Our secrets were invaded, as when the doctor grabbed your balls in the first school medical and twizzled them about before letting the elastic of your pants snap back with a sting. 'What,' asked Dr. Matthews 'are little boys made of? – Slugs and snails and puppy dog's tails.'

After it was all over the good doctor gave private sessions to any boy who thought he had 'a problem'; but I never went, knew my 'problem' was so encompassing it could never be solved by him, even if that had been my wish.

~

At ten o'clock this morning a huge fox trotted by the end of the garden before ambling off into the broom. I've seen him several times at night, caught in headlights; but this is the first time I've seen him in daylight.

~

Dungeness has been declared a conservation area, though much of the suburbanisation the Council wants to avoid has already taken place. Fences are up. British Telecom has replaced the old red phone box with a nondescript glass one. And those fishermen who do not live here continue to litter the beach and build very untidy rubble roads.

The Council's letter forbids all this, and also the building of extensions more than one storey high – so bang goes my Tower of the Winds.

Tuesday 25

The dead north wind still holds spring at arm's length. I walked well-wrapped along the shore beyond the Ness. The bluebell woods are in flower, and carpets of bright yellow rape chequer the marsh.

Here every flower follows a different rhythm. The purple irises, so bitterly hurt in the easterly, have still not bloomed, as if they have drawn in on themselves and are counting the days till summer.

~

Old houses guard their secrets behind net curtains, or beneath brown lino brittle with age. I found this letter carefully wrapped with a condom. The envelope was not addressed, though embossed with a tuppence ha'penny oval with the King's head. It almost turned to dust in my hands.

6.11.52
Dear Miss Davis,
  *After thanking you for your kind letter, hopeing you are quite well
again. I are O.K. What a wicked world we live in. You seemed ardly
old enough to leave your mother to me when I saw you, and here you
are been married and drifted apart. Now I feel very sorry for you, you
are so lovely. Now about myself, sorry my wife found the second letter
you wrote asking me to talk on the phone to you. She has played up
merry hell since then. She is so jealous, she has given me hell of a time.
You see I are 67 years of age and only ever feel 18. She is two years
younger than me, she has not slept with me for two years. I ardly dare
go in the bedroom in my own house, I have had no connections for
years and I are eager as ever. If only I had a night with you I should
fancy that I was in Heaven. I don't know when I shall come to
London now, but I hope to see you somewhere sometime. You see we
are an old established family and for peace and quietness I let her have
her way. Please answer this . . .*

~

At the very moment this last sad love letter was hidden for ever under the
lino, my mother was packing in the manor house of Curry Malet, preparing
to move to Pakistan. As winter drew in she was alone in the moated strong-
hold of Guy de Malet, William the Conqueror's trusted lieutenant. She
would hear the ghosts tiptoeing across the flagstones and up the spiral staircase that led from the great A-frame hall.

The ghosts opened and closed the heavy oak doors, lifting the iron latches
as they came and went. The previous occupant of the house had witnessed a
materialisation: she had been combing her hair in the dressing mirror when
a girl appeared, whose anguish was glimpsed before she vanished – condemned to wait beyond the grave for her sweetheart, hung by Judge Jeffreys
in the 'bloody assize' at Taunton.

Man hath still either toyes, or care,
He hath no root, nor to one place is ty'd,
But ever restless and irregular
About this earth do run and ride.
He knows he hath a home, but scarce knows where;
He sayes it is so far
That he hath quite forgot how to go there;
He knocks at all doors, strays and roams.
Nay hath not so much wit as some stones have
Which in the darkest nights do point to their homes,

By some hid sense their maker gave;
Man is the shuttle to whose winding quest
And passage through these looms
God orders motion, but ordained no rest.

~

With ghosts for company my mother finished The Inventory – a necessary part of Forces' life: counting the knives and forks. Meanwhile my father was a guest at another ghostly banquet: the H-bomb tests in Nevada, where he was being entertained as part of an armaments mission for the Royal Pakistan Air Force. And I was counting the days at school, and eating the unpalatable rationed food, 'Mrs. Monger's toenails'. We were all to be reunited after the New Year – and a boat ride halfway across the world.

~

Alone with my mother in the bleak functional rooms of our temporary home on the outskirts of Karachi I sensed her isolation. She arrived knowing no-one; my father had been delayed at the Test Site in Nevada. In this strange home she was faced with a large contingent of servants and their families, and a way of life (though she had been born in Calcutta at the other end of the subcontinent) that must have been a shock after the quiet seclusion of the stone house in Somerset.

Lost, bored and disorientated, I walked round the garden fortress, with its dazzling bougainvillaea inhabited by singing gekkoes. Outside lay a wasteland of dry stone gullies and thorn scrub, populated by starving wild dogs.

One night at dusk a swarm of locusts flew in from the desert, a struggling cloud, wave after wave of them landing in our green oasis. I watched them float in; they jumped out of plants and rustled in the trees. Noting my discomfort, the garden sweeper picked some of them up, snapped them in his fingers and ate them like chips. I turned away, and sat on the gate to watch the camel trains pass and disappear along the dusty road.

~

Shepway Borough Council is still 'anxious that Dungeness should not be suburbanised'. Their circular forbids fences, building in unsympathetic materials, altering the size of a house substantially and, of course, any construction more than a storey high.

The notice is very silly, as there is no group of houses in the South-East that could have grown in such an unplanned manner. There are old railway carriages, towers, breeze block houses – a shanty town of do-it-yourself: wood, bricks, metal, asbestos – a riot of building materials.

The notice, like all bureaucratic intervention, simplifies, is muddled and doesn't relate to the character of the area.

It seems that we the inhabitants are to be penalised while big bully companies are allowed to get away with it, building nuclear power stations and destroying old telephone kiosks. A letter has gone to Shepway to this effect as, after chasing through the labyrinth of Telecom, I found out that it was the Council's responsibility.

It is not the good manners of Dungeness that have made it so delightful, rather the haphazard growth and rusting past. The old army buildings, *PLUTO* pipelines, even the great nuclear power station gives this landscape its charm. The Council's notice should really read *Build whatever you want but don't demolish anything. Let it fall apart in its good time; or, like the railway carriages, find another use for it.*

Thus we would have kept old Gilbert Scott's red phone boxes and have the new beside it – the best of both worlds. For Dungeness is essentially a landscape of past endeavours: two lighthouses, two lifeboat stations, even two nuclear power stations. And these, we are told, won't be demolished either.

Wednesday 26
The hawthorn and birch are in bright green leaf; the pear is in blossom; the ash tree buds are breaking. The primrose and violets are disappearing till next year under invading nettles. As I walk past, the snobbish wheatears complain – *tch! tch!* – in the flaming gorse.

Spring dances on in soft white clouds.

~

Ministers attend a seminar on global warming.

~

There's a menacing sunset beyond the nuclear power station: livid yellows and inky blacks with a deep scarlet gash. As shadows close in, the landscape turns grey; the sky has sucked up all its colour. An icy wind gets up – rain before night's end is forecast.

~

They say the answer is more nuclear power stations.

~

Our little wood shivers. What of the earth below these angry skies? A tree goes, a road is widened, a meadow ploughed, more quarries, another house.

Thursday 27

My father's family left Coombe Farm, Uploman in the 19th century to farm the Canterbury Plain in New Zealand. My full name – Michael Derek *Elworthy* – retains a distant link with the Somerset village of that name.

Tyme tryeth truth.

My father told me that the Jarmans linked names with the Elworthys early in the eighteenth century when they married the last of the line. When he arrived here in 1928 he still had relatives in Exeter. Jarman is a fairly common West Country name. Sylvestre Houedard, the Benedictine, told me the name was Celtic – St. Germain was a distant Breton cousin.

~

When my parents moved to Pakistan in 1953, I was left behind to spend my holidays in Kilve, under the shadow of Danesborough, with Aunt Isobel in her cottage Great Beats – converted from old farm outbuildings which had sunk deep in the rich red Somerset loam.

Isobel was green-fingered, had the kindest country smile. *Oklahoma* on the gramophone, blue cotton dresses with polka dots, maidenhair ferns watered with cold tea, a cat and a boxer puppy, bulb catalogues, scented balsam poplars, a vegetable garden. And an elder sister, Helen, who had a black Daimler that roared along the sunken lanes of the Quantocks, clipping hedges.

~

It was almost 200 years since Dorothy Wordsworth wrote her journal in Alfoxden. Up the lane in the 1950s little had changed. I too gathered worts on Danesborough, which she often climbed with Coleridge. We also

> sat a considerable time upon the heath, its surface restless and glittering with motion of the withered grasses, and the waving of the spider's threads. On our return the mist was still hanging over the sea, but the opposite coast clear, and the rocky cliffs distinguishable in the deep coombe. As we stood upon the sunless hill, we saw miles of grass, light and glittering and the insects passing.

I would pick up my large drawing board, take paper and charcoal, and walk the lanes, stopping to make drawings under the singing telephone wires – then on down to the beach, past the ruined ivy-clad chantry with its enormous overturned poplars at the stream's edge. On a beach of grey slate I would find spiral ammonites in rock pools; and it was here that I built my first driftwood sculptures, and photographed them before the tide came in.

~

Three years ago I returned to Kilve. Stopping in the new drive-in café, I asked the waitress if Aunt Isobel still lived in Great Beats. She looked blank. I checked the phone book – she was not listed. The house was deserted. We drove down the lane, with its views of the sea and Hinkley Point nuclear power station, past the old mill, now a neat Youth Hostel. Even the poplars were tidied up and the chantry had become a busy car-park. The whole area had been declared 'of outstanding natural beauty'.

Today I called Telecom to see if they could find Aunt Isobel's number – perhaps if not in Kilve, Holford? 'There is no record,' they said.

~

The cold wind has fallen, the sea has turned an opaque jade. I rummage through my books – the Wordsworth still has some markers of faded red and blue papers, used for a collage all those years ago. Dorothy's journal captures the day:

I never saw such a union of earth, sky and sea: the clouds beneath our feet spread themselves to the water, and the clouds of the sky almost joined them.

~

I walk in this garden
Holding the hands of dead friends
Old age came quickly for my frosted generation
Cold, cold, cold they died so silently
Did the forgotten generations scream?
Or go full of resignation
Quietly protesting innocence
Cold, cold, cold they died so silently

Linked hands at four AM
Deep under the city you slept on
Never heard the sweet flesh song
Cold, cold, cold they died so silently

I have no words
My shaking hand
Cannot express my fury
Sadness is all I have,
Cold, cold, cold they died so silently

Matthew fucked Mark fucked Luke fucked John

Who lay in the bed that I lie on
Touch fingers again as you sing this song
Cold, cold, cold they died so silently

My gilly flowers, roses, violets blue
Sweet garden of vanished pleasures
Please come back next year
Cold, cold, cold I die so silently

Goodnight boys,
Goodnight Johnny,
Goodnight,
Goodnight.

Saturday 29

The weather lost its chill. For the first time this year I worked in the garden in short sleeves, slept with the window open and awoke at dawn. A white sea mist soon cleared for a bright sunny day, slightly overcast.

In spite of the cold April many of the flowers are well ahead of themselves after the warm winter: the first sea kale flowers are out and the sea campion, cranesbill and purple vetch are bright with bloom.

~

John Vere Brown drove over from Hastings last night. He's photographed the garden, says it reminds him of a Tibetan temple garden: the sticks and stones are the prayer flags.

In my poem *Under The Blue Sky*, which he's used in his article, he thought the idea of the eternal return was horrific. I read him a page of *Lux the Poet*, where the unfortunate Kali, cast out of Heaven, is condemned to perform a million good deeds in endless reincarnations. Everything she does ends disastrously.

I think stones can be reincarnated quite safely, but agree with John that we should quietly disappear. Though the dolt who keeps driving his Land Rover all over the shingle, destroying plants, should be condemned to return. Also the Borough Council, as reincarnation obviously employs a large bureaucracy.

The Borough Council, answering my letter, says the phone box is 'street furniture' and the responsibility of Lydd Town Hall. According to my neighbour, the officials there 'haven't two beans to rub together, not in their pockets, nor in their heads'.

~

This morning, Thomas, the big black cat that prowls through the brambles, caught a mouse. I went to investigate and found the poor thing half-chewed. I wonder if domestication and its special relationship with humankind has made dear pussy so cruel. It rolled around, legs in the air, flinging the poor mouse up and about for nearly half an hour before eating it. I can't be too upset with it. I caught dozens of the little beasts in traps two years ago as the autumn drew in – nine in one evening.

~

My front room is painted a clear translucent Naples yellow with a white ceiling, it's a great contrast to the other rooms which are all varnished tongue and groove. The door was removed, so it is now covered with old blue velvet curtains for winter warmth, the battered Knoll sofa is also covered with old purple velvets, above it Robert Medley's oil painting *An Autobiographical Incident* which he painted in 1976 from photos of the first scene of *Sebastiane*. Robert's paintings are dappled with woodland light, elusive as the fritillary, they tell their secrets slowly.

In the four corners of the room are sentinel posts, driftwood from the seashore, hung with necklaces of pierced stones, dedicated to the Hinney Beast. On the walls are several more driftwood pieces, a garlanded sheep's skull *Night Life at the Fifth Quarter of the Globe*, a gold and black painting from 1982 *Render Unto Caesar*, and the painting from my childhood in Rome, Nada's painting of Salita del Grillo where many years later I spent an Easter holiday.

The furniture is warehouse packing case, mostly from skips or derelict buildings, on the table is a crucifix that has been 'assisted' – one of a batch from Florence. This one has jewel like glass fragments, bullets and rusty nails; a small found sculpture of a hollow stone containing a gold ring; the large candle I used on the altar in *War Requiem*; and a jet black earthenware pot – the most perfect container for marigolds; oh! and lastly on either side of the fireplace are diamond paned Tudorbethan doors brought here from a scrapyard in London, covering alcoves packed with books.

Sunday 30

Shut your eyes and think of the ugliest seaside development you have ever seen, open them and behold! Greatstone. Nothing that any of you have imagined could be worse than the mean little houses that throttle the seashore here – a lasting monument to greed, aided and abetted by a mindless supine local government. Can you find in these four miles of houses one constructed with love or care?

This is not covered up by their names: *Ben Venue, Costa Lotta, Fort George,* and *Sea Drift*. Behind them, Hopeville: a scatter of concrete and caravans. Imagine for a moment a sharp agent advertising a holiday camp in

Siberia.

The beauty of the sea shore here has gone for ever. At this moment a Berlin wall of shingle hides the rape of the last wild expanse as it's gouged out for road gravel.

Beyond it the Listening Wall – a massive concrete semicircle built in the war so that we could hear enemy planes coming across the channel – is slowly falling into disrepair, surrounded by warning notices: *Trespassers Will Be Prosecuted*. But just who should be prosecuted for this mess? Perhaps several generations of pompous myops festooned with mayoral chains in Lydd.

I wonder how many crooked deals and backhanders the Listening Wall could tell of. But it, like the poor landscape, cannot speak, only listen.

~

The Listening Wall is the grandest concrete structure in the Kingdom – its scale Olympic, its symmetry Attic, kith and kin to the great Moghul observatories that listened to the stars. The Wall had its two ears tuned to earthly conversation, could hear a whisper over the horizon – or the shouts and curses of Dunkirk, the drone of enemy bombers in Normandy.

An Acropolis worthy of pilgrimage, its graffiti dedicates it to Haile Selassie, Lion of Judah. Even great Lutyens' cenotaph or the many monuments of battle lack its power. Here, lost in the shingle, reflected in the lake, beside this great monument falling into ruin, you can lament the heroes if you wish. Perhaps this is its finest hour, alone with nothing particular to listen to.

MAY

Monday 1

A cuckoo echoes across the marshes. I took a long walk this evening and in the dying light discovered a patch of periwinkle deep in the wood. Lady's smock was flowering by one of the old mine craters. I hadn't noticed it before. The island of bracken is unfolding.

May Day warm and overcast. Neither an indoor nor an outdoor day – strangely lethargic. My purple iris finally opened.

Before turning in, I watered the garden, as I'm away for ten days and the forecast is for warm weather.

Tuesday 2

Walking across the excavations in the precinct of Salisbury cathedral, I noticed Julian Sands waving to me in the sunlight.

In the cathedral I found myself in a corner with wooden shelves stacked with fragments of roof bosses and stone capitals gathering dust. In the queue in front of me was Robert Medley, looking very old: bareheaded, dressed like a monk, he was complaining about the ring he had been given – it did not fit, and was engraved with the name of some 18th century philosopher.

I sat down in the back row and waited for the service. The seats were in circular tiers; my row was upholstered in a faded blue material. I looked up at the gothick pinnacles disappearing into the dark. The young man in the row in front of me suddenly started to kick his heels. I moved, as he was hurting my shins – his mother turned and smiled at me with embarrassment.

I found myself mounted on a dappled grey shire horse with a middle-aged American tourist. We were crossing the ruined market square in front of the new cathedral. We passed a small child and some jugglers on stilts – small as the background figures in a Breughel.

The horse had grown enormously, and the American lady made some remark. I didn't reply but felt sorry for her: What had brought her to this god-forsaken town?

As we reached the other side of the square a black bull materialised like an incubus, and was wheeling around a matador, pawing the ground. Dark and menacing it grew like a thundercloud. The grey horse bolted, throwing the American lady off. I clung on for dear life, tried to talk to it, but couldn't find the words.

It was the violence of its bucking that woke me in the early dawn. The fog horn booming. I ran the nightmare through my mind and went back to sleep.

Wednesday 3
Back in London I woke to brilliant sunshine. I spent a couple of hours filming around King's Cross station – the grandeur of Cubitt's building still marred by 'improvements', glitzy pavements and the jumble of ticket offices.

~

Stations attract all those who have no journey to take; they provide warmth, a roof in a sudden storm, and the illusion of being at the hub of things.

Breughel would have recorded this: a shrunken man on a wheelchair driving around in circles; old men shuffling past in shabby suits, demob refugees lost in time; tense, pale, clerks, their ill-fitting trousers shiny with wear, threadbare briefcases; bleach-blonde mismatched office girls, hairdos and bulging jeans.

A boy with black nail varnish and tarnished jewels limps across the concourse. He stops and rummages through a litter bin. A bulky man on crutches with a lopsided theatrical turban heaves into view, cast adrift by a charity shop. A lean boy stripped to the waist walks back and forth with a pinched accusing face and wild darting eyes. A tragic tide spirals round gurgling like water disappearing down a plug hole.

I carry on filming. No-one notices, except the lonely ice-cream boy with a straw boater and striped apron. He is stuck under the large advert that reads *The Warhol Diary: if you're not in it, you're in it.*

Saturday 6
Three days of a May heatwave – the greenhouse effect sets in. Dungeness is to disappear in 100 years' time beneath the waves along with its power station – which, it's said, will take 100 years to dismantle. A meteor passes close to the earth, and the ozone hole shifts over southern Australia.

Monday 8
HB dreamed of Howard last night.

Tuesday 9
Donny left a message to say that Howard had died.

Wednesday 10

Glorious weather and three day shoot completed. A very happy experience, everyone excited to be back together again, all the good looking boys giving each other the gentle eye. David, who HB found at his gym, sparkles in the camera. Although he's never done this before, he does everything with the precision of one born to act. Asked to kiss Peter he did so without embarrassment – I explained to him how one screen kiss from a boy like him could set 1000 hearts free, he understood.

As we drove home I dreamt of a grand procession, like the Parthenon frieze, of naked young men with wands and torches, trumpets and banners, a triumph over death for dear Howard, figures draped in diaphanous silks with golden crowns and oiled torsos, naked youths on elephants, leading white oxen with gilded horns bearing all the heroes of history, Alexander, Hadrian, Michelangelo, Whitman . . .

Thursday 11

The *People* has a lurid article: *Movie Boss With AIDS – Glad to die in a shack!* What people do to sell newspapers! I don't know how they can live with their consciences – though, of course, out of use so long, they have shrivelled to the size of an appendix.

~

Laurence and Phillip's *Know What I Mean* televised at 11:30pm.

I think it was a little too near the knuckle for the programmers, so went out late rather than at 7:00 (the normal slot). I like the film, particularly the beginning with its word game, and the section at the end: painting in Dungeness. It seemed calm. The conversations about the films were breathless and defensive. I liked my observation that Section 28 was an attack on the family – I wish more people would talk down at the politicians, they have much too much importance. Politics combines all the seven deadly sins and is the forgotten eighth.

Friday 12

Several phone calls, all affirmative about the profile. Spent the whole morning with the *Folkestone Herald*: now the virus has reached the seaside let's hope this is the last of it.

One journalist had not heard of Section 28. This is how this government works, on ignorance. 'We had no idea this was happening.' Really, the *English* are a dozy supine lot, and spineless.

~

Visited the martello tower at Dymchurch. Not much for 80p: a few old postcards and a South Ken girl from English Heritage. Though the 'base-ment' was deliciously cool.

A sunny but very windy day. Read Richard Crashaw's *Hope*:

> *And he answered them nothing.*
> *O mighty nothing! unto thee,*
> *Nothing, we owe all things that bee:*
> *God spake once when hee all things made;*
> *He said all when hee nothing said.*
> *The world was made with nothing then,*
> *T'is made by nothing now again.*

Saturday 13

The hawthorn is in flower. The first elder blossoms are out; the wild pear has set fruit (my cuttings are thriving); the gorse is fading and the broom is coming into its own, the bushes skirted with gold.

The sheep's sorrel, no more than a couple of inches high, has turned the shingle a deep rust red as far as the eye can see, leaving the islands of dead brambles looking like mounds of bleached bones.

In this burnished landscape whites and greys are thrown into sharp relief. The sun beats down, though the wind has kept the butterflies in hiding; apart from the coppers I only saw a solitary white. In nooks and crannies the bird's foot trefoil, bacon-and-eggs, is beginning to flower; also the yellow rattle and treacle mustard.

~

On warm nights the drunken scent of the May caresses lovers under the sighing trees of Hampstead Heath. This is how I would remember it. Though others say its scent is cloying, the smell of the great plague of London.

My grandmother said it was unlucky, and should never be brought into the home. Her gardener, Moore, was married to May – which puzzled me as a child. Why should anyone have such an unlucky name? But the May could bring good luck: Wasn't the crown of England found in a thorn thicket? Here on the marsh, it was precious for building sea defences and protected by severe laws. You could lose a hand for cutting a bush. The blossom re-minds me of clotted cream and the heady visions of Samuel Palmer: *White in full power from the first – deadly dark browns laid on at once.*

~

HB's mam says May is unlucky because the crown of thorns was made from it.

Sunday 14

The cold wind that has blown for the last two days dropped. It rained in the night, and the clouds soon cleared. It was much warmer.

In the last week the garden has grown before my eyes. All the seedlings, dill, horehound, nasturtium, cornflower, Californian poppy and calendula, are planted out. A small pot of southernwood is a new addition.

Other plants fail to survive. Tarragon and thyme have died in the sharp winds. But rosemary has taken; also the purple sage, marigold and borage seed themselves. The sea kale are growing after months in which they seemed suspended – the huge plants from last year are in flower; the elder has recovered. Sea pea has germinated and poppies are in bud; the foxgloves I transplanted are also doing well. Most of the irises are flowering. All the lavender, curry plant and santolina are in bud. The clump of borage which started to flower in January is still in bloom. So are the wallflowers and aubretia.

After several false starts the garden is on its way. The roses are looking healthy – the exceptions are *Foetida bicolor* and *Frühlingsmorgen*. Last year's plants have established themselves: the burnet roses are covered with buds, and the pale yellow flowers of canary bird are out. In the front garden the bugle is in flower.

~

I chained myself to this landscape.

~

I find it difficult to write each day, but if I don't I'm swamped with guilt. Where does the compunction come from?

Perhaps I inherited it from Dad – he could never keep still for a moment; even when reading a newspaper he would tap his foot keeping time to silence. Back and forth I go into the garden, like the boy with anorexia who weighed himself every five minutes. At rest, a nervous pit quickly develops in my stomach and overwhelms me, forcing my mind to change direction.

I'm sleeping better, even have nights when I do not wake. But awake, I have the concentration of a grasshopper. Only the pressure of a film set keeps me focused for a day.

~

HB says I'm only content when under pressure or have something I can worry about. But what *do* I worry about? The garden mostly: the hurting winds and scalding sun. I worry about my stomach, as the crypto-whatever that's got hold of it leaves me with nausea. I worry about fire. I go round and round the house checking for cigarette butts and sparking switches.

I can sit for half an hour with a book – novels die in my hands. I'm left with poetry. History, biography or a new James Hillman will keep me concentrating.

An hour on a painting, fifteen minutes cooking . . . there's no time in a day. I'm up by seven, eight at the latest; I'm hardly washed and brushed up when midday is upon me. There is less time in the country than the city, Neil Tennant said last night. It surprised him at first.

Then there is the problem of work. When a telegram arrived on Wednesday from the opera house in Lyon asking me to direct the Strauss/Wilde *Salome*, I panicked: anything that removes me from Dungeness unsettles me.

~

How you can live in that bleak landscape? Asked the lady from the *Folkestone Herald*.

It's much more interesting than Folkestone, I said.

A nuclear power station in your backyard?

Yes. But it's yours as well. North Wales found itself the backyard of Chernobyl. At least I can see it.

It didn't convince her.

~

Dungeness has luminous skies: its moods can change like quicksilver. A small cloud here has the effect of a thunderstorm in the city; the days have a drama I could never conjure up on an opera stage.

Monday 15

Timothy Dalton called across the restaurant and invited us down to 'The Rose' to sign a petition against its demolition. The remains of the Elizabethan theatre are right alongside the site of my old warehouse on Bankside, of which nothing remains at all.

A group of young men I recognised from god-knows-where have mounted a vigil round the fence, which is decorated with ribbons and flowers and quotations like a pilgrims' shrine. I talked briefly to an archeologist, telling him of the many buildings and beautiful old alleys that had been swept away: Paris Gardens at Upper Ground; Horseshoe Alley. The most grievous loss: an almost complete bear pit, built into a group of ramshackle warehouses which had been a hat factory.

One old caretaker was still there. When he showed me around he told me that mercury had been used to get the shiny black of the Victorian topper, and the little old men who worked in the poisonous fumes had become as mad as hatters.

Tuesday 16

The AIDS charities' tie-up with the art world is in no-one's interest, as the big names like David Hockney and Gilbert and George, plastered across the press, are used to give the illusion that a caring society is caring. However welcome, half a million is a drop in the ocean, and the publicity lets the government off the hook. All these events should be prefaced by a rider on the part of the organisers –

In the face of continuing government inertia, we are holding this sale.

Friday 19

After three weeks of cloudless days, with temperatures in the seventies, the Ness is tinder-dry. The moss and grass are brittle and crunch under your feet. Thistles and plantain are wilting, and all the other spring flowers have withered. The shimmering colours of March have evaporated in the heat and the yellowing grasses are set off by the blazing broom, and white and red valerian. At the shoreline a white froth of sea kale breaks across the shingle, its delicious scent caught in the air.

The season is still in advance of itself: flaming May has brought June's flowers out in a rush. The sun's up – blood red at 5:00, and sets the same ruddy colour in an ominous haze at 8:30. The atmosphere is thick, but a cool breeze blows off the sea in the morning, clearing the skies by midday. Then, as it drops away, the haze returns.

The woods by the Long Pits are dusty with fluff from the sallow, which carpets the ground like cotton wool and makes you sneeze. Through it, red and black burnet moths flutter uncertainly. On the lake the swans have four very small cygnets darting about the yellow flag irises.

~

While watching a delicate blue damselfly I noticed a purple-grey plant at the water's edge, which turned out to be wild mint. Picked a couple of sprigs and brought them home to plant.

~

The yellow flag *Iris pseudocorus* is called locally 'segg', from the Anglo-Saxon for a short sword – known also as Jacob's sword, the flower with which he fought the angel. The flag is fleur-de-lys, flower of Saint Louis, the emblem of the Crusaders, the lily of France.

~

The savour or smell of mint rejoiceth the heart of man, for which they used to strew it in chambers.

In ancient Greece, where every part of the body was perfumed by a different scent, mint was used under the arms. In the Middle Ages it was used for whitening the teeth.

Menthe was a nymph whom Pluto loved – changed to this plant by Proserpine in a fit of jealousy.

Saturday 20

This landscape without visible boundaries is yet jealous of its privacy. Wandering across it, unhindered by fence or hedge, you stumble across piles of rubbish. Maybe that old car still belongs to someone. Who owns the corrugated hut blown sideways at the seashore? Its workbench is strewn with pots of rusting nails, spanners, rasps, an old vice, anchors, and coils of wire – a haven for ghostly ancestors to shelter from a brutish December easterly.

Time and tide have shipwrecked a huge tree, whose gnarled roots, bleached and bony, still grasp the rocks torn up with it. Who sat on those old canvas chairs, warped by the passing seasons, carefully placed alongside each other waiting for their owner's return?

I walk along the seashore each day, and it guards its secrets. Who plunged these anchors into their shingly graves? This rusting shadow on the ground was once somebody's bed. Old winches and hawsers, graves of toil and memories of angry seas – dissolving.

~

Worked in the garden all day. It was close, hot as an oven, the sun a dull red ball shrouded in heat haze. I repotted the geranium cuttings taken last month, and planted out the larger plants from last autumn. These old-fashioned geraniums, *Paul Crampnel*, are the only ones I'll have – all the modern ones seem muddy, bodged by some amateur colourist.

All the seeds I planted are now up: dill, fennel, horehound, pennyroyal and chives. The flowers as well: nasturtium, night scented stock, marigold, aquilegia, borage. The foxgloves are coming out, both the wild and cultivated ones; the irises are still blooming. The pale blue plant which has never produced flowers is particularly beautiful.

I lifted and divided the plants which have flowered.

The roses have taken – I've lost only three. The canarybird and burnet from last year are covered with blossom. The soapwort has many tiny dusty-pink flowers.

As the sun set I watered the garden.

~

I always thought of foxglove as a flower of the woods – deep in the shade, beloved of the bumble bee and little people. But the foxgloves of the Ness are a quite different breed. Strident purple in the yellow broom, they stand exposed to wind and blistering sunshine, as rigid as guardsmen on parade.

There they are at the edge of the lakeside, standing to attention, making a splash – no blushing violets these, and not in ones or twos but hundreds, proud regiments marching in the summer, with clash of cymbals and rolling drums. Here comes June. Glorious, colourful June.

~

The foxglove, *Digitalis pupurea*, folksglove, or fairyglove – whose speckles and freckles are the marks of elves' fingers, is also called *dead man's fingers*. It contains the poison Digitalis, first used by a Dr. Withering in the 18th century to cure heart disease. Foxglove is hardly mentioned in older herbals – Gerard says, *it has no use in medicine, being hot and dry and bitter*. The 'glove' comes from the Anglo-Saxon for a string of bells, 'gleow'.

Sunday 21

Where did the best of the gnome stories come from? I remembered it in the car this afternoon, did I read it somewhere? Or did someone, perhaps Tilda, tell me it?

The gnome garden was famous, and its prize, a particularly fine old gnome, stood in the centre of the lawn, staring into a lily pond. It had always been that way since time immemorial. One day, though, his owners were horrified to discover he had disappeared in the night. Nothing could console them.

A week later a postcard arrived from Switzerland; it read 'Perfect skiing weather with a good fall of snow last week, climbing the Matterhorn to-morrow, love, the Gnome'.

Some more weeks passed, 'Mount Etna, Sicily. Glorious weather and sightseeing, temples of Agrigento tomorrow, snorkelling in the straights of Messina caught between Scylla and Charybdis, love the Gnome.'

'Thebes, Egypt. Temples are grand, deeply moved by ancestral statues, Valley of the Kings tomorrow, Luxor, the great pyramids, in the lap of the lotus, the Gnome.'

'Kashmir. Smoking ganja with a view of the high Himalayas, marvellous view, the Gnome.'

'Bangkok. Sea food, beautiful girls, an idyll . . .' and so on.

Nearly a year passed when back in Somerset the owners of the gnome garden were surprised to see the gnome back staring at the lily pond. He was sporting a suntan and a pair of dark glasses and had left a note in the porch 'Glad to be home. Gnome.'

Wednesday 24

Went to the BFI to view the test of the second reel of *Jubilee*, reprinted from the old interneg in 35mm. It is in amazing condition. The BFI is ordering two new prints.

The film's a mess! And very rude. Hectoring annoying dialogue, or should I say monologue? The graffiti, though, are great. You could never see them on the TV, but on the big screen they shout out: *Is this sex or isn't it?* over a stark naked Jenny Runacre wearing the state crown; and over the sex scene, *Chelsea suck cock*. Healey's budget strategy in ruins.

~

Loathsome inept youth-orientated arts programme which drops any issue before it has picked it up. Devalues everything, all ideas, all values. How I hate this glup. What about Dada? said Julian. Well, Dada worked from ideas, had its own rules, threw out the artists who didn't meet its criteria. These stupid plastic presenters with hairstyles have a second in Eng. Lit. and a first in self-promotion. They are two-dimensional. Body art, tattoos and piercings thrown in with Yves Klein . . . though my Simon [Turner – composer of my film soundtracks] did the music, nothing could be more of a travesty. If *Mondo Cane* killed Yves' corporal self, this will kill his spirit.

Some weeks ago they rang me. I agreed to cooperate only if the work explained Yves and didn't turn him into a circus – perhaps an interview followed by as many minutes or seconds of blank blue soundless TV? Of course all they really wanted was to have me as a ringmaster whilst they stripped off some girl to offend the public – that was the measure of their ambition. All the time sheltering behind Yves.

Oh how I hate this unseeing. Yves' *Symphonie Monoton* and *Anthropometrics* were for a select invited audience, who were requested to show their respect by arriving in evening dress – this is the fifties, Paris, and that was what it was about, exclusivity.

The photos are the evidence, the performance a secret. The enemy is the spurious egalitarianism and lack of concentration of the media. Maybe the best way would be to black out TV sets. Furious phone calls: 'I've paid my license.' Yes but it doesn't give you the right to pry – this is a private programme of the void, if you wish to see it you'll pay the dues as well and if you fail you'll be fined.

IKB

spirit in matter

Thursday 26

At dinner last night Julian spoke excitedly of the night before at Poplar
baths, where, quite unexpectedly when the gates closed at nine, he found
himself in an orgy in the steam room, he was picked up by a young black
man and taken home. Something which would have never happened in the
daylight world. When I was young society seemed so totally restrictive I
found that the time I did not spend on the piers or bath houses wasted. The
heterosexuality of everyday life enveloped and asphyxiated me. I numbed
myself to this life – something which all gay men and women do even if they
bury the hurt of it.

~

Deep orange moon full and heavy in a sultry sky.

10:30, I take a deep breath, a double vodka and a taxi to 'The Heath' stop
outside Jack Straw's castle and walk down through the car park. It's here
that danger lurks – on the fringes. The dark woodlands seem by comparison
safe and friendly. Do the gangs of queerbashers who haunt the mind lie in
wait, thwarted and perverted guardians of propriety – or are they just in the
imagination? This year's stories flash past. Julian says he was hemmed in
this car park by a gang, armed with scaffolding poles, who drove him down
shouting abuse; he narrowly escaped being hurt.

Someone was murdered here last year, and for several months the police
staked out the place taking names and addresses, and one of my friends into
the bushes for a blow job before they let him go. Singly the police are often
friendly. For many gay men there is a thrill to the idea of trapping a policeman between the sheets. However, en masse they quickly turn menacing;
Richard said he was certain that a gang with torches and nightsticks he narrowly evaded were young, off-duty policemen. He said they were beating
people savagely, until a police car in the car park sounded its siren calling
them back to base.

All this said, I don't want to put any of you off, on the contrary, though
even among gay men I have to admit the Heath has a 'reputation'. It is considered by many to be off-bounds, for two reasons: as a symbol of the dark
into which the gay world has been driven by heterosexual censure, and also
as a reinforcement of the critics' respectability, that said nothing goes on on
the Heath that doesn't go on behind net curtains, the 'respectable' are found
in a smoke filled dungeon, such as 'Heaven' – a nightclub with an air con-
ditioning system that would please the Prince of Darkness, deep in the
bowels of the earth.

Location is the key to respectability, it's like cocaine in the boardroom
and the needle of the streets. But for those who know, the alfresco fuck is
the original fuck. Didn't the Garden of Eden come before the house which

hid our nakedness? Sex on the Heath is an idyll pre-fall. Did Adam mastur-bate until God hacked out his rib to create Eve?

All the Cains and Abels you could wish for are out on a hot night, the may blossom scents the night air and the bushes glimmer like a phosphorescent counterpane in the indigo sky. Under the great beeches some boys with gypsy faces have lit a fire, which they stoke sending sparks flying, smiling faces flushed with the heat. In the dark for a brief moment age, class, wealth, all the barriers are down. An illusion you say, I know but what a sweet one. Many of the men here lead straight daylight lives. There's a soldier from Aldershot in sneakers, training trousers and T-shirt; motor cyclist's studs sparkling in the firelight lounging against a tree. Others sit at a distance, someone has a ghetto-blaster, there's music.

At least two people recognise me and say 'Hello Derek', one says 'When are you ever off TV, Mr. Jarman?' Conversations are brief, though I have talked the night away, here it's quiet, none of the decibels that have invaded every other public space to drown a conversation. The Heath has its own plan you can soon get acquainted with it. Some stay near the car park, others move further down the path, and the leatherboys have their own sanctuary down the hill. But people wander everywhere.

Sex these days is as safe as you'll find it, few risk penetration, it's mostly confined to what my mum would call 'horseplay'. No-one who comes here need leave without an orgasm, though many come to walk and forget the frustrations of the day. A tall fine looking short-haired lad – ten spasms shooting come everywhere – we chatted for several minutes then he said he must be off home, but hours later he was still there. I paid the price of this sweet folly, unable to get a taxi back to Charing Cross at 3:00 in the morn-ing. I was so thankful I was walking down hill all the way.

After a week's absence I have visited the Heath several times recently, it is always exciting and joyous. The deep silence, the cool night air, the pools of moonlight and stars, the great oaks and beeches – all old friends. The saplings I've watched grow to trees forty foot high in the years since I first came in the sixties.

The place has changed, there was a time when any number of friends were out on a warm weekend. Sometimes it almost resembled a garden party, joints were rolled, hip flasks produced. People laughing and shouting, like a midnight swim. In the seventies it became even less inhibited, but, as always, once you are over the invisible border your heart beats faster and the world seems a better place.

Saturday 27

A cold easterly has blown through the last two sunny days making them surprisingly chilly. As there has been no rain for weeks, the ground, already parched, is like burnt toast. Each day there is less green in view, more faded ochre splashed with the white of sea kale, and the brilliant yellow broom.

At midday a hearse drives past piled high with flowers: Mr. Thomas, who won the pools last year and bought a Rolls, has passed by.

Two redstarts scurry through the dried grasses, and a small blue dives for cover in the soapwort.

The wind blows – it unsettles me. The constant buffeting scatters thoughts and concentration. This week has brought the summer flowers out in a rush. There are poppies and oxeye, honesty, woody nightshade, dog rose, convolvulus, and pimpernel, thistle, dock, and yellow horned poppy, mouse-ear hawkweed, and campion, curled dock, dodder, and stonecrop.

~

Nearly all the flowers that grow so abundantly on our shingle find a place in folklore or the herbals.

The petals of the red poppy were once collected on sunny days and made into a syrup; while the seeds are scattered over bread – the Romans mixed them with honey and ate them like jam.

The poppy is rarer than it once was. Gerard wrote *The fields are garnished and overspread with these wild poppies.*

Monday 29

At lunch today Nico said of David Hockney: 'I can't believe swimming pools are conducive to serious thought.' I said 'there were no shadows in David's work'. He replied, 'I'm certain Hades will be one vast subterranean swimming pool.'

Wednesday 31

Dinner at Jan's. I asked him which was the 'gayest' section of the orchestra – he said it was almost unheard of that the brass section should be, as he put it, 'friends of Dorothy'; oboes were so-so; perhaps the pianists.

~

In one of his newspapers Mr. Maxwell, retired chairman of the National AIDS Foundation, headlined me today as 'AIDS victim to stage Pets'. I mistakenly thought the *Mirror* a little more responsible than the *People*; but fact and truthful reporting are always the victims of money.

The night was cold. Walked up to the Heath and chatted to a 'straight' lad from Hackney, who said 'How do you know I'm not a murderer?'

'I don't,' I said. 'I don't really care if you are.'

Home by three.

JUNE

Thursday 1
Neil Bartlett called with plans for an installation next October at the Third Eye in Glasgow. He's translating *Berenice* and writing a novel about a happy gay couple. We talked about the *Mirror* and similar coverage he'd received in the *Independent*. They incorrectly reported he had AIDS, which caused his mum great grief; these things always hurt other people. I described to him the garden at Dungeness, my wooden table with its driftwood book – the table of the last supper, in front of the nuclear power station; and how last week someone had constructed an 'inkwell' out of wood and a feather, leaving it without a note.

When I told him old Mrs. Oiller's story of the two men falling from a plane in a clear blue summer sky, he said that it was the first shot from *A Matter Of Life And Death*; in Mrs. Oiller's story they had disappeared behind the Hoppen Pits, where the film was shot.

~

Blueprint becomes *Bliss* – dedicated to St. Rita of Cascia, patron of lost causes. Into the blue.

Wandered through the bookshops and bought *The Book of Changes* to construct the script.

Friday 2
David Lewis, a student at Canterbury film school, drove me across the marsh, the sky cleared – Prospect Cottage jet black across a lake of golden broom.

We turn the corner – so many flowers: white and red valerian, purple foxgloves, white campion. There has been no rain here – you can see the clouds building great thunderous ramparts over the hills. As the evening draws in the sea turns an unearthly sapphire, and the light lingers on long after the sun has set. The white shingle captures the daylight and stores it to light the glow worm's path.

~

I spent the day dreaming up the installation for Glasgow: the room turned in my mind from white to black, then blue, then white again. In the centre a tomb/cenotaph, 'Et in Arcadia Ego': two young men entwined in Rodin's *Kiss*, a shepherd with a staff and drapes from Poussin's painting. Near the tomb is a bed with two boys asleep – a scarlet counterpane painted with the number 28. There is a virus painting – crucifix, KY and condom – brightly lit. A pornographic video-tape, or a recording of telephone sex broadcast in the gallery – the visitors use their own money to pay for the service. A large painting, almost monochromatic, of condoms.

Saturday 3
Dungeness bathes in a pool of clear sunlight ringed by dark purple thunder clouds. Heat shimmers off the stones – there is no wind today. Breathless the bees' lazy flight through the foxglove spires.

My blue columbine is in flower, and last year's seedlings are thriving. The columbine – aquilegia, the eagle's foot – a wild flower, has crept into my garden, one of the herbs used against the Black Death in the 14th century.

The thunder clouds move closer – a hawk hovers so high it is almost invisible. Down here on the stones blue damselflies and butterflies mate. Gold cinquefoil and bacon-and-eggs catch the last rays.

The sun is overtaken by clouds; distant boom of thunder.

Cinquefoil boiled with the fat of children made the witches' ointment, spell flower for love potions.

It's twelve – my noon flower closes shop, Jack-go-to-bed-at-noon: *It shutteth itself at twelve of the clocke and showeth not his face open until the next dayes sun doth make it flower anew.*

~

The wind got up and within minutes it was raining so hard it dripped through the roof. Soon the drive was awash.

The effect on the colours in the landscape was immediate, as if someone had brushed varnish across a dull painting. This is the first rain for over a month; the grasses sigh with relief. When the rain cleared, ravenous slugs appear in their juicy hundreds to feast on the poppies and fennel.

~

Lynn Hanke, my friend from New York, arrived from London, swinging her car into the shingle nearly burying it. After lunch we tracked down lucky stones on the beach for a necklace, then took off for a long drive across the marshes to Old Romney, Appledore, Rye, Winchelsea, and the cliffs at Fairlight.

Lynn could hardly believe what she saw, thought such towns only existed in picture books – old houses submerged in roses and honeysuckle. We glimpsed peacocks through one garden gate, and a large white owl.

We didn't return home till seven, with books, biscuits, fudge, and two enormous pots to plant geraniums in front of the porch. In a lane by Fairfield church we gathered elderflower – Lynn calls it laceflower – which we fried in batter and sprinkled with sugar for supper.

Sunday 4

Gilded a small pocket book for *Blueprint*. As I walked along the beach I thought the film might follow the sound of footsteps, a journey with the continuous murmur of lazy waves, sea breezes, thunder, and stormy growlers. In the swell: dreams and recollections, the gemstone city of *Revelations*, brazen trumpets, the *Song of Solomon* – could all this be resolved with the *Tao Te Ching: great fullness seems empty?*

~

I must record the great display my sea kale put on. Its flowers are nearly over now and the seeds are forming. From *The Gardener's Labyrinth*:

> *Coleworts cureth the soreness of eyes, profiteth against the eating of venomous mushrooms. It maketh children to go speediller alone, cutteth the disease of the spleene and jaundise. It cleanseth the curse and leaprie, it amendeth the voice and grief of arteries, it cureth the bite of a dogge.*

The billowing white flowers along the shore are gone; but the mountainous white clouds in the blue sky and the horses breaking across a silvery sea cheer their memory to the echo. Today wind and sunlight fill the landscape with laughter. An old window opened in the wind and sent the cobwebs flying. The grasses are clapping – even seagulls loop the loop.

~

Picked dill, the first of the herbs grown from seed, and chopped it into new potatoes. The plants are almost a foot high, and growing strongly. Dill, like its cousin fennel, has a strong sweet taste used in pickling and with vegetables. The seeds have a soporific effect and were eaten in church to dull the agony of listening to sermons. The name of the herb is derived from the Anglo-Saxon dilla, to lull. Dill sent the witches flying.

> *There with her vervain and her dill*
> *That hindereth witches of their will*
> *A scarewitch stuffed with dill*

~

Sapphire and silver, jade and pewter, bright with sea horses under storm clouds. Chameleon changes – the white cliffs set like galleons catch the sun on the far horizon; bright as a shaft of light through a glass lens, it burns away the slate grey. The light is playing fast and loose: the hills are violet blue, the Ness a golden ochre, the broom Van Gogh yellow, with islands of blue sea kale and horned poppy.

Monday 5

Dinner at Colin McCabe's – Isaac Julien, Bernard Rose and his wife Alexandra. Film talk.

It was cold and wet and the journey to Alwyne Road took an age. Earlier I popped into Braganza, where they were having an art raffle for the Terrence Higgins Trust. Met various worthies, ducked out quickly. Kind but dire artwork, except for two Christo wrap-ups.

~

This morning I can't for the life of me remember anything that was said at the dinner party. Mostly sniper stuff: C4 'films', the Floyd concert which Bernard worked on. Poor Alan Parker, bright in his wilderness – everyone thought *Angel Heart* his best. I'm certain he would like to be like Terence Davies, socially sound; and as for the BFI, his criticism of its films (Tony Smith on the organ) is accurate but overemphasised, like bagging a sparrow on a tiger shoot.

Tuesday 6

Supper at the pizza place by the British Museum and the subject of Gilbert & George came up yet again. Julian, who is making a documentary about them, was put out by a remark of George's that 'the government was the best of his lifetime' – the yearning of a naughty boy for the strong arm?

~

The duo arrived one hot and sunny afternoon in the late sixties at Patrick Proctor's studio, self-consciously sipped their tea from his porcelain, while Alasdair and myself crashed out on the sofa looking like moth-eaten hippies. Then, they seemed the most peculiar embodiment of times past, a look and values to match a decade (the fifties) we'd spent demolishing.

They made their entrance like wind up dolls in their stifling tweedy suits, singing *Underneath The Arches*, defending petit bourgeois niceties with drunken belligerence in expensive restaurants. One morning in the early eighties they must have woken up to find themselves the spirit of times present.

Back then, sweating it out like two old colonels from a provincial cricket club, they looked plain silly.

Although I share many friends, who constantly emphasise their generosity and kindness – I still find myself maddened by their espousal of constricting values. 'Shit', 'Piss', 'Cunt' are not the language that attacks bourgeois values, but the language of the loutish conservative youth itself out on a macho stag night. I was told that George often ends his evenings legless at the L.A. [a seedy leather bar in East London]. This, if anything, underlines the bottled up sexuality. No feeling of liberation – dues paid in cash not spirit. Half a million to AIDS charities.

G&G's dream is as deathly-blanched as Burne Jones, their young skinheads as drained of life as those wilting maidens. The aggression is fake, and empty. We are all kind to friends who are dying.

This said I love their painting. They've created many an argument, endless attempts at analysis; and, like them, I can find strength in flowers, boys and childhood memories. They have also gallantly put themselves in the centre of their art at a time when you often wondered who was painting the picture.

Wednesday 7
The Chinese are queuing round the block to remove their money from the Bank of China. I spent the whole day working with Clive on Matisse – a video graphics paintbox – with 'photos' struck from footage of Christine Keeler for Chris and Neil's track from the film *Scandal*. Miss Keeler is shown getting into and out of cars outside court, at home, surrounded by pressmen. There's no other footage of her. In frozen frames she looks uncannily like Jackie Kennedy.

~

Comptons is a loud pub – no, the loudest bar in town. By eight you are pressed so tightly against your neighbours that to get out of the place is a major feat of concentration and negotiation.

When Sir Francis Rose brought me here many years ago, to find his lost son, it was dimly lit and half empty, a few Soho regulars propping up the bar. One of them, John, was a large man with a squashed face. He and Francis talked about the good old days before the war, when John had been a smashing boxer. The rubdown sexuality of those 'good old days' still pervaded the place, with its smattering of rent boys who had stopped off on their way to the Golden Lion from the White Bear in Piccadilly Underground (it was there that we later tracked down Francis' son).

Comptons had an underworldly atmosphere. You half-expected the Krays to drop in with cash to spare on a night West drinking with old friends.

Francis looked the perfect punter – though Comptons was not a renters' pub, just the sleazy mix of that Soho now almost lost in Brasserieville. A pub for old pro's of both sexes, its walls were covered with play bills and signed photos from the fifties: Tommy Steele, Henry Cooper, Diana Dors. That sort of thing. Here boys-in-the-band, faded stars of *Physique Pictorial, Drummer*, spliced themselves with busty blondes.

Nowadays at 6:00 Comptons is still quite empty. At this moment the bar staff pull down the venetian blinds to shut out the street and the curiosity of passers-by; the heat, nicotine count, and decibels gradually mount.

Much has changed – and then nothing really. The only real difference is the tidal wave of terrible music. I discover the pub is still used by *professional boys* on their way to work – though in Mrs. T.'s England, unlike Harold Wilson's, they are no longer waifs and strays from up North or the East End. These boys have passed their 'A' levels, have an arts degree and have opted for the easier life of the massage parlour and escort agency rather than a career in mortgageville.

Their attitudes and accents put the clients in Mayfair health clubs at ease, where for an extra £40 their hands slip under the towel. I have to admit I've never been interested in this world, except as a voyeur; even pushing fifty I would like to retain the illusion that I'm desired, if not for my body then perhaps for my conversation, or even memories!

I declined the offer of a young Portuguese lad who, as he rubbed his crotch against my thigh, suggested I could do with some healthy exercise in his club. With their Jimmy Dean hairstyles and frayed, faded blue jeans, these boys can make up to £1000 a week. They are forward and charming.

The Portuguese lad says 'I love your films' with an ever-so-winsome twinkle in his dark eyes – 'though I've never seen any of them'. The boy standing next to him chips in 'I'm going to see them all at the Scala tomorrow. I'm a painter and would love to talk to you.' Should I give him my phone number? I don't know. Perhaps they all were on the game, but it was quite exciting.

I left them all in the street debating whether to go to L'Escargot or an even more expensive Soho restaurant. I'm glad they can afford it; those places are pretty dull, and they'd cheer them up no end.

Friday 9

Completed two days and nights of extensive editing at Soho 601, the most sophisticated video house in Europe. In this twilight world, sucked into a TV screen, the hours slip by. Food and drink appear, one meal runs into the next and the digits flash past. Tristam, who is bringing the drinks today, is, I discover, the son of my uncle Mike's younger brother, who I saw a lot of in my schooldays, when he was the only member of our family working in cinema. He edited *The Abominable Dr. Phibes*. When he died he was working on a film of Chaplin.

~

The Pet Shop Boys' film wall is looking splendid – the only imponderable, the blow-up to 70mm. It's a medley that cavorts through the styles of the underground. Peter and HB have edited *King's Cross* like Bruce Bailies' *Ode To The American Indian*; at moments *It's A Sin* approaches Grünewald or Bosch; *Domino Dancing* is the most affecting, and has footage from Dungeness layered with its bullfights. There is a beautiful effect for *Always On My Mind*, like Monet's waterlilies and poppy fields seen through a kaleidoscope. Effects like these will never have been seen on film before.

~

Dinner with a young biochemist. She talked about genetic splicing, tompots and ligons, carrot genes for boys with red hair – all the possibilities under ethical wraps. Frightening and beautiful, like a Burroughs novel. Science catches up with art: baboon-assed boys frightening Mr. and Mrs. Average. Young ladies from Cheltenham with feather wings – 'cor look at that bird', flying in the ozone-free atmosphere, the ultraviolet glinting on their wings. No asthma or Downs syndrome. Oak trees covered with daisies.

Saturday 10

Drove with Julian and Joyce across the marshes to Fairlight in the evening. It is impossible to describe the strange beauty of the landscape, particularly the Ridge and Winchelsea Beach. A great silence had descended, only broken by the twittering of swallows. Light on every blade of grass, flowers, bushes, lakes. Such contentment. The wind rushed past as Julian drove recklessly along empty roads.

For minutes on end we sat in complete silence. Little rabbits, quite unafraid, looked at us curiously as we passed by; poppies and bugloss iridescent scarlets and blues. The world like a medieval miniature or one of the unicorn tapestries in the Cloisters; the gravel path – the road to an earthly paradise, above us a wild sky with a flaming sun in bands of violet, pink, and blue.

Silvery willows, reeds like purple smoke fringing the water, splashed with orange light, cascades of wild roses, honeysuckle and pink valerian. Walls of wild sweet pea and red hot pokers.

At moments in the deep lanes the car was swallowed in banks of lacy cowparsley and elder.

Sunday 11

Up at six, a sea mist hanging around the shore like smoke from a bonfire; at moments it completely veiled the power station. Awesome and frightening.

Drove with David to Folkestone to Maggi Hambling's show in the old palm court of the Metropole Hotel, a most unlikely place for an exhibition: poverty stricken spirit of hideously converted rooms, chipboard and fake mahogany over the beautiful old plasterwork, presided over by a loquacious arts officer in T-shirt and white shorts. He flashed his brochure.

Maggi, Spike Milligan, Melvyn Bragg and three Scottish poets – we all looked slightly bemused as the local press photographed us. An immaculate silver haired lady in a powder-blue suit talked to Maggi: she had left the Slade in 1920. She was the most informed of this ill-sorted group.

I'm certain the show will receive no more visitors – the apologetic manner in which the provinces engage artists was never more vivid. It sent me straight back to my schooldays in Dorset, and my first exhibition in Watford public library.

Hasty retreat home for fish and chips. The sun shone with a blinding intensity. Breathless day.

~

A letter from the *Folkestone Herald* alerted me: the *Sun* wanted to buy their photos of me. Meanwhile the lawyers' letters to the *People* and the *Mirror* have produced an apology and a correct reporting of my HIV status under the headline 'Del's Not Dying'.

A motorbike draws up and a hapless reporter from the *Sun* clambers off. This is his third trip down here from London.

'Do you mind if I photo you?'

'Yes, but since one way or another you're going to, we might as well do a good job of it. Not in front of the house, on the beach.'

We trek off across the shingle. I sense he wants to get this assignment over with as quickly as possible. I offer to carry his camera bag with a malicious smile. When we set up at the water's edge he says,

'I'm only a snapper.'

'Well,' I say, 'this is your chance to take a decent photo.' I fix him with a basilisk stare as he clicks away.

'You look uncomfortable,' he remarks.

'Not as much as *you* should.'

'Oh?'

'I'm writing a diary, which I'm publishing. You're today's entry. When all is said and done what I choose to write will, I expect, be the only trace of your life. Your memory is in my hands.'

Long silence.

'The *Sun*'s not kept by the British Museum, the paper destroys itself it's so acid. When you get back tell your editor to read the retraction in the *People*. Because next time I'm going for a million unless its right. Mr. Maxwell, the retired captain of the AIDS Foundation, has seen better to print an apology.'

I kept him snapping for as long as I could. I hope he remembers the session.

Tuesday 13

I've always loved working clothes: boiler suits, flying jackets, overalls, leather dungarees, jeans and T-shirts – most of them bought second hand in markets. I buy very little from clothes shops – the exception, my socks from Marks and Spencer. I find clothes shops intimidating, rarely venture into them, and then almost never alone.

The moment those self-assured assistants set eyes on me an overwhelming shyness swamps me. I duck and avert my eyes at 'Can I help you sir'.

I have never bought a pair of trousers or a suit unless accompanied by a friend, and rush through the process of trying clothes on behind those skimpy partitions. I would be surprised if I had bought more than one article of clothing a year in such places.

As a teenager all my clothes came from M&S, though Mum brightened it up by making me silk shirts – and brocade waistcoats, which I hardly ever wore.

At university in the early sixties I wore black polo necks – still from M&S – and duffle coats, the post-existentialist uniform. I grew my hair a little longer and bought my first Levis, wearing them in the bath so they dried tight as possible and, with a bit of rubbing, showed off my cock.

As for fashion, the editor of the *Daily Mail*, a friend of my father's, was far in advance with his elastic-sided Chelsea boots. And Stuart Hopps, returning from his summer vac 'kitted out', having worked in the first John Stephen's in Carnaby Street, made me almost die with embarrassment. He would have caused less sensation in drag.

With my sexuality repressed I was as green as they come, I had no idea then that one day I would fuck with boys like the handsome rugby player I met each lunchtime in the entrance to the college students' union.

I sensed clothes might betray me, but to what?

Only when, at 22, I tumbled into bed with Ron did I become aware that in the pubs and bars there was a look, a cut of the trousers, a flick of the hair.

~

Then I relied on youthful charm and would count the hairs invading my stomach as if ticking off the moments of a romantic life that would end before my thirtieth birthday.

~

I was never in fashion.

In '66 Ossie Clarke gave me a belt decorated in multicoloured leather, the prototype of a fashion accessory that was to take the sixties by storm. In Carnaby Street I bought an expensive pair of 'hunting boots' with zip pockets to match. At £8 they broke the bank, but on the whole I carried on with jeans and T-shirts – more fashion casualty than victim.

In '64 I toured the States with one of those Beatles' hats from Herbert Johnson. The summer of '67 came and went, I never bought a bright uniform from the doctor's wife who ran the stall in Portobello. Some 'deco' scarves from Vern Lambert at the Chelsea market, an earring and a pair of velvet pants with red stitching from Mr. Freedom, and a most beautiful velvet suit that Michael Fish gave me for *Jazz Calendar* – these were all strictly for best.

I also had a grey schoolboy suit, white T-shirt and plimsolls, a pair of bright socks à la Hockney and a string of pearls. With very short hair that put me in a class of my own. You see, I was vain.

Then you could not drink more than a weak Nescafé in the new bars, nor touch in a dance without someone coming up and separating you. 'Steady boys.' The seventies were more flamboyant. On more than one occasion I wore a cloak from *Sebastiane* down the King's Road – briefly dyed my hair bright orange to win Andrew Logan's Miss World. Bigger, brighter earrings, and in the long hot summer of '76 I carried a fan.

Then came the leather years, with a battered jacket rancid with Vaseline and poppers, and jeans split at the knees. Doc Martens, short hair again. Without this you could not get into clubs like The Mineshaft, where the doorman smelt you to make sure you weren't wearing aftershave. In fact so dark were the recesses of The Mineshaft all you could really do was touch and smell.

Now that world has gone. I jettisoned the jeans for battered trousers, and now try to look vaguely serious – as Mum would have liked – for the TV by adding a shirt and putting on a suit. Though I have never worn a tie, except one by the artist Cragie Aitcheson last week, and one at dinner at the Ritz many years ago with John Gielgud, when I was stopped at the door tieless and conducted to a small room where a tray of ties was presented. I chose a black tie, though I could have been a guardsman, or joined the RAF for the evening.

~

Midsummer and my little garden in the desert blossoms.

A hermit, with finches and noisy gulls for company, I watch the flowers. The first wild rose came out this morning; the sage is in bloom, and wild poppies blow and scatter their petals by lunch. In front of the house the dianthus is out, also the geranium; the last iris is fading along with the wall-flowers, which have bloomed for weeks on end. The lavender, santolina and curry plants are all covered with buds. It's been a dry year, so patches of green, with stakes and stones, spring out of the burnt grass.

Yesterday we touched 80°. Today, if anything, is much hotter, with just the slightest breeze.

Dill, rosemary, parsley and hyssop were all picked for the salad.

~

The children from next door bring more rocks and stones, shells and stakes.

~

In that garden be floures of hewe,
The gelofir gent that she well knew,
The flower de luce she did not rewe
And said, "The white rose is most true
The garden to rule by right wis lawe"
The lily-white rose me thought I sawe
And ever she sang , . .

This medieval poem, which probably describes *Rosa alba* – the white rose of York – could equally describe the dog rose, *Rosa canina*, of the hedgerow. Pliny says it grew so plentifully here that this island was named Albion.

The dog rose can live as long as the yew: there is one old bush in Hildesh-eim Cathedral said to have been planted by Charlemagne.

~

My rose outside the kitchen window is flowering for the first time. I wonder if it will see the nuclear power station out.

Wednesday 14
I finally identified a sticky, rather sad drooping plant that looks as if its flowers have wilted: the Nottingham catchfly. It grows quite abundantly on the shingle and has flowered in the last week, along with the mallow and willowherb.

Thursday 15

Took a taxi down to the studio to see the lighting plan for the Pet Shop Boys' concert. There is not much leeway for anything creative: it consists largely of flicking switches to the percussion, and choosing a couple of colours for each song. Technology out of control. All conversation revolves round the hardware.

So hot that the basement studio was a relief.

The 35mm print failed to turn up at 20th Century Fox, a real James event. We all sat round for half an hour, then went to Bertaux' for tea.

Later I spent a couple of hours reading the Bockris/Warhol book, which gives a good picture of NYC in the early sixties. It is more perceptive than the usual art book, though the index is weighted a little too heavily towards the Duchess of Windsor and Boy George.

Simon Watney's book *Taking Liberties – AIDS and Cultural Politics* is spot on. Simon is the most perceptive writer on the health crisis.

On the Heath someone choking in the dark giving a blow job, said loudly: 'The ghost of Christmas Past.'

Picked up a tough looking skinhead who said: 'Fuck me.'

'OK,' I said.

'That's a bit risky.' he said, and had a good laugh.

'I was only thinking it.' I said.

'Fuck everything.' he said.

Friday – Sunday

Three days blur in anguish. The sky fell in leaving a blank page filled with tears. Then, clenching his hands and staring skywards behind dark glasses, HB started to turn the dark back, and a chink of light appeared. A twitch in the eye became a miracle. At the lowest moment he sat under a towel in the bathroom and said 'Please don't look at me'.

HB looking as if the light had been put out. Like a sad Picasso Pierrot, big blank sad eyes, no growls or shadow boxing. The thrombosis left him practically paralysed down the left side, his face screwed up involuntarily in a strange silent grimace. He said a muscle relaxed in his ear had caused his hearing to become so clear. It was the hearing of the gods.

I walk on his right side so he can talk. He says Ron should give him the part of Montgomery Clift (after the accident). High on codeine he walks slowly. A sense of our fragility on this sunny afternoon.

~

Nothing had prepared either of us for these terrible days. The sun left its course, time went in a scramble. Our happy years were punched off course by the gods. HB said it was a punishment for looking at them. But now, on

Sunday afternoon, after watering my garden with tears in my eyes, I find a pattern returning. The logic with which HB is fighting will, I'm sure, win through – if anyone can rewire the brain he should be the one.

At lunch he was talking of frightening American tourists with his ruined features, of Foucault's concept of the family, of Hubble's Atlas of the Galaxies, and Lewis Carroll's work with logic. He feels my finger traced across his face, says he will be training in the gym next week. Every cell in my body wills his regeneration. HB's arrival in my life has saved me from collapse in the past two years. I wish to do the same for him.

Sunday Evening

Sat on the steps at Capper Street Hospital watching the ants on the paving stones. Asked HB about logic: 'Tweedledum and Tweedledee.'

A girl came out of the door and stepped over us: 'Give us a fiver,' says HB. She laughs. His doctors come out of the building, both young and good-looking in T-shirts and beach pants. It's so hot this evening.

Gerard arrives – we walk through Fitzrovia looking for a restaurant. All are closed. We eventually have an indifferent 'Greek' at a seedy kebab house in Percy Street; then down to Old Compton Street to buy cakes for the nurses.

Walking back through Soho Square, we read the memorial between the plane trees that commemorates the Great Storm, now nearly two years ago. When we get to the hospital HB is locked out – we've arrived so late. 'Go under the tunnel' says a voice behind the barred doors. HB growls as he dismisses us. Everything seems set to get back to 'normal' as soon as possible – 'Two weeks,' he says.

Monday Morning

HB here prowling up and down – he noticed a joint in the ashtray, said the whole flat smelled of it. Growled at me again when I said he was OK on the telephone: 'Tell the truth.'

All this sounds optimistic. His sudden stroke at the age of 24 has shocked everyone, it seemed so arbitrary. I still can't believe it has happened.

Off to put Chris and Neil's show together at the Brixton Academy.

Monday through Thursday

The Brixton Academy is a barn of a cinema, neglected, cast off, statues, and moorish architecture covered with a peeling cream paint. It's only just big enough to contain the Pets' show, which we have rehearsed here for the last four days in sweltering heat.

I've been dreading these days for weeks, as unlike a theatrical show there has been no 'home'. The bricks and mortar of Massive (which owns both

Bros and the Pets) is a chic office in Covent Garden. Song, dance, costume, lighting and film were all contracted out and allowed to go their own way after a series of discussions in a foyer.

So any detailed control has been out of the question; though I have made certain that everyone worked on a theme. I 'directed' these days as un-obtrusively as possible – quickly realised that everyone had done their best, quietly stopped anyone from changing anything, and tried to make what we had work.

At the dress rehearsal last night my reward was to see the show run smoothly, and the audience – Jon Savage, Tom from Massive and assorted 'relatives' – all congratulating Chris and Neil when it was over. We have a song and dance show of considerable sophistication, put together in a mere four days – unlike the weeks spent on a musical. All was made possible by the advanced technology of the music itself – stored in an elegant computer which has liberated the stage from sweaty performance.

I expect some of the music critics will react against this 'cool', but they will be wrong. The argument has been tried against the electric guitar, or Warhol – that he didn't paint his canvases, therefore they had no validity or passion. The 'live' performance at a rock concert is a myth.

The show would have been impossible without Neil's good humour; although denying he's a showman, he has an acute sense of what's possible; he displayed the patience and charm of a true vaudevillian – not the aggro and angst of the movies. We were as unlike *42nd Street* or *A Chorus Line* as possible: no tantrums, broken legs, or drunken dressing-room scenes.

All through the week I prayed that things would go smoothly as I couldn't allow the show to go to Hong Kong in an unfinished state and was desperate to stay here. I knew both Neil and Chris wanted me on the tour, but they both understood that I couldn't really leave. Nothing was said to twist my arm.

Annie's costumes were very well made, and Caspar's dancers (he invented the Moonwalk for Michael Jackson) had no problem with them. The dancing is spectacular throughout the show, and so well rehearsed that this after-noon we were able to spend time on Neil's performance, which has im-proved by leaps and bounds as he has gained assurance.

Friday 23
HB wiped the sleep from his eyes and declared a miracle: the slightest move-ment had returned to his face, he can twitch a smile. He looks composed, says it takes enormous concentration. A fortnight after the stroke he's in control.

At midday I left for Dungeness with Julian to water the garden. As I turned on the hose Julian said there was a £400 fine or two months im-

prisonment. Fuck it! I thought, my flowers also have a right to live.
Jon says the weather is 'chemical'.

Saturday 24

Woke at five to the sound of the fog horn. A white sea mist had closed in
during the night. It hugged the house close, covered the flowers and spiders'
webs with sparkling dew. I thought I had seen each twist and turn of the
weather on the Ness, but each day it springs something new.

The sun clears the mist by nine. The poppies and bugloss emerge from its
shadows, the chrome yellow broom is fading. But these scarlets and blues
have taken their place: the poppies *P. hybridium* – a deep double scarlet –
and *P. dubium* have interbred to produce an intermediate type. One by the
front door, has scarlet petals with a deep chestnut base.

~

Bugloss is less in evidence than last year except in those parts of the garden I
have watered. There it has grown strongly. Of bugloss Culpeper says

> It is a gallant herb of the sun, it is a pity it is no more use than it is.
> The gentlewomen of France do paint their faces with these roots, it is
> said.

Two to three foot high, it is covered with clear blue flowers, and of all the
plants of the Ness is the brightest:

> Viper's bugloss has its stalkes all to be speckled like a snake or viper,
> and is a most singular remedy against poison and the sting of
> scorpions. – Cole's, Art Of Simples – The water distilled in glasses and
> the roote taken itself is good against the passions and tremblings of the
> heart, as also against swoonings, sadness, and melancholy.

~

At 9:30, Derek Ball who has moved into Windshift, up near the lighthouse,
arrived and we push start Julian's car to get us back to London for the Gay
Pride march at 2:00. On the way back Derek tells us some more stories of
the Ness's past inhabitants; of a 'Lady' who brought her rough trade down
to one of the railway carriages incognito; of the Messerschmitt that his
friend Steven used to play in at low tide back in the fifties; and a fabled
society fortune teller. I told him of the gay sea captain who'd lived next
door. The Ness it seems is not quite as sleepy as Jack at the corner store
would have us believe, more detective work is needed. Derek promised he
would find out more of the Lady.

Afternoon

For the 20,000 gay men and lesbians who marched this afternoon from Hyde Park to Kennington 20 years and as many thousands after Stonewall, the Pride march is the most joyous day in the calendar. Nothing can compare with the elation as the street becomes 'ours' for a few short hours, the whistle blowing, cheering, waving and songs – *She'll be coming with a woman when she comes*. The wry humour of it makes the sad old October march as out of date as its totem, the macabre secular icon in the mausoleum. Our march is the true May day, however much other dismal factions squat it, the strictures and structures of heterosex are banished, boy meets boy, girl meets girl, in a shower of anarchic kisses, even the police must sigh – a sigh of relief, how much nicer it must be to be the butt of 'what are you waiting for sister, come and join us' than the sticks and stones of many another march.

Pretty policemen are targets for whistles and cheers and a 'photo opportunity' and the march as it winds through Parliament Square is greeted by a Margaret Thatcher impersonator who waves and bows to 'Maggie Maggie Maggie, out out out!'

It all ends up in the park with stalls, bands and dancing. The girls and boys on the march are without doubt the handsomest both in mind and body. They have the moral high ground. And each year in spite of Margaret Thatcher's delinquent government, they are happier and more relaxed. Nothing shall turn the tide back now. Clause 28 is a clarion call to unity, and has given us new purpose. Next year there will be 21,000 on this march.

There are a million psyches to win, and nothing but loss in store for the seedy guardians of the moral majority. Dear Jesus, innocent begetter of an evil and corrupt tradition, we know you would join this march, our entry into Jerusalem, would kiss John and consign the born again to the bottomless pit, or rather enlighten them and put them to bed with their brothers and sisters. For we know that the castle of heterosex has its walls of tears and dungeons of sadness. We can laugh at the house of cards called the Family. We demand one right 'equality of loving before the law' and the end of our banishment from the daylight.

Evening

Martin John, HB's old school friend from Newcastle came down to see him. In the evening they went to the cinema. Nothing on earth would get me to *Hellraiser II* . . .

~

I only go to the cinema now out of friendship or nostalgia. I cannot watch anything that is not based on its author's life. Acting, camerawork, all the paraphernalia, bring me little pleasure without the element of autobiography.

~

So, drunk and slightly stoned – Dutch courage – I went for a walk on the Heath instead – and stumbled on the worst film production of the personal kind you could imagine: a collegiate version of *A Midsummer Night's Dream*, in modern dress. The director was a young American who covered his insecurity with a great deal of shouting. They had set up at midnight on the path under Jack Straw's Castle, under a full moon. I approached the blinding lights cautiously – perhaps there had been a murder. An elderly man coming towards me stopped me and said, 'I've seen everything up here in my time, but this takes the biscuit.'

Further down the path a group of lads had built a large bonfire round which they sat in silence, adrift in the night. None of them spoke a word, though one kid broke the silence to say he had never seen anything so amateur in his life: 'They don't have any characters.' Back 'on set' Puck was leaping about putting his magic flower on some fallen tree-trunks, on which a young woman with slicked back hair draped herself in an outfit by Yohji or Katherine from Sloane Street.

Further on a group of young men were making love under the trees. Others walking back home were stopped by scouts and pushed back in the bushes, before they stumbled across the set. I wished I had had my own camera. The film of this film would have made the finest *Midsummer Night's Dream* that had ever been recorded – and to think they missed all those *real* fairies.

Sunday 25

Unbearably hot day. I slept off my late night, hadn't returned home till sunrise. HB was so hot he got up and spent the rest of the night on the roof.

In Camden Lock I bought three fine silk saris. HB tried them on – the purple one looked magnificent.

More movement has crept back into his face.

Monday 26

As HB seemed much happier, and feeling he needed a break from my worrying, I came down to Dungeness. In the evening he phoned to say the doctors expected him to get back all the movement in his face and arm, though it might take a year. I went to bed early and slept soundly.

Tuesday 27

Woke at five, a gentle rain falling – the first for over three weeks. Much cooler. Walked along the beach collecting stones. At midday there was a violent thunderstorm with purposeful shafts of lightning. Hurried back to Prospect and spent the rest of the day reading.

The rain brought an immense relief.

Wednesday 28

I woke with a slight chill. Spent the morning cleaning and tidying the studio. Bright sunlight streaming through the window hurt my eyes.

The sun was soon lost behind grey clouds. I took a slow walk through the woods – in sheltered glades a myriad meadow browns and coppers, one tortoiseshell, and a battered red admiral.

I met an old man who collected 'aberrations', only butterflies, no moths – moths were too great a subject for one lifetime. He complained that the butterflies of Dungeness were true to type, 'as if minted from a printing press'. He'd had no luck.

~

Walking across the shingle I mark my way by a thorn bush or pear tree, a stone or clump of nettles. Vague disquiet.

~

The AIDS programme on drug users and prostitutes used 'theme' music from *Sebastiane*. Perhaps it was a compliment, but it made me sad. I wonder if the people who made the programme chose it deliberately. They used it on the night shots around the red light districts of Plymouth and Birmingham.

Thursday 29

A strong gale got up in the night and the day dawned ash grey. Now the sun has gone I feel dejected. Perhaps my summer cold has brought on this depression.

The phone crackles even more loudly so I can barely hear shouted conversations.

I always fall prey to these withdrawal symptoms here, especially when the phone dies.

~

Matthew rang to say * * * * council – I couldn't hear for the crackling – had banned all its school children from attending a Glyndebourne production of [Britten's] *Death in Venice*. If anyone on 'the other side' still believes we don't live in an idiot land . . . he said he'd ring back with details.

~

Retired into my workroom and completed a gilded canvas in the manner of a relique: a coffin nail, locks of hair, a broken comb found on my walk yesterday, a diamond, gold ring, ruby blood drop, one lucky stone hanging from a string and a pale pink condom.

Nick, Robert, Terry, Howard, David.

~

At low tide I walk in the rain along the shore; drops of water gather on my eyebrows and blind me. Stranded on the sands are violet jellyfish the size of dinner-plates.

Back home the phone still rings – bringing indecipherable static. In it I hear Patrick shouting from Hong Kong that the Pet Shop Boys' show had finished to a standing ovation.

Friday 30

Hither and thither, restless as a mosquito larvae swimming across the stagnant pool of my dreams, I wrote out the script for the *Blueprint Bliss* all morning. The sun was out. At 12:00 David arrived and we drove to New Romney, bought food, a phormium and a good strong holly.

We spent the evening reconstructing the front garden. David said it lacked verticals, so we placed several stakes, including a large central pole with a glass lens that caught the sun and turned the world upside down.

At ten Alasdair arrived on his new bike.

JULY

Saturday 1
Quid sit futurum cras fuge quaerere et quem fors dierum cinque dabit lucro appone, nec dulcis amores . . .

Try not to guess what lies in the future, but as fortune deals days enter them into your life's book as windfalls.

Sunday 2
The rain has brought the garden to life; each morning the poppies bloom and scatter before midday. I pick the dried flower heads of the foxgloves and sprinkle the seed.

It seems strange that many of the flowers on the Ness grow in a small patch, sometimes singly. Maybe they were brought here in the earth and rubble used to build tracks out to the boats. There is one ivy-leaved toad-flax, a square yard of scabious at the roadside, a patch of golden samphire by the Long Pits. I've found one broom rape and a small group of St. John's wort.

Other plants are much more plentiful: hawkweed, hempnettle, lesser knapweed and sheepbit; also, white clover, and haresfoot, which grows on the verge.

The range of colours in the poppies is astonishing. On the shingle at Lydd-on-Sea there is a plant that is such a deep red it might be called 'black poppy'. I'm keeping an eye on it for seed.

The groundsel is infested with the orange and black caterpillars of the burnet moth. Some plants have been devoured to skeletal remains.

Monday 3
Wash day. Packed for London.

At 7:00 Mr. Drako arrived at the pizza house near the British Museum, and ordered a 'vegan pizza' after scouring the Venezianas and American Hots through gold pince-nez. A vegan pizza turned out to be a slice of white bread with olive oil. He does not eat white bread, so in the end he was reduced to some lettuce leaves with a squeeze of lemon. He looks uncommonly well on his diet.

~

Cousin Bev phoned from Ibiza – I haven't seen her for years, not since she was headmistress of Leeds Girls' School. Way back in the fifties, she took me to a matinee of *The Way Of The World* – my first 'grown up' play – and then along the Charing Cross Road to Pooles' second hand bookshop to buy me *The Cloister And The Hearth*, and *20,000 Leagues Under The Sea* in an edition of the classics printed on bible paper and bound in red leatherette.

All those shops are now buried under the ugly brick ziggurat next door.

Tuesday 4
News filters back from Hong Kong: the censor is up in arms over the two boys kissing in *It's A Sin* and the large cock the flasher reveals.

Friday 7
Violent thunderstorms through the night brought three days of stifling weather to a close. Opening the windows and doors at the flat admits a tired breeze and a lot of traffic noise.

Saturday 8
A quiet withdrawn day swathed in mist through which the sun glimmered.

Peter and his friends from the Royal College hung my painting in the martello tower at Dymchurch – the cool circular windowless room was pitch black after the bright sunlight.

~

Dymchurch is a strange little seaside town. Built on the old Roman sea wall, it's a bric-a-brac muddle of old cottages sunk deep in sandy soil, a ditzy amusement arcade, shops selling postcards, pink rock, and shells. There are old-fashioned drinks – dandelion and burdock, cream soda – and candy floss and lurid cakes in shocking pink and green. All guarded by three martello towers, built in the early 19th century to ward off Napoleon.

This little village once ruled the marshes. Here the jurats made 'deme', erected the gallows, and carried out royal orders to fight back the sea, building defences right to the gates of Appledore.

You can see each end of the high street if you stand at the tower in the middle. It is strangely old-fashioned – holiday makers braving a nippy sea breeze.

In the evening I drove with Derek Ball in his old Citroën along the hills that border the marsh from Port Lympne to Hamstreet. Everywhere the harvest was baled; golden fields and dark green trees and a mist so thick it swirled around the car in the twilight.

On the road to Brenzett police vans and arc lights diverted us along the sunken lanes to Snargate, where tens of thousands of bikers had set up a tent city around a large sign, *Wall Of Death*. We crawled along the lane at walking pace, surrounded by bloated beer-gutted figures, black with leather and blue with tattoos.

As the dark came it seemed like an encampment on the edge of another world, some vision Wyndham Lewis dreamt up for *The Childermas*. All we needed was the devil in the back seat pronouncing doom on the mutated tide of humankind – 13,000 we were told, though someone else said 40,000. Countless bikes and multicoloured tents, wave upon wave, in arcs around a scaffold (the bandstand). The whine of the bikes, each pub a hive, the last swarm of summer.

Sunday 9

Planted a triangle of three holly bushes and two tamarisk at the back of the house. Filmed the garden, as the purples and yellows of the lavender and curry plant are at their best.

A dull overcast day, only the sound of the flies breaks the silence. Not a breath of wind. In the mist a tallship with sky blue sails, deathly still.

Monday 10

Lazy high summer. The drowsy bees fall over each other in the scarlet poppies, which shed their petals by noon. Meadow browns and gatekeepers flutter wearily across the shell-pink brambles disputing the nectar with a fast bright tortoiseshell. The bees clamber hungrily up the sour green woodsage. Drifts of mauve rosebay and deep yellow ragwort studded with orange and black burnet caterpillars.

Blue damsels dart here and there, a great brown dragonfly hovers. I pick dead heads off the poppies and scatter the seeds.

Walking home I stumble across a wild fig, more bush than tree, hugging the ground. I take a slip from it, and two cuttings from the sea buckthorn. The lone fruit on the wild pear is already the size of a hen's egg.

At three I water the roses, then fall asleep in the heat, waiting for the telephone to ring me awake.

Tuesday 11

The garden is invaded by grasshoppers, which leap about and make such a din. Sylvia's pet crow wheels about the roof of the house. She says the twitchers spotted a raven some years ago and crept up on it in the night. It didn't budge from its perch; but when they got too near, at dawn, it politely said 'Good morning' loud and clear.

~

Left at five on the slowest strikebound train for London. There the phone rang continually – Lord Olivier died this morning. As *War Requiem* was his last film they wanted a comment, 'Have you heard the dreadful news?' the first words of each conversation.

~

Death in the media has to be terrible to drum up custom. His death was peaceful and in his sleep.

~

My own brief encounter with Sir Lazzers, as we called him on set, was with a charming, rather quiet old man full of reminiscences, hardly aware of the present. Tilda said it was touch and go when she was wheeling him around. But reading *Strange Meeting* he was as clear as a bell.

~

Spent the morning reading *Matthew*, and *Wisdom*:

> *Our name will be forgotten in time*
> *And no-one will remember our works*
> *Our life will pass away like the traces of a cloud*
> *And be scattered like mist*
> *That is chased by the rays of the sun*
> *And overcome by its heat*
> *For our allotted time is the passing of a shadow*
> *And will run like sparks through the stubble*

Wednesday 12

A strange coincidence. HB and Gerard put a personal ad in *Square Peg*:

> Twins, 24: Dave, builder, plumber, electrician; Kevin, painter
> decorator. Do anything.

They received a reply which said 'What do you mean when you say that you "do anything"?' This evening HB picked up a fan letter I had received in the morning from the same young man. It shows, I said, how small the world is, or that he's a very prolific letter writer.

~

How does one reply to deep confessional letters of an artistic nature? Usually I write a serious reply, but this morning my letter began *Do you make it a habit to write to strange men?*

~

Spent the afternoon with the Pets, organising – or rather discovering that filming a concert is a straightjacketed affair. Time and money lead to five fixed cameras in Wembley – manoeuvrability blocked by finance.

In the morning a cheque arrived for the show: a sigh of relief, as I have received no money from film since *The Last Of England*. Last year the great *War Requiem* produced one old £10 note for the script, no fee or even expenses. I even had to pay for a driver and bought most of the props. If Dad hadn't died so timely chaos would now hold sway in the Nat West, Northwood.

Thursday 13
Colour is the eye's music – Lorca.

Friday 14
The French government mounted a most inapposite procession to mark the 200th anniversary of the storming of the Bastille – designed by Grace Jones' hairdresser. Some young fashion models dressed in funereal black, like enormous tops, pirouetted unsteadily down the Champs-Elysées embracing embarrassed young boys dressed as Pierrots and Samurai. A dilapidated black conductor, looking like an illustration of a cocktail shaker in a twenties *Vogue*, hammered at a drum surrounded by girls flopping around in a pastiche tribal dance, black willies in classical tutus.

Two bored commentators came and went in the haywire sound, with comments like *All the worlds' tribes are meeting here tonight* or *The more uncomfortable your position, the better view you will have of the parade.*

This included: several British military bands waving the Union flag, clog dancers, Soviet bandsmen goose-stepping in a snowstorm, a contingent of Senegalese recruited from the unemployed in the Paris suburbs. We saw the backs of an assortment of uninterested heads-of-state at a dull reception – behind, as the commentator repeatedly told us, bullet-proof glass. Mrs. Thatcher, wielding an enormous pair of binoculars, was eating cake with George Bush.

In the Place de la Concorde, at about 10:00, Jessye Norman, wrapped in an enormous tricolour duster, with blue hands, suddenly appeared at the foot of the Egyptian obelisk to belt out the *Marseillaise*; before this – the climactic moment – the sound on my TV faded in an eerie wind, the sort you get in horror movies. After it had blown through the proceedings for several minutes the commentator informed us that this was the official soundtrack.

I can't have been the only one who had thought the gods were blowing cold on so much wind viewed from the 190ft crane. The interminable programme was delivered to us by the perpetrator of this *ennui*, a Mr. Goude, who was editing it in some distant video suite. For myself and 500 million other viewers.

An event almost as big as Live Aid, said the commentator. I decided it was no coincidence that Mr. Goude's name resembled the dullest of Dutch cheeses, the tedium was increased to hilarity by constant reference to his *avant garde* status.

Saturday 15

The fennel which runs wild along the roads from Lydd is covered with yellow flowers; and the seeds I planted some moons ago have formed healthy-looking plants nearly a foot high. In the woods the teasels are in flower. On my walk I saw a peacock butterfly feasting on a clump of nettles, the first this summer.

A glorious summer day with a cooling breeze. At night the stock came on with its delicious scent.

Sunday 16

Up before sunrise, the first light of dawn still and mysterious. A sea mist blew in, and the fog horn sounded till eight. Then gradually the mist melted away in bright strong sunlight. The garden is invaded by butterflies: whites, meadow browns and peacocks.

Painted and tarred a bible – open at *Leviticus* with barbed wire marker.

Monday 17

Even on this fleeting visit, Glasgow is a surprise, its elegant architecture far more delicate than the eighteenth century classicism of Bath; the sharpest Greek detailing on the terraces. And in spite of postwar development, the city is intact: cleaned, and restored, its ruined spaces planted with trees. The docks have vanished but the city's business area has fine grand buildings, which escaped a sixties' ring road by a miracle. The art school is the finest secular building in the British Isles, and sits like a fortress on its hillside. The Third Eye Centre is a gem by Greek Thompson.

Glasgow seems to be taking hard times with resilience and imagination. The smoke-black city of memory has disappeared. Sure, I'm forgetting the concrete housing estates; but central Glasgow shines, bathed in sunlight under a parasol of white clouds – a crystalline light that is the enchantment of the North.

I find Glasgow irresistible, a city that is 'home'.

Tuesday 18

Long indigo shadows of trees fall across the hills. A swollen yellow moon lit up far below as we flew from Glasgow late in the gathering shadows of a scorching day, rose-red and purple.

We had spent the day walking through the city: smiles and autographs and a long interview with Richard Jobson in the park.

Richard has the face of a recluse, a media hermit. He spent his wild days quickly, between 15 and 20; now, at 28, he's already lived nine lives. He's just returned from a week gathering herbs in a monastery garden, though you're just as likely to find him late at night on Venice Beach. In conversation the camera soon disappears.

Wednesday 19

A barrage of phone calls. HB seized the infernal machine, stopped the bell with putty, left a message saying 'you have reached 8367454, this machine does not take messages'. Robyn Archer, who had come to tea, laughed herself silly. HB said the phone was ringing and I picked it up silent. Three times I intercepted calls by chance. But that's not a miracle – the phone rings all day.

~

Rang Donny in NYC and asked him if he could ask his friend Matt Dillon for the sound of his heartbeat for *Blueprint*: it would be a great first credit.

~

Sleepless night spent dreaming up the exhibition: the beds, no longer on the floor but placed as constructions on the wall, tarred and feathered sheets, quotations from Aquinas and the *Sun*, skeletons, KY tubes, Vaseline, condoms, a tarred and feathered TV set with a tape of sex and Mozart's Masonic mass.

~

Last night we saw *The Vortex*. Noel Coward put his sexuality in a little silver box and sniffed it.

It's a ghastly play, dahlings truly, brilliant but defeated – harder than Cocteau but flawed. Coward, drugged up in a kimono, pouring coffee from a silver pot, reverted to type like Bunty, dear. Confession as innuendo: weekend parties with the fast fag set – Mountbatten, 'the sailor boy who had it all'.

This precious trivial world, magnified by boredom, has trapped poor Rupert for six months at the Garrick. The play is still infinitely contemporary, all the idiocy of the established classes mirrored in the audience – the lady behind me squealed 'The girl who plays Bunty doesn't have an English name, dear.' Another took out her compact and powdered her nose vigorously.

Cigarettes, lipstick in public, all the ritual of the social swill caught brilliantly. Phillip Prowse's set and direction paid a distant bow to Pasolini's *Salò* in its modernismo. It was all very well done and frightfully upsetting. Coward remained firmly stuck in act one for the rest of his life.

Rupert sweated through the piece with style, and we met later in his dungeon of a dressing room. He said he'd fallen out with the theatre set, and its oh-so-nasty niceties: 'the so-so English THEATRE, darlings, is deadly.'

The whole world of royal fagdom has sat for weeks applauding – snappers and flappers and the deadbeats. You know, dear, that the Duke of York caught the Prince of Wales in bed with a Cuban ballet dancer who was given a one-way ticket to disappear in the Bermuda Triangle, where a little later his lover followed him. And later on Noel went too. And that, my dears, is just the tip of the Koh-i-noor. Cocktails everyone?

~

Why do people read novels when they are only written in the hope they'll be made into films?

History fascinates me, letters, autobiography; so this is why I answer your question about swinging London. Though if you rummaged through the fading colour supplements you would find the sixties happened in NYC. Manhattan was everyone's goal, most of the painters and designers I knew ended up there. Sex and money, in that order.

Where's the party?

. . . must be the epitaph of London. The party was always somewhere else, at someone else's place.

I was just eighteen years old in 1960, so if a decade belongs to youth, the sixties were mine. I missed National Service by a few months; even now I can hear the sigh of relief; a whole generation of pretty boys forgot square bashing, and beat a trail to Carnaby Street. Art was my passion. The Slade still a centre – its yearly dance the only place where you could let your hair down, dance with your hands on another boy's arse, open his flies and slip your hand in, and rock the place. Art was very heterosexual, beards and billiards at the pub. Rauschenberg, Johns, Hockney and Warhol were to change that.

Gay? Well we were still queer, with nowhere to go, just two or three unlicensed bars that held a hundred at the most; coffee bars with dance floors where you were forbidden to touch: 'Now lads please, you know the rules.' So you sipped lukewarm Nescafé in a Duralex glass cup and stared and stared.

Victim on release and some years to legislation. Fucking was fucking once you were in bed in the 'privacy of your own home'. Drinking clubs like the Rockingham for the Quentin Crisps; the Rockingham! – the name was enough to put you off; our clubs were La Deuce, the Gigolo and the Hustler, the A & B – Arts and Battledress – a memory of the war, a mere fifteen years ago.

~

David Hockney won the prize for Young Professionals at the London University Art Competititon in '61, I was classed as an Amateur and took my £5.00 prize along with him.

We were the ones who swung, out and about at 4am – cruising. Sort of high class renters, though no-one got my arse for a dinner. A large cock was an advantage in this world. I thought myself dead butch. It was not until the end of the decade – shorty after the first meeting of the Gay Liberation Front at the London School of Economics – that I turned over and got fucked – at the hot end of the Gigolo; no words will describe how exciting that was.

Clothes. Carnaby Street was cheap and egalitarian, art school clothes at Pauline Fordham's Palisades were on the way. My friend Ossie Clark who swung London, and lost a collar or two to the sound of the Doors, founded the King's Road. Meanwhile David's friend, Mo, painted the large blue skies and swimming pools in the background while David held the foreground with charm and a toothpick. 'Blondes have more fun.' David was constant, unlike Rudolph, who danced right off the stage of the Opera House, down the King's Road in the small hours 'till he turned a trick. Patrick Proctor gave up and redecorated 'Moroccan'.

Where's the party?

I fucked with my first man in the basement of 64 Priory Road, Kilburn. A student hanger-on, bystander.

David and Patrick seemed so rich, rich and old, though we were only separated by a few years. Peter said we were there to protect them from the confetti of purple hearts at La Deuce – social shields. We ate upstairs at the Casserole and after 11:00 dived into the scrum in the basement of the Gigolo, whose owner had nearly a dozen large Francis Bacons on the third floor which you might be invited to admire.

Finding sexual partners was difficult and they were often transitory – hardly bothered to take their pants down before buttoning up. And the police might raid, send the prettiest ones in as *agents provocateurs*. They had hard-ons, but didn't come. Just arrested you.

Where was the party?

It might be Tony Richardson's whose metallic rooms echoed to the cry of a pet toucan; the Guinesses, where we talked to David Niven and rolled joints in a corner; or Isabel Aberconway's where we behaved and admired the Picassos, gingerly accepting grapes dipped in chocolate at tea time.

Snobbism in large helpings sunk Patrick's leather boys and Joe Orton's; their place taken by the Buckles and Snowdons in increasingly transitory watercolour. David painted lurid Western art collectors and opera directors sitting on Breuer chairs.

A private view? Where's the private view?

... was still the place to meet the interesting rather than the interested, but after ...

Where's the party?

A drunken mistake with a boy who turned out to be middle-aged when he removed his Beatle wig and doused me with phials of poppers that sent me dizzy for my jeans. I slept in them. That was no party.

Cuba, the assassination of Kennedy, Martin Luther, Vietnam.

I slept with a handsome young black man in '64 on a pile of coats in a Manhattan bedroom, that was a party.

Tinker√, Tailor√, Soldier√, Sailor√, Rich man√, Poor man√, Beggar-man√, Thief √ – counting the tricks – Mass Murderer √ (that was later).

New York was more adventurous and older, Swinging London? Pop music, the Beatles, Stones, and the Who. Paul McCartney's £250 million suggests that even then sobriety paid; Lennon and his swinging heroin addiction vanished to New York, and David Hockney to the West Coast, Rudolph to Paris; others disappeared without a trace.

The sixties: clean streets and dirty buildings.

The eighties: clean buildings and dirty streets.

Flower power soon faded.

Sex, and drugs, and rock and roll were the seventies.

Then, the last great smog that blackened the churches and public buildings, crept into your bedroom along with *Lady Chatterley*.

Laurence suggested sex might be described as a euphemism: I slept with him.

Clinically: we had sexual intercourse – not very gay that, definitely heterosexual.

Or as profanity.

My sex was certainly that – he was a great fuck, phallocentric, selfish, and fun.

Love came later.

Thursday 20

Filmed the Pet Shop Boys' concert at Wembley. It had rave reviews in all the music papers and listings; only the qualities have poured cold water. Whatever the shortcomings, it's entertaining – spectacular dancing, colourful costumes. And the film backdrop – Super 8 blown up to 70mm -- works.

In *It's a Sin* the show crescendos and the whole thing fuses together. *Shopping* has choreography as stylish as Gene Kelly; *King's Cross*, with HB's beautiful black and white film, is heartfelt. *Sin* and *Paninaro* (which I don't like) are the audience's favourites.

Filming it is a contradiction as there are five cameras mounted in fixed positions to interfere with the sight lines of the least number of seats. Loss of contact with the cameramen is almost complete, the music so loud you can barely make yourself heard through their headphones. I sat with Matthew and HB in a van outside monitoring it all.

My paranoia of technology mounted through the day, so I let the two of them direct the whole thing and was a back seat driver throughout. It was the best thing, as knowing the show so well I would have been carried away by detail and missed the broad canvas.

In this lies the contradiction: it is impossible to capture an audience of 10,000 on film. Distance destroys the light show: it is reduced to the size of a postcard on the TV screen, or cut off in close-ups, either way dwindling into insignificance.

On film the close-up is always more interesting, but this is not how the live audience sees it. Filming a theatrical event can produce sudden horrors: in the *Rake's Progress* the clowns among the middle-aged Florentine ladies of the chorus had invented a punk make-up – which the audience at the opera house never saw as they were too far away.

~

Got Neil to tone down his make-up: in the test run last night he looked like a sweaty panda, with two huge black eyes. Throughout the whole event (which must have been nerve racking, as he has never performed to a large audience before) he has shown the most remarkable calm. Without this the show wouldn't have worked; his astute decisions and support carried the day.

Friday 21

At Wembley by 9:00 – to run through the concert for the cameras. A gruelling hot day. In the evening I stood by the ticket office to help friends get in, so great was the crush, there were no guest tickets, even though they had been promised.

Stood by the mixing desk next to George Michael. He left after six numbers. When it was all over I pushed through a scrum of kids round the stage door, and smuggled in Ian McKellen who could not pass the barriers.

Joined everyone at the party at Westway Studios for a couple of hours. All the lads after the Bros boy, a shining suntan ad. Gerard was given the eye. Tilda and Rupert arrived and we all took turns on the roundabout. Left at two.

Saturday 22

The temperature climbed into the mid-nineties, a close heat-haze shrouded the horizon, oppressive clouds appeared from the west and the evening turned a sour grey smudged with an angry sunset. It rained heavily in the night in short bursts.

After a week's absence there are casualties in the garden: the rosemary has died and the marigolds have wilted. Hose pipes are banned so I have to use the old watering can I bought for *War Requiem*. The marigolds picked up within minutes, and by the time I'd finished, at ten, the whole garden was awash with the scent of night stock.

Exhausted from the week in Wembley, I was in bed early, though up at dawn. The bees were already in the lavender, which is in full flower. Another hot day, the fields harvested. I don't remember a year like this.

Sunday 23

Tarred Güta's garden seat to match Prospect Cottage. It's an 18th century seat made for a lady in a pannier, just like the one in the Gainsborough painting of Mr. and Mrs. Andrewes. It has been rebuilt, as the original timber rotted. Garden furniture of this date is quite rare.

A disturbed day after a week on the run. The silence has left me winded. The sun shone down relentlessly.

Tuesday 25

David arrived at lunch with an enormous block of pitch.

After swimming, we built a brick hearth, lit a bonfire, and melted the pitch in an old tin can. For an hour we rushed back and forth to the house for brushes, gloves, barbed wire, crucifixes, prayer books, bullets, a model fighter plane, even an old telephone, which we tarred and feathered. The results were instant and extraordinary. The hot tar splashed everywhere and set like shining jet; the half-buried crucifix looked like a Medardo Rosso sculpture.

Working with the tar had all the excitement of building sand-and-water pinnacles and spires on the beach as a child. An old pillow provided feathers.

Wednesday 26

Spent the day beachcombing, discovered an anchor and wooden oars for the garden.

Friday 28

A cool dry wind blows across the parched landscape. Crickets sing in the grasses. White butterflies congregate on the lavender and lay bright orange eggs in clusters on nasturtiums and cabbages; within days they hatch into crowds of little caterpillars which nestle together and hide themselves from the fierce sun.

In the bone dry landscape there are splashes of yellow ragwort. Ragwort was believed to cure speech impediments: *Under the command of Dame Venus, it cleanses, digests, and discusses.* It is the only plant flowering; the sea peas and valerian have long gone. The wounded landscape waits for the autumn rain – blood-red berries of woody nightshade scattered like rubies.

Saturday 29

Overcast and much cooler.

Made myself toast and coffee, then into the garden to clip back the dead flowers of the santolina which have faded from bright yellow to brown. It was a pleasant job as the leaves are lightly scented.

Picked up the dead poppies, so dry they rattle as the last seeds fall from the brittle heads. At the base of the elder, the borage has sprung up waist high from the seed of the plants that flowered last winter.

The dog rose is covered with hips and has put out strong new shoots; the purple sage doubles in size every few weeks and is a flourishing two feet across. My lavender cuttings have grown into little bushes.

~

David here at midday. After a trip to Rye we built a bonfire from the drift-wood and carried armfuls of props – crucifixes, prayer books, barbed wire and shattered glass, and several old paintings, including the construction with Boecklin's *Isle of the Dead* – down to our tar pot.

All this was a good excuse to empty the studio, which has lain idle for months – almost impossible to move there for the mountains of old iron and driftwood collected during the last two years.

Working in a frenzy we completed eight new paintings – three with crosses; others have old tree branches, prayer books and glass. The Rood Dreaming. The tar glitters so brightly, forms are lost.

In Rye I spent nearly £60 on a couple of books of 17th century poetry, which I read out loud as we bowled along the road from Camber, passing the military base with its red flags flying.

Sunday 30

The bunches of dried curry plant and lavender scent the house. It wafts over as you nod off in the dark. In the garden the yarrow is blooming – *Herba militaris*, achillea, a wound herb used to staunch blood. Woundwort, knight's milfoil, nosebleed, staunch grass, bloodwort, sanguinary – also known as devil's plaything – yarrow was brushed over a victim as the dark one cast a spell.

Monday 31

As we worked yesterday I remembered a fairy tale I wrote in the 1960s of a blind King who, dressed as a beggar, travelled the world to find the Springs of Aqua Vitae, where poets gathered with tape recorders to catch each evanescent phrase as it bubbled to the surface and burst, releasing its secrets.

As if by magic there was a telephone call from Guy Ford, who lived with me in the 1970s; during a long conversation, he said he had discovered over a dozen notebooks I had written as a student. In one of them is this fairy tale. They also contained hundreds of drawings. He promised to send them.

~

A long walk to the woods, after which I spent the afternoon jewelling a photo of Mick Jagger for the magazine *20/20*. I gave him a Salvador Dali moustache, which branched and ended in bunches of flowers. Then slapped the broken record from the sleeve of *Let It Bleed* on his head like a beret. 'Thanks Mick' – this record supplied the soundtrack for momentous old Super 8s at Bankside, 'you can't always get what you want' – how true!

~

There is the suspicion of rain in the air, but a dry wind blows. The downy seeds of the willow herb float by. The black seed pods of the broom split with a crackling sound.

At the end of the garden the sloes are turning purple, and the blackberries are ripe. My wild pear tree wilts in the drought, and the nettles are dead and rattle in the wind.

By the lake a large grass snake curves silently across our path through the withered grass. Swans stand forlorn on barren stony islands that have emerged from the water.

Everything is waiting for rain: the great burdock, purple with bloom, flags like a thirsty dog; the grey moss crumbles like ash under my feet. Only the yellow ragwort, bright with tortoiseshell butterflies, is happy with this long summer; while an angry cloud of smoke from the burning fields hangs in the bare blue sky.

AUGUST

Tuesday 1

Woke before dawn to find Venus framed in my window, diamond bright, and a blood-red sun rising on a grey sea. A cool fresh breeze had blown away yesterday's clouds leaving a blue sky. As the sun gathered intensity the sea turned silver. By 7:30 the dazzling light burnt my face.

~

Idiotic phone call from some colour supplement, with a long list of questions: Where or what would you like to be?

Then blessed silence again – only the crackle of the broom's black seed pods bursting in the sun. I picked a handful and scattered them round the telegraph pole.

~

The sea has turned perfect blue, set off by the pale yellow grasses and pink shingle. For painters the colour of this grass is the elusive Naples yellow, a colour which I have always loved.

Sylvia's crow, Jet, arrived and danced up and down the tar pot viewing its reflection. Then it flew on to the table and stole a piece of blue glass, before flying up to the telegraph pole where it stayed a full minute, before plunging down into my clothes pegs. It picked one up in triumph, carried it off – and nearly got run over by a passing car. Like St. Cuthbert I should teach it to do something useful – hang out the washing or polish my shoes. But it's much too full of itself. Each time I chase it it swoops round the house, then pops up behind me with its strange croaking laugh.

~

August brings the butterflies. Clustering on the ragwort are peacocks, red admirals, and tortoiseshells a bright mosaic. The wild hops are covered with pale green flowers. On the willows huge yellow and black caterpillars hang in downy bunches, with sharp Y's etched on their bulbous faces.

At 5:00 David arrived and we drove to the Little Chef for a brunch breakfast. Returned through Greatstone as it is usually full of good looking boys with suntans. Today only one to delight the eye, spreadeagled across the bonnet of his car with split blue jeans.

~

We lit the bonfire with driftwood and boiled up the tar as the sun set.

In the gathering shadows we completed new paintings: a mirrored Coke can surrounded by demons; and a ship in a bottle – filled with black gold and smashed. The glass fell on to the canvas like a tallship in full sail; the tar eddied about it, the broken masts of the ship swallowed in the black – black that breaks down forms and distinctions, swallows shadows.

Wednesday 2

Up at six.

I sleep on the floor; so the first step of the day is a giant leap upwards, during which my mind is on hold. Along the corridor to the bathroom – ritual splashing in front of the mirror, my face barely visible in the condensation. I shave with my favourite razor, a simple silver T which the blades slip into. I bought this in Rome in 1978 when I was writing *Caravaggio*. More splashing – shower – clothes thrown on for decency and the postman. Breakfast – coffee, the same hot Boston from the Algerian Coffee Store in Old Compton Street, whose packets announce *Individual orders despatched by post to family and friends in Great Britain and abroad*. I discovered this coffee fifteen years ago. With it and my razor I can face the day happy. Two slices of toast.

I hang last nights' paintings, clean the kitchen cupboards which gather spider's webs, and water the front garden, write the diary up and handwash a few clothes. It's another perfect summer's day. By 8:00 I'm ready to walk along the beach, gathering stones for the garden.

Today the tide is far out and the sand flats are deserted. I walk at the base of the shingle bar, jumping the fast-running rivulets that carve deep furrows in the sand. The postman brings a surprise, my garden's first gift – fenugreek, thyme and balm seeds, beautifully packed and labelled in silver foil – from a lady who stopped off and admired it last Saturday.

I walked to the woods and filmed the butterflies on the ragwort; then back to find Jet had wrought merry havoc, descending out of the sky like a dive bomber into my cornflakes. In a flash he was onto the roof, marching up and down talking to himself – before a second attack, throwing my neatly arranged painting materials to the ground. Today the bullets are flying, and the clothes pegs. As I wash up he sits on the drain and stares at the water splashing from the pipe. Then he's off, leapfrogging across the posts.

At 3:30 the producer George Faber arrived with the writer Penelope Mortimer, and we brewed tea and talked around a film to be made of Penelope's novel *The Handyman*.

Took photos of the garden and noticed the first painted lady butterfly. Then, after a walk to the beach, cross-country to Sissinghurst, where they are filming *Portrait of a Marriage*.

~

Even without the charabancs the place seems desolate, too immaculate. In the white garden the art's too artful. Shadow of Vita through high mullion windows – and a film crew with walkie-talkies, seriously communicating.

Drove Penelope back to the truly deranged Great Danes Hotel – a schizoid structure, half barracks, half Victorian country house, thrown together by planners who'd shopped through the most vulgar arcades with their eyes closed. Signs everywhere. One huge one, on what looked like a water tower, proclaimed *Hotel*; the entrance also had a huge sign, *Main Entrance*, and a large warning sign, *Lock Up Your Car*. Four identical scarlet bridesmaids looking like glee singers – perhaps the Danettes – passed us in the lobby, where a sign read *BBC. Please note, no jeans*.

The theme park philosophy of the white garden descended into chaos. More urns here: they're cream, with false flowers or chrome. Gold carpets like melted ice cream, crazy crystal chandeliers, chocolate brown smoked glass walls.

Back home to London. George drove like a maniac, the car drifting all over the place – rather like the script. The central character lacks definition. Have I let myself into something crazy, casting for the handyman my favourite Marcello Mastroianni? He can be so funny, the epitome of a spiv.

Thursday 3

A parcel of my old notebooks arrived from Guy. Apparently I gave them to him 13 years ago after making *Sebastiane*, when I was homeless. They have all the rough sketches for Ken Russell's *Gargantua*, which I had forgotten. If the film had been made it would have been my best design.

~

The Russell designs included an altar with Coke bottle candelabra. There is a detail of the king's porn palace, a window made with pink marble legs and those ruched theatre curtains like a Can-Can dress. The notes also have precise descriptions of style, e.g. Pompadour Gimcrack. There's an avenue of monumental hammers-and-sickles, a swimming pool with a Warhol soup can li-lo, a gold raft with a sail in the shape of a silver fish. The Abbey of Thelema is a ziggurat with a double spiral staircase built like Hadrian's tomb – with woods, and surmounted by a two hundred foot ornamental urn sprouting a tropical garden . . . On and on, page after page. My favourites were some carriages in the form of sailing boats – sails painted with hearts, clubs, diamonds, and spades.

~

3:30, Paul Bettell's film, *I Have Seen The Deflatable Man At The Olympia*. This is the second time I have seen the film: it grows on you, a little classic.

Friday 4

Meeting at Zenith films with Scott Meek and Robyn Archer to start the ball rolling on a film of Robyn's show *A Star Is Torn*. Walked back through Soho with Robyn to the Bar Italia. The show follows the tragic lives of stars like Billie Holliday, and Marie Lloyd – suggested ghostly deserted locations, bars and stations, even a theatre with a soundtrack of people enjoying themselves.

Dropped into Comptons, my local boy bar. A cocky lad in a white T-shirt and jogging trousers bobbed over and got into a conversation. He was, he apologised, an actor, but also a Punch and Judy man. I asked him to come and perform in *The Garden*. 'Will it fit?' he said. 'Doesn't everything fit in?' I said. He smiled, 'Well yes.'

Filled in a questionnaire for the *Sunday Correspondent*:

Q: How would you like to be remembered?

A: As a flower.

'A pansy!' shouts HB. 'No, a red hot poker.'

Q: Your virtues?

A: My homosexuality.

Q: Vices?

A: Inconsistency.

At nine I went to Hampstead – no attractive lads there, but an energetic police raid to make up for it. Artfully dodged through the boys in blue, but got myself ready for a full front page in the dailies: *Pets' AIDS victim exposed*.

Rolled into bed at three in the morning. The traffic roared through the night, gathering in decibels down the Charing Cross Road – almost unbearable after the silence of Dungeness. Moaning destitutes crashed out in doorways, drunk nightclubbers tripping over them. Cars roaring along with mindless muzak at full volume.

Saturday 5

Given a video of *British Boys*, a porno tape that is slower than my *Angelic Conversation*! These boys can't act, let alone fuck. Crashingly boring, though it has several surreal costumes: cricket pads, gloves, jockstraps; and one scene sports an unlikely member of the Household Cavalry licking boots. Inept SM scenes with swagger sticks and cricket bats.

Q: What most depresses you?

A: Film.

Q: What most upsets you?

A: Other people's film.

Who cares to possess *British Boys* electronically? It's at moments like this that I regret for myself and everyman, as I toss off in the sheets. Perhaps the British boys could learn a thing or two about their art and the camera from their American cousins; their sex patter sounds as convincing as a tired lettuce, 'shove that hot cock up my arse'. Even their groans are agonisingly simulated.

Gerard says they throw safe sex orgies in Amsterdam, advertised pushingly by gay organisations like COC – patron: Queen Beatrix. I wonder which member of our royal family should extend their patronage? Perhaps the Queen Mum, who is reputed to have found one of her footmen trying on one of those hats and to have said sharply, 'There's only enough room for one old queen in this house.'

We bowled into the Little Chef on the way to Prospect and queued for hours for 'brunch breakfast'. The sunny side eggs had a total eclipse.

Prospect bathed in sunlight. Walked down to the beach and swam, the beach completely deserted on a hot August Saturday.

In the evening I watered the garden. Brian watched me as I rescued my poor pot plants, and suggested the lighthouse should be the star of Bethlehem. Packed in watering at 11:00 for a second viewing of *British Boys* to see if I'd missed a trick. Sadly I hadn't.

Sunday 6

A hummingbird hawk hovers over the lavender. Jet, hellbent on moving everything he can lay his beak on, ignores it, and hides his treasures in nooks and crannies. He has carefully covered a strawberry with sticks and stones. Ten minutes later he re-discovers it. Chance or memory? He's a beady-eyed little monster. There's sticky spaghetti shoved into my drying shoes.

Cut back santolina and helichryssum and planted dozens of gorse cuttings. The sea buckthorn I potted up a few weeks back has rooted. Planted out the iris and the slips of my old pink, Mrs. Sinkins; also the great mullein. Sprinkled seeds of the purple sea pea all over the garden.

~

The seed heads of the dill have turned a deep bronze. The purple burdock flowers are covered with tortoiseshells, and the wild fennel is bright with yellow flowers. The thrift in the stone circles has formed strong plants which are flowering, and the blue borage is in flower again under the dog rose. As I write, a wall butterfly is sunning itself on the marigolds. The woundwort has flowered, which can 'cure many grievous woundes and some mortale'.

~

The great mullein was the herb that Ulysses used as a protection against Circe's enchantment. These flowers were used by Romans to dye hair yellow: *The golden floweres of mullen stiped in lye causeth the heare to war yellow being washed withal.*

The plant had many uses: it drew splinters, cured earache; dipped in wax, it was used as a taper – *the whole toppe with its pleasant yellow flowers sheweth like to a wax candle or taper cunningly wrought.* Verbascum *is of the latines called* candelaria *because the elder age used the stalkes dipped in suet to burne wether at funerals or otherwise.*

Cole in his *Adam and Eve* writes: *The husbandmen of Kent do give it to their cattle against the cough of the lungs.* It was called 'clown's lungwort'.

~

Alasdair bowled down on his motorbike for tea; followed by Toby, who showed us his first film – dreamt round Millais' *Ophelia.*

Unsuccessful walk to find butterflies. The ragwort is dying. Had a meal at the Greek restaurant and then watched old movies: *In The Shadow Of The Sun,* with the flamenco singer Almadien.

Monday 7
A yawning lethargy sucked my footsteps all day. Each time I sat down I fell asleep. Slept through the afternoon – a close, hot day.

Alone after the others had departed to London. The phone brought tedious requests: 'I'm not interrupting am I?' Even Jet annoyed me by stalking into the kitchen and overturning everything that sparkled.

Hellfire and damnation in a book called *The Unacceptable Vice.* Here the madness of Christianity can be followed in its fight against the physical body, waged with increasing violence through the Middle Ages. The council of Nablus held in 1120, the year Henry I's homosexual sons drowned in the white ship, marks the turning point. Now adult sodomites were to be burnt. The denunciation of William Rufus, was preceded by Mempricius, a fifth century British king of the time of David, who, the chronicles say was devoured by wolves after giving himself over to buggery. Malgo, a sixth century Saxon was drowned in his bath at Winchester, for the same offence: 'who ever dwelt in a building where sodomy was practised should be burnt along with the house.' Pederasty punished by castration in Florence. A boy of fourteen who voluntarily submitted to the act was beaten and driven through the city naked. A procurer had his hand cut off. And when it was all ended who can show one soul saved for the thousands mutilated and murdered? A murderous tradition which still contrives to legislate against us.

Tuesday 8

There were half a dozen painted lady butterflies on the purple flowers of the knapweed in the woods. Though all the other butterflies have disappeared even this number seems small in comparison with my childhood memories. There was a buddleia in the courtyard of the old manor of Curry Malet, where at any one moment on a sunny afternoon five or six butterflies would be drinking nectar – peacocks, red admirals, tortoiseshells, hummingbird hawk moths. These insects are now rarer.

~

When I first came to Dungeness one old man down the road made a point of saying that we had the purest drinking water in England. Dungeness is a natural filter. Today's report from the Friends of the Earth says it contains unacceptable levels of lead and aluminium. A water board official says the levels are safe. But surely pure drinking water should have no impurities, and he should have said he was working to achieve that.

~

Agrimony and purple loosestrife are in flower. Agrimony,

> *If it be leyd under a man's heed*
> *he shall sleepen as he wer deed*
> *he shall never drede ne wakyn*
> *till fro under his heed it be takyn.*

The yellow flowers of *Agrimonia eupatoria* are named after Mithridates Eupator, a king who brewed herbal remedies. It is known colloquially as 'church steeples' and yields a bright yellow dye. 'A decoction of the leaves,' says Gerard, 'is good for them with naughty livers.' 'A herb of princely authority,' says Pliny.

Thursday 10

Spent the small hours round a bonfire with the gypsies on the Heath as the weather closed in. Woke this morning to find the world awash, the first rain for months. Put on a stout pair of leather shoes from a dozen I've collected over the years from second hand shops, cleaned and polished the rest. HB in the bath said I should change my name to Imelda.

Spent the morning rewriting *Blueprint* and afterwards caught the 24 up to Albert Road to see Simon Watney, who has the most complete archive of media disinformation. I have decided to dedicate each of the tarred and feathered beds to a newspaper, *Mirror, Star, Sun, Guardian, Times,* they've stolen the best of names and all of them have put out dangerous and false information.

Simon has an astute grasp of our situation, a true and incisive attitude, and can put pen to paper like few others – in the sad wasteland of print his voice rings out. For me it often seems the only voice, as he not only publishes in the academic journals, like *October,* but also in the freebies like the *Pink Paper* – read in gay bars and pubs. He attends endless conferences and symposia – where the experts' lack of knowledge about our lives is truly monumental.

Last week a doctor in the mainstream of research with a leading drug company said that looking for drugs to combat the virus and to prolong the lives of those already infected posed an ethical problem, as keeping them (read *me* here) alive only exacerbated the situation. Better we should all die quickly.

Every day, in many little ways, we are subject to this terrorism. Our relationships unsanctioned, beyond the law. Meanwhile the *Sun*'s medical correspondent, flying in the face of all facts (the vast majority of HIV cases are heterosexual) wrote for his readership that they had nothing to fear, the 'facts' were a conspiracy: only gays were ever infected.

We need Burroughs' gay soldiers. As I write, only the niceties and constraints of an English upbringing stop me reaching for a gun.

~

The walls of the gallery will have several beds, mattresses, sheets, discarded clothes, all tarred and feathered. In the beds could be bibles, condoms, the clothes – jeans and sweatshirts, sport clothes; uniforms – a fireman's or policeman's. Quotations from the newspapers, photos of loved ones and families, found photos, alarm clocks, a telephone, a tarred and feathered TV.

In the centre of the gallery an oasis: a bed with two young men surrounded by barbed wire; on the wire, press cuttings, as if blown by the wind; and a tarred and feathered skeleton wearing a concentration camp uniform, spreadeagled as if shot trying to enter the space.

Friday 11
Telecine of the Super 8 footage taken this summer in the garden. With the exception of close-ups on the new camera, it all came out perfectly: jewel-like colours dark and mysterious forms dissolving – much magic.

A meeting to discuss the Tilda sequences, Madonna of the photo opportunity.

Saturday 12

Cloudy, with a warm dry wind. It had hardly rained here, which surprised me, as the deluge in London felt as if it must have covered the whole country. More damaging than the drought is the strong wind, as it dries out the plants.

With the hosepipe ban the view has become a desert, everything left to chance and the isobars. The sloe bushes are heavy with purple fruit a full six weeks in advance of last year – we picked them in early October. The rosemary bushes are dying, and most of the flowers are over – the geraniums and marigolds, scarlets and reds. The brave bugloss is at a finish. Picked up the dead flower heads of the sempervivum and night scented stock, trimmed lavender flowers. Repotted seedlings of foxglove and great mullein; also sea buckthorn and the wild fig.

> To prove there was a life after
> A man had himself buried six feet under
> In a lead-lined coffin, holding a fig.
> He said, 'If a life after exists, the fig will grow.'
> The fig grew. That's quite certain.
> As a child I ate the figs of eternal life;
> They were unripe and gave me colic.

Dungeness might seem the least hospitable environment for a fig tree to take root. Cut back by biting winter easterlies it is a mere couple of feet high, dwarfed but thriving. Sycamore and oak have established themselves in the same way.

Monday 14

A band of rain blew over at dawn. Warm sunny day which clouded over.

Before the sun disappeared we filmed David out on the shore amongst the fishing boats, lying in huge coils of rope. Then, as film was running low, we made a trip to Rye; but by the time we returned the sun was lost.

A sullen evening: parched flowers dying, menacing clouds mounting above burning stubble, ploughed fields drained of life – the only movement, the silvery grey leaves of the willows along the drainage canals.

Julian swung the car along the empty roads like a rally driver, in silence. Dark by 8:30. Evenings drawing in.

Tuesday 15

Feelings of frustration and dissatisfaction – detachment from friends – life wrenched apart – all the sourness of Fellini's *Ginger and Fred*'s tired and rubbished landscapes washed over and overwhelmed me. As I looked through the tapes of my films for David I couldn't bear to watch any of them, ghostly memories.

Sandy rang to say Paul is now very ill. I feel furious and impotent, why should this happen? Lovers shrivelled and parched like the landscape.

~

The handyman who was to help me put in new windows doesn't ring – I wonder if it is my reputation.

HB rings in a panic to say the song he is working on isn't cutting – I knew instinctively that it wouldn't. I lost my temper briefly with everyone at the shoot: all the cameramen framed the same dancer, and shouting over the intercom in that rat-trap Wembley didn't change anything. A replay impossible, as time was out.

What am I doing?

Julian and David left at 10:30. The clouds dissolved in the strong winds and by two the sky was clear. Still no rain, though a few drops fell out of the blue sky.

~

Chattering in the kitchen told me Mr. Crow was back; as I turned the corner he was tucking into the bread and was damned if he was going to give up. Carrying a large slice, he eventually made off, only to be pounced on by two large seagulls. Then all hell broke loose – he chased them up and over the house, right out of eyesight and back again, making a terrible racket. They gave up and left him sitting on the chimney pot in triumph.

~

The dew of the garden was mixed in the morning with the sweet fragrance of his memories. The flowers are his mouth, the breeze his breath, the rose had been moistened by the dew of his cheeks. Therefore I love gardens madly, for at all times they make me remember him who I love.

~

I sat and wrote this poem, the bright sunlight through the window hurting my eyes.

No dragons will spring from these circles.
These stones will not dance or clap hands at the solstice.
Beached on the shingle,
They lock up their memories,
Upright as sentinels
In the dry grass.
Rolled by the sea down the centuries

They wait the great Tide
That shall come a second time
Recalling them to the depths
Where the salt sea will unlock their silence.
Then they'll talk of their time here
To strange creatures,
Telling them how the postman came up
The path with your letter,
How I couldn't conceal my happiness,
And walked backwards and forwards in the garden, skipping.
How, when you came, we set off under a full moon,
To watch the patient fishermen,
And then turned home,
Throwing handfuls of pebbles
In showers of sparks
Under the starlit sky.
Of your face, lit by the beam from the lighthouse,
Every ten seconds,
A smile,
A little frown,
Green eyes,
A wink.

~

Planted out santolinas and fig tree cuttings.

Sat in the deck chair and watched the sun set and a full moon climb over the lighthouse through bands of iridescent cloud.

The stones reflect the great circle of the moon. They can hear me singing in the kitchen.

Wednesday 16

The smallest gestures are amplified on film: a shaking hand holding the camera can make an earthquake, a speck of dust becomes a beam in the eye, a scratch a super-highway. In epic film – except in the hands of a master like Eisenstein – all is lost: a half-smile, a nod, a frown, are invisible in the juggernaut moves of the camera. *The Garden* is a simple domestic drama, a document. No fiction. The smallest gestures.

Christopher Hobbs rang. The Madonna's crown (modelled on Van Eyck) is now completed; and he is off to Oman to paint a mural for the Sultan. I sip my tea and watch Mr. Crow drinking from the blue-green leaves of the sea kale, which catch the water in sparkling pools. The stalks of these leaves form little conduits to draw water to the plant.

Annie Symons, the film's costume designer, phoned, said the Virgin comes in all colours besides the traditional blue – pinks, scarlets, even emerald green. A green earth Virgin, as opposed to a blue sky Virgin, seems contemporary.

It's grey and overcast, a spattering of rain.

Back in London a bright full moon dazzled the eyes. Fresh breeze and the clouds scudding past.

Thursday 17

Anselm Kiefer's painting, covered with the dust of centuries: frozen, inert burials, firestorms, cinders, great leaden tomes, spidery nervous wires, odd submarine encrustations, amphora from the wrecks of memory, monumental ruins beached between the Tigris and Euphrates, strange alchemical angels hovering over the ancestral skip – echoes – the 20th century ashes, awe-inspiring in the vast studio at the Riverside. Felt kinship.

~

Deborah at Working Title asked me why I always appeared so happy. Because I am the most fortunate film-maker of my generation, I've only ever done what I wanted. Now I just film my life, I'm a happy megalomaniac, I added. Making films our way makes all others seem fabricated; most of the directors can't even pick up a camera, let alone a pen. And the pretentiousness! Who is worth their salt, or has even a chance to throw it over their shoulder? There's no Mastroianni or Bette Davis here, they are all somewhere else.

~

Meeting with James, then up to Pollocks' theatre shop where Robert showed me his Punch and Judy booth – then down to Richard Salmon's to meet Roger and his daughter. He bought five small paintings. He now has forty from the last 25 years.

Richard Salmon has an impressive life-size crucifixion painted for Philip II of Spain, a copy of a Van der Weyden. It is standing next to Gilbert and George's blood-spattered *Bad God*. They bleed in unison.

Back home Tilda arrived; and we spent the rest of the afternoon at the edit and eating cakes at Bertaux'. Arranged to bring the Moscow horse chestnuts – taken from the graves of Khrushchev and Chekhov – to her parents' home in Scotland; talked about the possibility of Daniel Day Lewis being in a Super 8 film. My nerves stop me asking him – he would only need to work for a week. I can't afford to unbalance the project with stars, pay Equity minimum! It wouldn't keep his agent's racehorses in bran.

Did nothing. I have little ability to cope with the world of success, either in myself or in others. My dynamo runs backwards quickly.

Tilda left for Scotland, seemed troubled but happy.

On-line video edit on the Pet Shop Boys' concert movie till five in the morning. We put together *Rent* in a series of multiple *Come Dancing* dissolves. Could this be Hell? I had a sudden flash of it going on relentlessly, through hundreds of years.

Crawled into bed at 5:30, the sun already up.

Friday 18

'You're not as dumb as one thinks.'

At the Kiefer show a little boy, in long white shorts and a white shirt, perfectly silent in the vast space, stared along the railway lines in a painting, captured a dandelion seed that blew across the floor. He performed a strange dance with it, leaping into the air, crawling about catching it. No-one except an old lady noticed, and she smiled with me. The painting of the tulips has just such movements (coup de vent), the petals blow in the air. How do you paint the wind? This is how. The little boy could have leapt from the paintings.

~

'You're not as dumb as one thinks.'

As I passed the bag lady with fine chiselled features, nut brown under a huge bonnet made of a paisley shawl, she spoke these words in a clear voice, not loud enough for anyone else to hear. It seemed she addressed me, although she could have been talking to herself.

At 12:00, Alex, a young art student from Canada – my cousin John's son – arrived. We went to the Kiefer show, then had a pizza.

I liked him a lot – the younger generations of Jarmans seem relaxed and attractive. I told him about the mad generation of grandparents: Geoff, who was court-martialled for getting the National Servicemen to work on his boat rather than square bash – who made everyone happy except the Air Ministry; of Marshal of the RAF Elworthy, the proper one; and dear Dad.

All of them were casualties of the war, and went into the sad peace of the fifties: drinks parties and all the niceties; fitted carpets, double glazing, mink coats, pearls; dreams of something different that they could not grasp – as they could not imagine anything different. The clubs, the evenings when they donned dress suits and medals, and when the mums put on their best and splashed on the treasured Chanel No. 5.

A week later a large photo would arrive of a group of uncomfortable strangers round a dinner table: frozen smiles in the hard white light of a flash.

~

Kiefer's paintings. I see so much of myself there, the finer part. His *Tulips* made me blissfully happy. A sparkling grotto filled with treasure.

The sun's out with a cool breeze – perfect weather.

Saturday 19
Drove down to Dungeness with Sandy Powell and Paul Treacy.

Paul is dying, has lost nearly three stone. He says people treat him with the most extraordinary insensitivity. They collide with him on the street. They can't believe someone so young is walking with a stick. Others are so curious they are speechless when he talks to them. One ghastly inquisitive at a cocktail party badgered him with questions. How did it feel to be dying? It so distressed him he had to escape and cry in the corridor, as he had only been diagnosed the day before with Karposi's Sarcoma, on top of all his other problems.

A homeopathic doctor quizzed him about his sex life: 'You've never been to bed with a woman?!' he asked incredulously; then 'How long do they give you to live?' – before banging him a bill for £68 for some pills he had made up. And a further bill for the consultation. For this he had waited in the heat for over an hour. I'm glad to say he threw the pills back in the quack's face.

~

It was another beautiful day here. We made an enormous salad and sat in the garden. It should have been happy and carefree. Maybe it was.

A sunset covered the sky in pinks and violets. The landscape shimmered a deep orange and now in my window a full moon looms above the sea.

~

Last night I dreamed many dreams. In one a clay man crumbled into dust at my touch at the entrance of the great library between the Tigris and Euphrates.

~

Gathered seed: scabious, sea kale, and sea pea. Along the perimeter of the nuclear power station the samphire is in flower – herbe de St. Pierre, dedicated to fishermen. I wonder if the fishermen of Dungeness know this? It was once widely collected, picked and eaten as a delicacy. Much of it came from the cliffs at Dover – 'the dreadful trade' as Shakespeare called it. Its bright green and yellow flowers make a fine contrast with the dead grasses and burnt shingle along the shore.

Sunday 20

I collected cuttings of samphire and bought two tree lupins and a dozen wallflowers – very sturdy plants for £1 at the Boot Fair on the Parade at Greatstone; also an old sickle and a small mirror. Derek Ball, who drove me there, wisely bought kitchen equipment. I found a Dylan album, *Blonde on Blonde* – everyone sighs when you mention the 'Born Again'; but his voice echoed through a sixties summer almost as idyllic as this one.

Tuesday 22

Drove to Rye – god-forsaken spot, all the shops closed, all the boys wearing Bermuda shorts and bright tops. One tried to short-change me in the ice cream shop that used to be Radclyffe Hall's living room. A grumpy lady in the greengrocer's said the samphire never flowered. Geriatric drivers all over the place, minds filled with deathwatch.

Found a model boat to 'capsize' in the tar, and a 'Van Gogh' landscape. Wandered across a desert-scorched Dungeness with the smoke of burning wheat fields in my nostrils.

~

The Garden creaks on in typical 'Jamesian' manner – nothing, as ever, foreseen. No meetings equals No money. He has acquired a ghastly video of the Pets' show to pay his phone bills, and lost my film, for the time being ...

Beleaguered on all sides, the great library between the Tigris and Euphrates will not be dreamed on to the white page.

Transplanted tansy and gathered seed. Oh fuck everything! The phone is going again.

Escaped with the camera to film close-ups of rocks and weathered wood for the bluescreen backgrounds in *The Garden*.

Wednesday 23

Walked down to the beach in the moonlight. The tide was far out, the sea almost inaudible; a wide band of silver across the wet sands. Today has been warm and dry.

~

An enthusiastic Italian lady from Ferrara invited me to stage or film *A Midsummer Night's Dream* in 1991 – in the reedbeds and flatlands of the Po, where *Ossessione* was shot.

No-one has made a successful adaptation of the play; both Lindsay Kemp and Reinhardt went for bust in glitter and glamorous faeries – at the expense of *ossessione*, the love compulsion in the play.

Thursday 24

Long production meeting with James at Basilisk to organise a shoot for next Friday; then over to the edit of the Pets' concert film. HB and Peter hacking through endless material – once and once only! Chris Lowe's delivery of the words 'Sex, money, death, religion' are more punk than Rotten: *deadpan* say the fans, *deadly* say the detractors.

~

Hot and tiring day, without the excitement that I felt back in London last week. I can't muster the energy to write letters. I am getting more absent-minded – forgot where I had stored the green sari for Tilda. Rather like Mr. Crow.

Friday 25

Lying in bed in Bankside I would watch the river ebb and flow. Barges and containers, the old tugs and pleasure boats passed through Southwark Bridge across to the huge iron-grey Doric piers of Cannon Street rail bridge; at low tide I would walk by the river bed and scout for coins and pilgrims' badges. I have a fine medieval ring from the 1340s, patterned in golden pinchbeck, that came from the river here.

~

Late lunch at Mildred's vegetarian restaurant. A young man from Chicago started up a conversation; it turned out he knew friends of mine there. I told him about M., who is heir to a great fortune, and whose mother, disapproving of his lifestyle, 'buried' him at a society funeral: her way of telling him to disappear. Now he can visit his own headstone and contemplate immortality.

Another conversation struck up with someone who worked for the dreaded Murdoch's Sky TV. I suggested he did an interview, 'Sky is Blue'.

Mr. Murdoch is in the news criticising British TV. He is quite right about it and its awful costume dramas: hideous design and indecent acting, reinforcing class, snobbery, all that the British consider valuable. The young man from Chicago, after his year at the Architecture Association, made the same criticism. It had taken him this year to grow to hate London: 'Everything has to be measured by the past here,' he said. 'If you make a criticism it falls on deaf ears. People are so convinced they are superior.'

Sunday 27

Brought in seeds of alexanders, burdock, hawkbit and yellow horned poppy. Replanted seedlings of the poppy and ivy-leaved toadflax; also the periwinkle from Phoenix House.

Everything dry as a bone. White groundsel seeds like pearls in a desert. Teasel, thistles, and the burdocks scorched and dying – nothing left for the rain to save. Even the willows rattle with drought.

A cool northerly brought the skies back. Fast-moving low cloud over bright silver with shafts of light. The sea running high, white capped; shimmering dead grasses. The summer's back broken.

~

The sun has picked out the white cliffs, like a vast iceberg in a dark blue-grey sea. The crow followed me out to the Long Pits and saw off the small dog of a couple of surprised hikers. Took cuttings of the dog roses, slips of yarrow; scattered seed of the white poppy from the seashore at Greatstone. Built windchimes from metal rods and two baulks of timber from the beach.

Just before sunset a rainbow glowed across a dark sea offset by violet-pink cumulonimbus clouds. Back home I painted a notebook cobalt blue and pasted up the script.

Monday 28

Eno's *On Land* is the music of my view: a crescent moon under a dog star, clouds scudding in the grey dawn.

I tidied the wood from the back of the house and spent the afternoon picking blackberries for jam. Noticed very few butterflies at the Long Pits, which have almost dried up; but a host of large dragonflies. The blackberries are just ripening and cascade across the light green bushes, blood-red like raw meat. It was hard work and I got torn to bits.

~

In Somerset we used to pick blackberries for jam along the hedgerows, and worts, in the Combe above Holford.

Butterflies and flowers, the deep red earth of the Quantocks, and little whitewashed houses in the woods. Days without end, no purpose but to wander wide-eyed across the fields to the sea and wade through rock pools. Why can't my film return to this Eden?

Perhaps I should celebrate the 1990s with a descent into what was once called 'the underground'. With 21 people arriving on Friday I have all the paraphernalia of 35mm with none of the advantages, and no money either!

Tuesday 29

At seven last night, as the sun was setting, Aiden and Marcus arrived with lights and camera equipment; we spent two hours taking photographs in the garden, which they had decorated with flowers and mirrors. It was hard work, as they had me stripped to the waist; and as the weather has changed, it was very cold.

~

Today I can hardly lift the knife to butter my toast. At breakfast I drink gallons of hot weak tea and feel sorry for myself. The postman arrives with a letter full of information on the Warhol show – the best lecture title: *In the future everyone will talk about Andy for fifteen minutes.*

~

I'm not certain what effect Andy had on my generation. Anger's films were more effective. Anthony Balch's film of Burroughs preceded the Factory. Warhol was a discovery of the *late* sixties.

I fought shy of the Factory, although embracing some of its ideas. For a young gay artist in NYC it was, of course, difficult to avoid. I imagined Warhol had a greater influence on my work than he really had. My Super 8 of Andrew kissing his friends was a spoof. Anger, Burroughs, Ginsberg and Rauschenberg were the influences – Andy, the court jester.

~

I first set eyes on a Warhol (a small silk screen of a dollar bill) in Richard Smith's Old Street studio in 1964. Mark Lancaster, who led the hip brigade of transatlantic artists with David, had invited me round. The new art was exciting; but it had a brittle *joie de vivre* at odds with my gloomy depths.

My first visit to the factory was to see Nicholas Ray put on his 16mm films. I met Richard Bernstein, who airbrushed the covers of *Interview*. And then later still my friend Mark Balet became art editor of the magazine.

But by that time it was all over – my only contribution an interview of Andrew Logan. You will not find my photo there, I never stood in the queues for an autograph, or spoke to the guy; the parade went by without me. I was too vain and insecure to allow myself to be snapped by the master.

~

My solitary companion today is a seagull which has perched on the telegraph pole facing the wind. I walk across the Ness and bring back slips of restharrow, hempagrimony, wormwood, plants of yellow horned poppy, teasel.

At two the glazier arrived and replaced the windows.

Wednesday 30
A chill coming on after lying naked on the shingle for the photos. Restless night, shivering and hot by turns. Woke feeling very fragile.

A dull cloudy day, colourless. Read the Lorca biography.

Thursday 31

Still unwell. Washed all the bedding and T-shirts and pottered round the garden. Dreamed all morning of escape. To where?

Will go back to London on Monday and try to work out a plan for the film.

James rang to say funding was on the way for *The Garden*. I feel it is too late: the summer's gone.

However hard I try now I find it almost impossible to connect with others, let alone myself. Was it ever any different? Was I gifted, or was it as a burden of proof that I took to film?

Still can't fathom it. The moment the engines failed, becalmed I started to row for my life – was it always like that? Such a feeling of disquiet overwhelms me. Are others happier? More content? I rarely feel moments of self-pity, but when they come they roll over me.

~

The ragwort *Artemesia vulgaris* was used once as a substitute for tea or to flavour drinks. Placed between linen its dried branches warded off moths. *Cingulum Sancti Johannis* was worn by John the Baptist as a girdle in the wilderness; it also preserved the traveller from fatigue and sunstroke, pixies, elves, and wild beasts. Make a charm of it and wear it on St. John's Eve for protection against the evil eye.

This tall silvery herb grows deep green by the wayside despite the drought. Culpeper says: *A very slight infusion is excellent for all disorders of the stomach, prevents sickness after meals, and creates an appetite, but if made too strong disgusts the taste.*

I'm going to wear a crown of the wort tonight, not wait for St. John's Eve. And put a leaf in my shoe, as this will enable me to walk 40 miles before midday without getting tired.

~

The mugwort leaves are the deep Brunswick green of the paintings I made on an old wooden easel in my friend Güta's attic in Northwood in the 1950s. Heady scent of linseed, turpentine and camphor – a ray of bright sunlight falling across my table from the dormer window. Down below, huge clumps of white and yellow iris surround the disused tennis court. In her apron and miner's wooden knee protectors, worn for weeding, Güta is making tea.

We sip tea in the library under photos – yellowing and fading in the sunlight – of marble busts of Homer and Socrates, Virgil and Hadrian, which hang above the bookcases on hessian walls.

Güta's garden seat now sits tarred black behind Prospect Cottage.

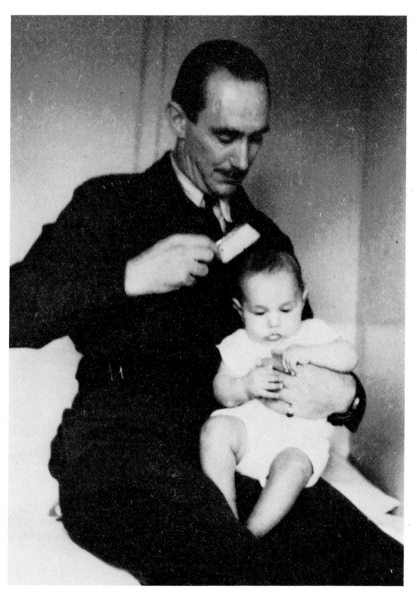

1943: my father spruces me up for the camera.

Right: My
mother, RAF
Witan 1943.

Below: My
grandmother's
garden, Manor
Cottage, with my
mother and sister,
1945.

Left: RAF Northwood, 1957.

Below: Merryfield, with my sister and parents, 1959.

64 Priory Road, 1965.

Greenhouse bedroom, Bankside 1970.

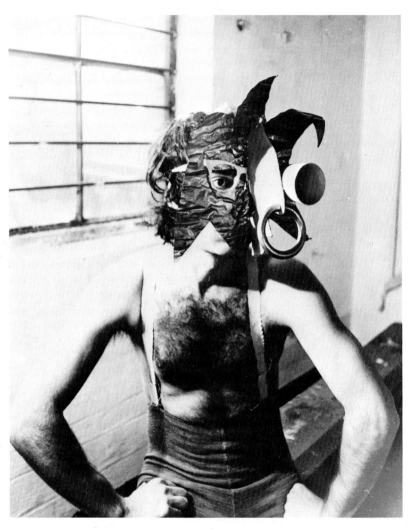

Above: Wearing a mask made for theatre design, about 1969. *(Photo: Karl Johnson)*

Opposite: Jubilee, 1977. *(Photo: Ian Charleson)*

Above: Howard Brookner, 1984.

Opposite: 1990, St Mary's Paddington.

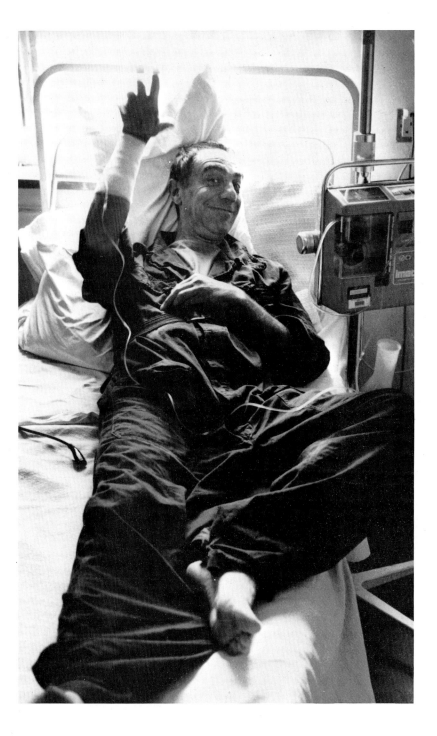

Above: 1989:
from *The Garden*,
a happy
Christmas.

Right: 1989: Jody
and myself –
centurion and
dunce – on the set
of *The Garden*.

H.B.

Pouring tar for the exhibition at the Third Eye, Glasgow 1989.

The garden at Prospect Cottage, 1989.

Above and opposite: The garden at Prospect Cottage.

Prospect Cottage, 1990.

AUGUST

~

In front of me a jade sea is running wild.

~

Güta cuts delicious slices of Otello cake – layers of strawberries and cream with the thinnest sponge. At Christmas dinner she sits upright at the head of the table, in a black silk dress with a necklace of uncut diamonds. Güta is descended from the mistress of a Danish king – the exquisite furniture, bleached ivory by time, had been made for her in Paris. Chinese bowls are filled with flowers from a garden which is slowly returning to the wilderness. The ground elder creeps in in spite of all our efforts. We sit round the Christmas tree alight with candles – more candles in chains overhead, each bearing somebody's name; the first name to burn gets a present.

The kitchen is old, a far cry from my mother's electric, modern one. A gigantic gas cooker, all dark metal angles, heats the steam kettle. I help in the garden to earn my studio and a little money for paint.

~

Güta is my gardening soul mate – she's planted a pale blue clematis by the front door; but her strength ebbs as she slowly withers away from cancer through the long summer. I keep the lawn mown and the beds weeded in front of her window. She does not know the ground elder is growing up through the path to the front door.

A few days before Güta is taken my sister comes over in her wedding gown to show it off.

Then she's gone. With her, my attic. She leaves me the fine ebony writing table with the winged griffin mounts in brass. But it's too heavy and my parents fail to bring it over the garden wall. It's sold to an unscrupulous dealer. I try to get it back, but it's lost – in the window of a Bond Street dealer correctly priced and labelled 'French Directoire'.

The garden is destroyed, bulldozers tear down the lime trees along the drive to make a 'close' of a dozen little houses. Not a brick remains of the old house. Güta, who fenced for Great Britain before the war, and who during the blitz kept the VADs going in Mount Vernon hospital – fighting mock battles with knitting needles – is remembered here no longer. She was the most elegant gardener, thin and wiry, nutbrown from the weather. Güta – upright in the candlelight, singing Danish carols, with those fiery diamonds given to her great-great-great-grandmother, the mistress of a Danish king.

139

SEPTEMBER

Friday 1

Up at seven, waiting for the dread invasion. It came in a medley of bright old cars until, by ten, the whole crew of 21 were here and Prospect Cottage was piled high with mirrors, make-up and costumes.

Christopher arrived early in his taxi and we walked round the garden waiting for the others. The lighting van was next, and then a donkey.

Among the last to arrive were Johnny and Yolanda with baby Oscar. By this time Tilda was crimping her hair with John Egan. This took nearly two hours, while clouds scudded past and grew larger and blotted out the sun.

Made up like a ragamuffin, Robert set up his Punch and Judy in front of the experimental radar station near the lighthouse. Richard Heslop drove us up there, on the wrong side of the road, in his bright red car, music blaring. Nick was despatched to my next door neighbour with £100 to rent the hut that we are using as a stable. Jo busied herself in the kitchen with piles of soggy samosas, KitKat and enough Evian to drain the spring.

James arrived last! The donkey shut in his box brayed loudly and sadly. Hector, Steve and Liam put on the terrorist-photographer outfits – the sun disappeared for good, and were we ready to film? We'll lose the film for a hairstyle. Christopher buried himself in a book on the martyrdom of Thomas à Becket.

By 1:00 the crimping was complete.

Oscar decked in gold embroidered trousers.

Windmills, crocodiles, sausages.

And Punch was ready to perform – hee hee hee whack! ho ho ho – we were off.

The sun peeped out, then gave up.

Mr. Punch wheezed malevolently. Policemen and crocodiles were dispatched. The crown toppled, the sari tangled and Oscar cried. But the indestructible Punch went on – whack bang bang! Perhaps he is the genius of this film – ha ha!

God what am I up to? No script!

Is this OK, Derek?

Yes!

Is that OK, Del?

Yes!

I feel so old today, everyone is so young on this set. My hair is silver grey. I'm not filming – nor looking through any camera. My hand shakes too much.

A hasty lunch is prepared.

Then: Madonna of the photo opportunity, with the three wise men transformed into terrorist photographers.

This way Mary, give us a smile. – Over here Mary. – Lovely.

Richard says film against the bank of bright lights. Tilda glitters in the grass-green sari holding on to the wobbly Van Eyck crown. Yolanda is wearing a pair of sunglasses. I grab them and put them on Tilda, everyone laughs. Oscar is crying. The photographers jostle, 'This way Mary.' 'Nice one girl.' James is coming up the road with the donkey.

The chaos of a Super 8 shoot is a finely choreographed dance, everyone dodging this way and that. I walk the donkey across the set. Is this a farce? Buñuel would have laughed. The Madonna pouts and looks sulky, the child screams, and then she's up chased by the photographers. Far away, almost out of sight, a battle ensues on the shingle.

A cop on a motorbike has arrived, he looks bemused, no-one tells him the old story.

At five we call a wrap. Is it 'in the can'? Who knows.

Now the serious part's over Thelma and John do a ghastly make-up job and I cram on the crown of thorns and lie in the cabbage where Richard pours a bucket of cold water over me.

Saturday 2

A journey across the sepia marshes: the last wheat field burns – the hawthorn bushes blood-red, heavy with berries; the jet black of the burnt fields; and elephant grey skies weighed down by motionless clouds. Deep green rushes in the ditches. Appledore – an oasis across the fields, its church swallowed in trees.

I buy a shepherd's crook in the junk shop and talk to the blacksmith about a wind vane for Prospect.

At seven a recce arrives for the filming here on the 12th. The note put through my door several weeks ago that said *we are looking for a location* has brought Gabriel, who lit and operated on *Caravaggio*, and Lucy, who designed *War Requiem*. They scout around for the right shots. Meanwhile Alasdair rolls up on a motorbike.

We all have an excellent supper at Windshift to celebrate Derek Ball's birthday and walk back under a stormy sky along the shore.

Sunday 3

Up early, a clear sunny day. I gild the old army helmets, fix a new shaft to the shepherd's crook and a handle to my pruning knife, then dig out the last cape from *Sebastiane* in the attic.

Got Peter up and we walked to the seashore, where the tide was on the turn – deserted except for Len mending his nets, the sea a strip of silver; on the horizon, a tallship with striped sails.

~

Peter is so shy I am almost tongue-tied asking him just to walk on the mud flats or point to the horizon. He is terrified of the camera.

His shyness is a gift. He looks as if a complete stranger has walked up to him and said, drop everything – which is what I asked him to do on the phone. To my surprise he rang back, and after an initial hesitation, came here.

Having filmed on the sands we walked over to the Long Pits and I threw the cape over his shoulders, handed him the crook and knife, and had him cut the red hips from a jewelled rose bush. He hid himself from the camera behind the cape. I filmed this, and later him sleeping in the sun. Felt Pier Paolo smiling over my shoulder. Secret camera work.

> *On that I love most entirely*
> *Gelofyr Gentil or rosemary?*
> *Camamill, borage or savery?*
> *Nay! certenly,*
> *Here is not he*
> *That pleaseth me.*
> *'I chese a floure, freshest of face.'*
> *What is his name that thou chosen has?*
> *The rose I suppose? Thine heart unbrace.*
> *That same is he*
> *In hart so fre*
> *That best liketh me.*

There is a romance in the camera that I touched in *The Angelic Conversation*. I see it all over the Pasolini films – something vulnerable, an archaic smile. I see it in our films, nowhere else. This is all I really want to film.

At midday the sun went in and we came home. The boys spent the afternoon flying a kite high over the fishing boats. At five they came in for tea and then returned to London.

Fell asleep early. Three exhausting days over. But a feeling that events were moving on.

Slept well and awoke clear-headed, no night sweats.

Monday 4

An almost unbearable silence. The sun came up a fiery scarlet with a halo of black clouds, but these evaporated in a clear blue sky. I carried on the hopeless task of watering and planting out the cuttings. Strands of thought crisscross, but one thing is clear: the film must show the quaint illusion of narrative cinema threadbare.

Tuesday 5

To Rye, where at three you can't get lunch – everything closed. We all hate Rye, twinned with Ypres – soulless shoppers, cobblestones that hurt the feet. The curry we tracked down in the nice ice cream parlour next to the citadel of Lesbos reminded me of school fare, cost £15 for the three of us. Microwave soggy.

~

At Hordle House, my prep school, Mrs. Monger's toenails: tough apple cores swimming in a sour translucent mush, were gulped down – holding our noses – along with the pilchards frozen in their 'tomato' sauce; or the congealed Saturday herrings. I am reminded of the ghastly institutional cooking of the fifties, ancestor of this curry. RAF camp food was bliss after school fare. There we had choice!

Food has never recovered its position in my life: I still gulp it quickly, as a penance. *Laus domine.*

Here I come serving up the dyed-green mushy peas from a huge aluminium container – once dropped them on to the lap of my housemaster. Scrubbing the tough remains of eggs off plates at 6:30 on a December morning, using the cold water in the lavatories called Nineveh. Fagging would horrify modern health inspectors. Dusting, polishing, ironing. Could I ever forget all this? I am still tidy under my scarecrow appearance.

~

The system left me with such a profound dislike of my own. I would be quite happy to see the young businessmen who sit behind their papers on the Ashford train liquidated, with the Xeroxed boys from the city wine bars. Spoilt baby faces, loathsome suits, ties and collars, ordering people about. I can't abide the English system that has everyone queuing except those that have no need to – as they jumped it long ago. Nor can I abide the values of this repression, its false houses, marriages, families, the Church of England, sport, all the rotten paraphernalia, the anger fizzes on below the surface waiting to explode . . . destroy. How many feel the same way?

Wednesday 6

The fog horn sounded through fitful dreams.

An autumn sunrise: blinding light trapped in a dazzling mist, all the garden soaked with a crystal dew that sparkled. Cool, not a breath of wind. A flock of bright finches in the blackberry bushes.

Made myself breakfast with the blackberry jam I cooked last night. I was alone for two hours last night by the Long Pits, alone except for the crow, who swooped so low over my shoulder I fell into a fearsome bush. Long and painful minutes extricating myself while he hopped about on top of the bush laughing.

Picked several pounds of blackberries – very firm through lack of rain.

At 12:00 David Lewis arrived and we drove for the next six hours to Oxford – along the south coast to Winchester, before turning north. It was a glorious day. We stopped at the Piltdown, a pub with a sinister black and white skull on its sign. Here we had an excellent lunch; then on into Wessex.

At Winchester we paid over £1.50 and walked through a deserted cathedral. The great Romanesque transepts take your breath away. Discovered the tomb of Cardinal Beaufort, the son of John of Gaunt and red-haired Katherine, Chaucer's sister-in-law – heroine of a historical romance by Anya Seton that thrilled me as a child. Corpulent and middle-aged, the cardinal was laid out in his vestments.

~

At my sister's. All who remain of our family were gathered for my Aunt Moyra – mother's younger sister, who lives in South Africa. We had a surprisingly merry evening, everyone pleased to see each other and my sister looking elegant. If Mum had been there she would have had to swallow her words that neither of us had inherited her good looks.

~

Moyra confirmed all sorts of details of family life, especially Gran's sister Doris, who offered herself at the age of eighty to the tabloids as the 'first woman in space'. When she was five Doris had bundled her into a taxi one morning with a huge bunch of red rubber roses and said 'Buckingham Palace'; then after a little while leant forward and quietly added 'Back door, not front'. Queen Mary had the Palace decked with Doris's roses, which were scented.

Moyra also filled me in on Doris's practical joke at the Dorchester – in which she had managed to get the best table for a Christmas Eve dinner after having been turned down. She had her son impersonate the secretary of an Indian maharani on the telephone. The hotel's 'mistake' was rectified immediately – Doris arrived wearing a tablecloth.

The hotel ignored this, the waiters said nothing and she left without paying. Royalty does not handle money.

She *did* pay for the meal, however, by appearing on the front page of the *Express* wearing her tablecloth; and poor Moyra, still a child, was dispatched to settle the bill. She said she was treated like a VIP as the hotel couldn't quite believe what had happened.

The enormous silver handbag that Doris gave me when I was twelve – the one she used for her sewing – was the one that Q.M. used at the Delhi Durbar, and yes, they swapped knick-knacks and gewgaws.

Nothing you could imagine about Great Aunt Doris could be exaggerated. Gran ordered us to avoid her – she had the royal habit of descending, broke, and staying indefinitely. The whole family was ex-directory and had an elaborate system of cover addresses. Moyra herself had pretended to be a French maid the last time she telephoned. Whenever they unwisely let her contact them she was almost always on the verge of 'suicide'. She outlived all her generation.

Pegs saw her last as an old woman. She had let her hair grow its natural grey, she looked like Grandma, very fine. She was no longer red or blue or pink.

After the war she ran a boarding house in a bombed-out mansion she bought next to Harrods; it later became the Guatemalan embassy. Here she entertained demobbed officers and gradually restored the rooms. Moyra worked there as a receptionist one summer; and it was here that, propped up in bed, Aunt Doris gravely handed me Queen M's handbag. Doris had always been my favourite. And by the way everyone joyfully contributed their stories, she had certainly left her mark.

~

My Aunt Pegs said I was the apple of Granny Mimosa's eye. She would douse me with Edwardian patent medicines, Collis Brown, gripe water, brandy and warm milk – as I snored she thought I was adenoidal. I slept on a collapsable military camp bed in the living room.

Mimosa was also an adventurer, Pegs added. After my uncle was born in 1914 she upped and left to join my grandfather in India.

Later she took the very first air flight from Calcutta to Paris – the first in the family to fly. Harry Lytten, my grandfather, who Pegs said was small in stature, spent the whole war in India. The sisters were born Reuben and orphaned – brought up, according to Pegs, by wealthy guardians who educated them in Europe. Though I had heard they were Barnardo's kids.

~

The whole evening revolved around the past. Moyra said my memory of

Italy in 1946 was accurate and quite astounding. Gaye, my sister, says I romanticise the past, especially my Jarman grandmother's Maori blood. But all my life no-one had believed I was English; even at school I was ragged and called Wog for my dark colouring. It would be great to find out if I was one; if not, a Yid (the other term of abuse) since Jewishness descends in the female line. Where does Reuben come from? Surely buried somewhere is a middle-class cover-up.

Friday 8
Three-hour telecine of last Friday's shoot. Same problem with the Beaulieus (cameras) – Chris's camerawork on the Isle of Dogs okay, less sure of himself on the shoot – the terrorist photography gauzy, out-of-focus shots of Tilda just usable.

Saturday 9
Terrible nightmare. Found myself at the wheel of a jet-black car careering out of control along a highway lit with sodium lights. Unable to drive – remembered to take my foot off the accelerator as I swerved into the oncoming lane. Nothing happened – discovered that the car had no pedals. Don't know how I came to a halt, crashed into the pillows.

HB sleeping peacefully. I woke him up by staring at him.

Sunday 10
In Soho we are shoved and jostled by the varicose crowd outside *Anything Goes*. Derelicts clutch at the turn-ups of the fortunate young and slobber abuse – which is returned in an amused manner as the latter count the change in their pockets and dole it out, cracking jokes at the expense of the staggering unfortunates.

~

I find all the new machines quite incomprehensible, can't operate the new ticket machines in the underground. The old ones were easy. With crowds pushing down on me, I give up and, embarrassed, wait nearly three minutes at the counter.

'Do you put money in those Mercury telephones or use a card?' I asked a taxi driver.

'Haven't a clue how to operate them,' he said.

So I'm not the only one. Oh for the simple pre-decimal life, where distance was measured in feet and inches, temperature in Fahrenheit. I know I can never adapt. Six foot is a tall man, 70° a warm summer's day; water will always freeze at 32°. I measure out my garden one foot in front of the other, country feet, as intuitive as writing.

SEPTEMBER

~

Robert Medley said the gigantic con job of the Thatcher years had been successfully sold to a country illiterate in its own traditions and history. Everything about this 'new England' appalled him.

'What's the picture about?' he asked, and added 'It has to be anarchic; that is the only way to deal with this. The whole propaganda exercise about helping the little man was so transparently fake, everything was sold to the great companies. They'd sell the water under Christ's feet.'

~

In the newspaper today retromania rules: Mr. Branagh, who has not had an original theatrical thought – *Look Back In Anger, Henry V* – is hailed as the new Olivier; and Emma Thompson is Vivien Leigh. Lego theatrics with the Royal Seal – according to their article they asked Prince Charles's advice about their film of *Henry V*.

As for Olivier – Robert, who founded the Group Theatre, has *Dog Beneath the Skin* dedicated to him, had Britten compose incidental music and Henry Moore as his set designer – said: to his generation Olivier was nothing but another old ham. He never could speak poetry, 'He was terrible Derek.'

Monday 11
Expedition to M&S 'lifestyle' food hall; then down Berwick Street market for fruit and veg, before David arrived to drive me down to Dungeness.

~

Silence for only ten minutes, then two camera crews invaded: Sony Video magazine; then the commercials crew with Gabriel Beristain.

Up at the lighthouse the Pretty Things, now very long in the tooth, were distressing a drum kit to the amusement of the lighthouse keeper. A media blitz on the Ness.

Tuesday 12
Mr. Crow arrived with the Winnebago, and twenty other vehicles to make the Hi-fi advert with Prospect Cottage as their location. An hour into the invasion I threw up my hands and left. Huge awnings and lighting rigs had sprouted all over the garden; in the shingle, a wooden road.

Drove into the marsh along misty lanes – blood-red hawthorns fringed the golden grass of parched water meadows, olive-grey willows vanishing in an opal haze.

When we returned the garden resembled an archeological site – at least next year the poppies will bloom in the disturbed ground. A deep trench dug beside the house, lined with boards, provided a road for a hapless model-girl in a velvet mini skirt to drive her Volkswagen.

All day Gabriel fought the failing light, until at eight he gave up. The local kids swarmed around the food truck, led by Kes, the wild eleven year old. He skidded his dune buggy to a halt amongst us, and chatted about his kestrel. The kids were fascinated by the odd collection of cars, particularly the Porsches, which Mr. Crow hopped over quite fearlessly.

~

The crew was incredulous that I had allowed this invasion – my studio ousted for a movieola, doors off hinges, window frames repainted, nails hammered in here and there.

By evening I was not certain either. Perhaps it is a good thing for a film-maker to have his house invaded – just as architects should have to live and work in their buildings, so should film-makers have to open their doors.

I have never made anything like this – the budget is more than my next feature. To the local kids, the crew were a gang of millionaires – a far cry from my Super 8 enthusiasts perched on the edge of social security. Here were the smart cars, the paraphernalia of affluence.

The afternoon left me breathless. Little things I treasure, like my drift-wood doorstops, I discovered way out in the shingle – everything in the house travelled ten yards. Windows were opened, curtains drawn, lights taped up, clothes removed. But everyone worked with immense charm, and when it was all over, nothing was harmed at all.

~

I asked Edward, the kid next door who had declared the model-girl 'a yuppie', whether he thought I was one. He replied, 'Not on the outside, but I'm certain you are on the inside.' His sister added, 'We are just common, and people who speak well like you have everything.' This was in earnest. Nevertheless, I am getting on well with them, they are very shy.

The Dungeness leaseholder's association received the fee of £200 for the day. Sylvia, the treasurer, said it was a fortune.

Wednesday 13
Jehovah's Witnesses crept up the garden path, dulcet voices, crippled minds, deformed bodies, *Watchtower* and *Awake* in their hands. Today's *Awake*, September 8 1989: 'Homosexuals who want to serve God must do so on His terms. Deaden their body members as respects fornication, uncleanliness, and sexual appetite.' *Colossians* (35).

Watchtower ends with a heading: 'Revolting Sexual Mores.' *The un-leashing of the full fury of the sexual revolution has not yet produced any measurable benefits to the country as a whole, unless we think in terms of monetary gain. But with its emphasis on sex as a recreation and spectator sport the revolution has produced a host of problems that threaten us with social chaos. Venereal disease for one. VD is not a new scourge, but it has now become a plague, giving rise to new strains of exotic bacteria and virus-like agents. Genital herpes, incurable in adults, has caused infant deaths from Meningoencephalitis. AIDS has found its way into the mainstream of our society and into the bloodstreams of innocent victims via contaminated donor blood . . . they promised joy, liberation, and good health, they've de-livered misery, disaster, even death.*

As I sweat it out in the early hours, a 'guilty victim' of the scourge, I want to bear witness how happy I am, and will be until the day I die, that I was part of the hated sexual revolution; and that I don't regret a single step or encounter I made in that time; and if I write in future with regret, it will be a reflection of a temporary indisposition.

~

Tilda, Roger Cooke, Spring and David here at lunch time.

We went on a recce up beyond the power station, and came to these de-cisions: that *The Garden* should have menacing terrorist newsmen; that at moments the film should be theatrical, that naked angels should light scenes with flares; that Drako and Spring will be the devil and his disciple; that the week after next we should film Christ walking along the great empty road into the sunset beneath pylons crackling and buzzing with electricity, that he should be confronted by a jogger – Graham – who is swearing about the state of things.

Other sequences: we will place the bed on the sands and light it with flares as the tide comes in. We should have a sequence in the studio – writing. That we will film the childhood of Christ outside the railway carriage, and Mary Magdalen at the Listening Wall.

~

At Camber we met up with Gabriel Beristain on the set of his advert, then took off to the Little Chef, where James contacted me on the payphone: hys-terics about the BFI. Tried to calm him down.

The film is up in the air again, the BFI have adopted a wait-and-see policy – at the same time suggesting that the £50,000 they were going to invest might be used for two shorts by new directors. This is a false economy – I've received less than some, and my name helps keep the flag flying abroad. They have a reasonable chance of making the money back.

The original intention of the Institute was to foster experimental film. I'm the only director of my generation in features who might just still fit into that category.

I told James I'd pay the £13,000 for the two day shoot from Dad's cash so we can get ahead; perhaps with a few more feet in the can we can persuade everyone.

James's strengths are also his weaknesses. The BFI has never liked him, and he doesn't fit into the old boy network. The 'gang' who make the decisions are graduates or public school men. They talk to each other – even if they dislike each other and play the field together and eat in the same restaurants.

I have a similar problem: I could never become a 'film director'. Not 'class' this time but sexuality and a lifestyle that doesn't fit into their watering holes. What's possible for a photographer, painter, writer, is quite impossible for a film director. *Colossians* (35) made its mark: you had to deaden your member to shine in the studio.

Life overwhelmed a career in my case, and then went on to add further twists. It seems that 'gay' films made by straight directors – Stephen Frears' *Orton* and *Launderette* – were a good step. But it never occurred to anyone, not even the 'gay press', that perhaps these films would never have been funded had they been suggested by gay directors.

Don't think I could have done a better job, that is not the point. It would have been difficult, even unacceptable to suggest that the hero of the Orton film was Halliwell – a much more attractive character than Joe. He wrote the plays and was forced into the shadows by the egalitarian priorities of the sixties, and Joe's youthful good looks, aided and abetted by Margaret Ramsey.

Thursday 14

The sun shone out briefly before disappearing behind the clouds. A grey drizzle set in. Spring and I filmed along the lanes and canals of the marsh.

Ben Gibson rang and put the BFI side of the story: he said James had flown off the handle. I know! I'm always having flaming rows with him myself. He had produced a minimum of material. That, I said, was my fault. I don't want to be funded on a script.

~

If only Howard Brookner could have called out from his grave: 'The Last Of England is the greatest film to be made since the move into sound.' It details a whole new way of looking in film. Matisse said you judge a painter by the amount of new signs he invents. Howard said The Last Of England did that with profligate genius.

~

As the storm closed in Drako arrived. Immaculately dressed in a grey suit and gold pince-nez, he is a perfect Devil, performing his life in a series of entrances and exits, talking nonstop about Dali and Gala, the new moon, the Living Theatre, Gerard Malanga, prison, and dancing in Beirut.

By the time he leaves a howling gale has sprung up. But the fires are lit.

~

I've asked Drako to play the Devil; his blue mascara frightened the lady who sells fishing tackle.

Friday 15
Another uncomfortable night with no sleep. I don't feel ill, but weak, and my temperature fluctuates. When I stoop in the garden I feel giddy and take a minute to recover.

~

Rang Lorraine about making a will. This is forced on me by the project to buy Gerard a boat in Amsterdam. HB says it's tempting fate.

~

Dark thoughts invade – I make tea, do the washing.

Saturday 16
Restless night. Fell asleep at dawn as the sun cast a rosy glow into this room. Across the marshes a full moon, white in a pale blue sky.

My fever has brought a deep, almost comforting lethargy. Spring remarked yesterday that I was unusually calm – it seems ridiculous to worry.

Four years ago I wouldn't have thought twice about it, just made a trip to the doctor and come away with a prescription. Now I will myself to get better without the aid of antibiotics, feel almost ashamed of pottering off to the Kobler centre to take up valuable time.

I refuse to believe in my mortality, or the statistics which hedge the modern world about like the briar that walled in the sleeping princess. I have conducted my whole life without fitting in, so why should I panic now and fit into statistics?

When the doctor first told me I was HIV positive, I think she was more upset than me. It didn't sink in at first – that took weeks. I thought: this is not true, then I realised the enormity. I had been pushed into yet another corner, this time for keeps. It quickly became a way of life. When the sun shone it became unbearable. I didn't say anything, I had decided to be stoic.

This was a chance to be grown-up. Though I thought I ought to be crying. I walked down Charing Cross Road in the sunlight, everyone was so blissfully unaware. The sun is still shining.

The perception that knowing you're dying makes you feel more alive is an error. I'm less alive. There's less life to lead. I can't give 100% attention to anything – part of me is thinking about my health.

~

Drako said that as a child he had watched a beautiful blue damselfly emerge from its chrysalis, watched for hours as it unfurled its wings; and then, when it finally took flight, a bird swooped down and scrunched it up. The memory horrified him to this day.

~

The swallows swoop over the garden catching flies.

~

Drove home late across the marshes, the land shrouded in low cloud and a misty drizzle. The drought has taken the leaves off May trees, the horse-chestnuts have turned gold. The elders are losing their leaves. Swallows fly low over the fields.

~

The flat seemed so empty without HB. He flew to Newcastle for the weekend.

Supper at the Amalfi was slow, half-cooked, and delivered by harassed waiters who made an extra show of being overworked by cleaning the tables with a self-conscious clatter. This is the restaurant where years ago a mouse pursued by the house cat ran up my trouser leg.

Tonight there is an ill-assorted crowd washed up by the weekend; Dutch tourists to the left, a lesbian couple to the right.

Later Gerard and I spent ten minutes in Comptons, but the music was so loud we gave up. We walked down to the Coliseum as he wanted to see an opera – something he had never done. Then home with the listings.

Spent nearly an hour opening a pile of unsolicited mail: water privatisation, a glossy mag from the Nat West, and a copy of *Elle* with some incoherent blurb – hastily copied from a telephone interview. Opened the front door to a group of students from the North who were taking snaps of themselves under the Phoenix House sign. I could do nothing but be polite and allow myself to be snapped along with them. The flat is staked out as if I were a pop star.

~

Vomit-coloured faces of Saturday night revellers lurching from one short change joint to another. Queues round the paper stands for the Sundays.

Sunday 17
This morning the streets are empty, except for the derelicts and piles of rubbish. One man huddled in the doorway asked 'You know what day it is?' 'Sunday.'

Today I will do nothing. The aimless nightlife for the daylight people, who have no idea how to behave after the sun has set, has evaporated in this empty dawn.

A quick journey to the market at Camden Lock: bought wooden models of fighter planes for a painting of a child's bed in the Glasgow exhibition; then over to the nursery to buy tulips, narcissus, and hyacinth for the balcony garden.

At eight I went up to Hampstead Heath and walked in the moonlight until midnight. The full moon was so bright it blinded my eyes. No bonfires or gypsies.

Worried about the film. Insuperable barriers of subject, finance, the weather, my health.

Back at 12:30. HB's voice on the answerphone.

Monday 18
Slept soundly.

Bought Keith Vaughan's *Journal* and collapsed on the bed with it. Sharing his troubles made me aware how lucky I am. I wish now I had got to know him – but when you are young you do not realise your youth is an asset. I never thought I could do anything but bore him – felt tongue-tied, unsophisticated. He mentions he was coming to my exhibition, but never made it. How he would have spent a pleasant afternoon with a group of us.

The last years of the journal are so bleak – the description of the wasps devouring the pears in his garden, flying like bullets; and he, barricaded inside, unable to enjoy a perfect autumn day.

~

Unlike Keith Vaughan, I'm not out of love with myself. I still retain vain illusions that I am desirable. I hardly drink – unless out on some escapade. Smoke the occasional joint. Last night I went to the Heath without either, though I took a bottle of poppers – a habit I acquired late. I have successfully given up smoking. I still retain a strong sense of self-preservation, though I feel in tune with his depression. His diaries gather in strength until the suicide: 'I've taken the pills.'

Tuesday 19

Little time for depressed introspection, meetings all day. First at Basilisk for next week's shoot. Then a long walk with Derek Brown through Covent Garden, where we found a puffer fish for the child's mask and a silver water pot of biblical proportions. Ice cream at Neal's Yard, then back to Basilisk and the Pets' edit, which is coming to a close.

The highlight of the day was HB's edit of our little promo for the film, in which he had put the constellations over the sea at Dungeness.

I bounce back, the sweats have passed like a shadow. I shivered as someone walked over my grave. When the hurly-burly of the week is over the quiet at Dungeness will bring few of these shadows. Sometimes at night the noise of the Charing Cross Road is unbearable; and lunch today at Mildred's was a torture of chatter so loud I felt pressed up against the wall.

~

I'm as much obsessed by sex as Keith Vaughan, though few opportunities present themselves. I enjoy recounting escapades and listening to them – like fishermen's yarns they are always whoppers.

~

Corners of the city bring memories – though I've never been quite as bold as A. who was giving a boy a blow job on the Fulham Road, propped up against a traffic light at 4 am, when a policeman stopped and said 'What the hell are you doing?' A. replied, without looking, 'What the fuck do you think? Push off.' The young policeman was so embarrassed he did.

Wednesday 20

Riots and tears. Caught between the Pets and PMI – the production company. I warned everyone what would happen. Poor HB, after hours of care and late nights putting this concert together, full of serious anguish for Chris Lowe – who walked out saying he hated it. I wish he had stopped to listen to himself, when all about are doing their best with material that was botched from the start. I suggested in our final pre-shoot meeting that perhaps we should leave it; but everyone decided to carry on.

No-one could have made a better job. The video cameras are 'state-of-the-art' – but still do not have the quality of film.

PMI is a company lined with gold but leaden-hearted. When I told Martin (the producer) that I did this for the money he lost his temper. I never wanted to be put into this situation, but everyone begged me to do it.

It was as if I were to hand Chris five notes, inferior recording equipment, and two hours with people shouting to get it over – and expected to get a number 1 hit.

I wonder how a jobbing PMI director would have reacted to 'You're never going to work again'.

Perhaps Chris really means *I* don't want to work again. I think Chris expects to be entertained by a conjurer like a small child.

Thursday 21

I walked to Neal Street East, held my breath and spent £1,000 on three lengths of fabric – I need an extravagant present for myself after yesterday. Adam and Eve and Christ are clothed for Tuesday in the finest transparent silk saris – I hope that gesture will bring us luck.

A Mildred's lunch; then another deep breath and off to the clinic at St. Mary's.

Saturday 23

Caught an early train to Ashford after a coffee at Bar Italia.

The trains, as usual, run in mysterious ways. No Ashford trains from Charing Cross today: one of those treacly charm school voices B.R. employs announced a string of stations, causing confusion and laughter. Read the *Independent* on the train: the magazine had a tragic article on the homeless boys of Mexico City, renting and glue-sniffing to numb the horrifying poverty – now dying from AIDS with no advice or medication. Everything aggravated by deathly Catholicism.

Monosyllabic taxi driver from Ashford to Dungeness made me feel rather uncomfortable – three attempts at conversation withered. The sun was out over the marshes, so I contented myself with the view. The reeds are dying back along the canals – everything is greener. At Prospect I noticed thousands of seedlings had germinated in every nook and cranny. Red admirals flying fast in the sunlight.

Planted out the samphire cuttings. Opium and Californian poppy.

There was a heavy downpour here a couple of days ago, but the earth is still bone dry. Hawkbits, sea campion, and bugloss are still flowering, but autumn has tucked up most of the flowers.

Sunday 24

Spud Jones down to film.

I have no luck with the weather again: grey and overcast day.

We went blackberrying, picked mushrooms, and four more cuttings of the dog roses. I noticed a mullein growing wild out at the Long Pits – my own in the garden are now very large plants, about a foot across. Their silver leaves startling in the shingle.

Rearranged the studio for filming. Took a couple of minutes of film of Spud holding birch twigs against black velvet.

David came at 5:00 and took Spud back to London.

~

I forgot to check the times of the Warhol seminar in London at which I was expected – found it was in the afternoon, not the evening. Left futile excuses with a Sunday receptionist.

It's a pity, as I had decided to pour some cold water on all the adulation. I'd thought of kicking off with Andy's quote: 'The scripts and lighting were bad, but the people were great.' And that was his first mistake. Most of them were quite dreadful.

~

The parochial nature of the Factory – Bill Burroughs and Kenneth Anger were in London, like anyone else switched on. The New York art scene was middle-aged – all the artists in their late thirties. London was ten years younger – only the New York art snobs in the English scene beat a path to the Factory and offered their services.

The truth is none of us had anything to offer: the Factory's most lasting contribution was not film but the music of Nico and Lou Reed – Andy's Judy Garland complex: star-worship and insecurity. The conventionality of recycling the famous through the silkscreen process, and the rise of sophisticated advertising in the sixties, made Andy the right man in the right place. His work reproduced so well in colour supplements and books that landed in their thousands on glass tables.

~

It was this graphic linear quality, the bright colours and cloudless skies of LA, that made Hockney famous at the same time.

~

In NYC, I found the boys on the piers made the Factory look like a cocktail party. Although its success fascinated me, it was boring watching boring films. It was of its time but captured the least interesting aspect of the sixties – the knowing complicity with trash.

I remember the sixties underground treating Andy with disdain: 'a terrible opportunist'. Now old men, they are falling over each other to associate themselves, hoping a bit of the tarnished glamour will rub off. I've done this myself, made too much of my visits.

Monday 25
A sea mist shimmers in the dawn. Still air. Dew sparkles on the shingle. A solitary magpie perched in the driftwood.

The chill soon warmed away by the sun. Nico singing *Little Valentine*. Gild the angels' helmets.

Tuesday 26
Usual Basilisk chaos. Chris (the cameraman) phoned me before eight to say no-one has arrived to drive him down here.

~

One of those nauseous film breakfasts which turns your stomach over – soggy toast with half-mouthfuls of grabbed tea. The generator has not arrived. Nick says it is very old.

Up to the railway carriage, 'Westward Ho', where Pat lives surrounded by clutter, says it should be that way: the carriage was blown up by a film crew two years ago – she still hasn't received any compensation. This is the carriage I was going to buy when I first came here. It has a spectacular view.

Nine o'clock. The generator still hasn't arrived but Annie and baby are now setting up a costume department in my bedroom.

Wednesday 27
The two days have passed in a delirium. The violation of the house, the chaos and extreme fatigue leave me lurching backwards and forwards. I feel as tangled as the sheets which move through the hurricane of my dreams.

Thursday 28
By eight this morning the house was cleared of the last of the camera equipment. I walked dazed through the debris, before I called up a second wind and, armed with buckets of hot water, soda crystals, and Jeyes' Fluid, scrubbed the floors and polished the furniture. By midday, when David arrived, only the kitchen remained to be done.

We loaded the car with 15 exploding sacks of rubbish and dumped them at the tip in Lydd. The sun came out and lit up the white cliffs. Silence returned to a spic-and-span Prospect Cottage. I sat for ten minutes looking at the view. Then we loaded the car, stopping at the white house on the corner to drop off a cheque.

As I opened the car door I almost stepped on a large grass snake writhing at my feet – it opened its mouth in agony. The car had run over it. An ill omen. We hadn't seen it – the snake of wisdom who brought the knowledge of good and evil, man's best friend, serpent of memory, great figure of eight, lying with its back broken and its mouth open, crying in silence.

We talked of Duncan Campbell's attack on the people involved in THT, Positively Healthy and alternative therapy. I liked him very much when I met him last year, but he seemed under a great deal of stress, he said to me, 'Nice to meet the other most hated man in England.' That had never crossed my mind. I've always been under the impression, or should I say mis-apprehension that I am liked. Duncan's war on unorthodoxy sits strangely with his past.

~

Back at Phoenix House three silent phone calls, then an excited voice: M., who played the sacrificial youth at the beginning of *Sebastiane*, and who I haven't seen since that day, invited me to Corfe Castle tomorrow. 'I can't possibly,' I said. 'I'm off to Glasgow.' He was very insistent, quoted from Eliot's *Quartets*, said he had so little time for expression. He asked about video cameras; at one point his voice cracked. I talked to him calmly for an hour, then put the phone down.

Time present and time past. In the dark, alone, I shivered. He'd insisted I came alone. Underneath the welcoming voice I sensed despair and desper-ation. Perhaps I should have asked him outright what he wanted. Looking back at that scene in the film it is very violent. I hope it didn't trip him up, like the young boy who played Kes in Loach's film.

Friday 29
More sad news on the answerphone. P.P. says in a long message that Andy has returned from the U.S. in a state of collapse. He has reached rock bot-tom and has to decide whether to climb out or go under. Andy was round last night and talked poor P.P. into the ground till 4 am, threatening suicide. P.P. is at the end of his tether: thousands of pounds and hours of support are getting him and Andy nowhere.

HB won't let me get involved any longer. I know he is right about this but feel guilty. One last time? But the last time was the time before and the time before that. 15 years of mistakes.

P.P. says that on the night Andy was attacked and stabbed – after years of aggressive behaviour – all the venom leaked out with the blood; and now it seemed nothing would staunch the flow.

Saturday 30
The day dragged out as we waited for Gerard to arrive with the car to drive us North. He has a bad cold; the car was vandalised last night – the window smashed and the stereo taken. That and the loss of the houseboat which was called *Eau de Vie* have made him depressed.

He arrived at four in the afternoon; and after packing a mountain of luggage, paintings, video, film into the car, and the two horsechestnut trees, 'Chekhov' and 'Khrushchev', on the roof-rack, we took the A1 North.

The long wait was enlivened by a scaffolder who put up the third scaffold behind Phoenix House that has been built this year. He was a beautifully built redhead with a sharp haircut and a little gold earring, wearing a loosely fitting navy blue track suit. He whistled his way through the day with his mate, strutting about showing off his body. He had fine features, a handsome open face. HB, driven to distraction, videoed him from the kitchen window and walked back and forth to the door with little sighs. In the end he got so excited he had an asthma attack. Meanwhile the scaffolder worked, ignoring the comings and goings. I asked him what they were doing, he said they were to strip the ventilation duct of asbestos – after years of neglect with the stuff flying everywhere, they repaired this duct only six months ago. As he told me this he put his hands behind his neck and stretched back, enjoying the attention.

We arrived in Newcastle at ten. The horsechestnuts survived, but their shredded leaves resembled gigantic cannabis plants.

OCTOBER

Sunday 1

HB in the bathroom dousing himself with cologne as if he were tossing a salad. Morning newspapers. Cats and kittens pouncing everywhere. At twelve we left for Kimmerhame to deliver the trees.

As we approached Berwick the sun came out, lighting up Holy Island. The further North you drive the more beautiful the country: the broad rolling hills and woodlands of Northumberland, unspoiled by developments, show how violently the South has been ravaged. Poor ruined Kent with its ugly commuter towns, there every field and hedgerow is under siege.

At midday we arrived at Tilda's parents' castle, placed the horsechestnuts, labelled *October 1984 Novdevechy cemetery*, alongside the front door. Politics: 4 feet 3 inches – poetry: 6 feet 6 inches.

~

We had a picnic lunch in the kitchen and then walked to the walled garden. The greenhouse was hung with delicious purple grapes.

~

At 3:30 we left for Edinburgh across the moors. The sunlit landscape under vast skies stretched into the distance, the farthest purple hills imperceptibly joined the banks of cloud. The road was empty.

This drive has been the most enjoyable I can remember. We have encountered no delays and precious little traffic. The South that we left behind decayed and polluted, with smog-pinched skies. There's a desperation on the roads round London, a feeling that you will not escape. After Newcastle the *Little Chefs* – roadside cafes with greasy interiors and filthy egg-stained staff – disappear.

I felt that we had escaped when we arrived in Edinburgh. Time played a part as well as distance.

We stopped at Richard de Marco's gallery with the ten paintings for the show, where I was cornered by a French archeologist; she talked at me in incoherent English for nearly half an hour as I tried to make the arrangements for the show. The words 'fabuliste' and 'magician' were used – she stared at me with such passion, with eyes of machine gun intensity. Then she was gone. I didn't see myself anywhere in her barrage of words.

~

The Central Hotel, next to Glasgow's station, resembles the Peking in Moscow, with over 500 rooms. But there is no babushka at the end of each faded corridor. The bath has a plug – a rubber tennis ball which leaves black marks.

The room was in the *Kentish Town* style of my student days: green walls and purple lights. It has a spectacular view over the station's glass canopy, which is bright with orange light.

I expect the hotel was shabby even in its 19th century heyday; it suits me fine. HB found it gloomy.

Men, pink as Pacific prawns, barely covered by their small bath towels, stroll along the ancient floral carpets to the bathrooms – many of the rooms do not have running water.

There is a grand staircase, suspended over a precipitous drop, wide enough to march an army. The hotel opens right into the station, which has been renovated. Filled with music it is more like an ice rink.

Monday 2

An aimless day wandering through Glasgow in search of indigestible meals. My second impression of this city is very different from the first. It moves at the slowest pace. Today at lunch nothing arrives in a recognisable order – perhaps reflecting our state of mind. People set themselves on course to bump into you with deliberation. Traffic lights float in a timeless zone, change wearily and unwillingly.

Glasgow has preserved a pace and way of life long since vanished in the South. Was London like this thirty years ago? The city has its glitzy shopping malls; but not the brasserie culture to go with them.

Night. The empty streets resemble the Soho of yesteryear, a time before Londoners became tourists in their own city. At midnight we sat in Bennet's watching the boys go by.

Back in my room I read the Ackerley biography: drear descriptions of sexual encounters – though his guardsmen seem a great deal more seductive than the clientele of Bennet's. Fell asleep on it.

Tuesday 3

Pulled out the first mattresses from the railway arch – the workshop at the Citizen's Theatre. And with tar and feathers we put the first four beds together by lunch. One of them has a policeman's uniform and a football shirt in the local colours.

As we were pouring pitch over them a dustcart passed along the alley; the young man on it registered such shock he looked paralysed.

Wednesday 4

Opening at Richard de Marco's in Edinburgh. The small black paintings looked fine.

William Wilson, who set all this going in his gallery in Lyth, invited us out to supper in his flat on the Royal Mile. Conversation slipped back to the sixties: William said I should write more about a decade that has fallen victim to its myths. Young people are thinking of it as a Golden Age. There is a club here in Glasgow called Love, with Andy Warhol look-alikes and all the old tunes.

~

The nostalgic dancers would be shocked to find themselves in the poky holes of sixties' Soho, with no alcohol in their mits, just weak Nescafé in Duralex cups; surrounded by pill-popping transvestites, high on amphetamines – beehives and mascara.

William asked after K. who I haven't seen in years, his bedroom had a scum line of KY floating across the dingy wallpaper, above an unmade bed with physique mags scattered across the twisted sheets. Once admiring one of his football pin-ups I stepped back onto a full tube of KY that exploded and spattered the far wall.

~

A sixties' weekend. As the bell rang 'Time' frenetic enquiries to find the evening's party. Once there, you would stand uncomfortably in the corner of a strange room full of the tongue-tied getting drunk on sour wine; the kitchen full of sharp queens who eyed you up and made you feel uneasy. Impossible to have a piss as two guys were locked in, taking an interminable time to reach orgasm.

Negotiating the bodies on the staircase, the centre of conversation, you would look in the bedroom for your coat, which was lost under a drunk or a boy who was being gang-banged. Cigarettes on expensive carpets. And the 'owner' (as William described him) – some elderly man who had said 'I can only stomach the working classes one at a time and backwards' – imploring some thuggish boyfriend to close the whole thing down as his neatly placed possessions were scattered and trampled.

~

One Saturday night with no party, returning from the Kings Road on the number 19 I stepped on to the pavement at Centrepoint, where a tough looking bloke gave me the eye and when it was returned spun round and shouted 'What the fuck do you think you're looking at?' Terribly embarrassed I crossed the road, but before I had gone a further ten paces a piercing wolf whistle summoned me back; after a moment's hesitation I crossed the road.

'Are you a queer or something?' he asked.

'Yes' I replied.

'Can I talk to you?' he said. We walked twice round the block passing a magazine shop full of straight soft core.

'You got any mags?' he demanded.

'Yes' I said thinking of K.'s bedroom where I was staying. I took him upstairs and shoved a handful of gay hard core at him, and without waiting to see his response disappeared into the kitchen to make tea – which was never drunk; as when I came back he had his trousers down and a hard on protesting he had never done anything like this. Afterwards he said it felt great, buttoning up, saying his friend – a plumber's mate in Leytonstone – would not approve. I tried to start a conversation, but he left hurriedly saying he would send me his poetry. I never saw him again, he was the sort of lad dreams are made of, who came and went sadly leaving no name or address.

Roy Hattersley put on the most deplorable show at the Labour Party conference, rejecting proportional representation. He said only the Labour and Tory parties had an ideology, the parties of the centre were a nonsense and democracy would be ill served by giving them the light of day. It was a statement well to the right of Mrs. T. as hard-line as any Stalinist could wish, tight-arsed little dictator, god help us if after her we have him and his boastful master with his continual macho reassurance of his toughness. Kinnock exudes a bullish beery heterosexuality; ugly to look at. We have only the frying pan and the fire to choose from. The party is prepared to make any compromise for power. After its most successful conference the Labour Party is far to the right of Edward Heath's old Tory Party. There is no longer any decency or consistency of vision in British politics we are left in the tender hands of these loons of Right and Left. I find it small consolation the age of consent might be on the agenda. Hattersley's statement lost my vote. Why could he not say the Labour Party has no interest in proportional representation as we wish to win an election outright. Is there a politician who says it like it is?

~

The *Sonnets* and the *Symposium* are a cultural condom protecting us against the virus of the yellow press. They also relocate the way we view the old photos from this fifties *Physique* magazine. Another photo of two boys giving each other a blow job records a moment of beauty. Or the photo of the two young men who have caught each other in their arms and a flashlight which has a sweet naïveté, poignant under the damned soul from Michelangelo's last judgement.

I finished the Ackerley book – John Vere Brown said he was a tiresome queen. What could be worse, than to be a middle class, middle aged failed homosexual? Do I feel any sense of failure? Young men on street corners still make my blood race, though approaching fifty it would be a bit indecorous and importune. No dog Tulip for me.

At Bennet's last night three boys chatted me up; one for solidarity – he's been diagnosed HIV positive. I lost my heart for the evening to a young man with the looks of a Belmondo, who flashed his eyes at me more than once and weaved in and out of conversations. He had a shock of short black hair, a dressy black suit, a great smile. The only lad in the place with charm and trouble on his face. A middle-aged man and a woman in a leather mini were his companions.

Saturday 7

Wearily down to the breakfast room after a very late night. Walked to the street market – shop fronts blazing with light and bright lettering. Nothing like this down South. Several near-perfect locations: cafés and stalls.

Discussed working in the theatre. Phillip invited me here to direct in 1991; he suggested a Greek tragedy. Could I write a play? Perhaps around the *Sonnets, A Lover's Discourse*, a chorus, a small orchestra, two or three actors.

In the evening we went to a performance by Keersmaeker, a Belgian dance group. Chic little black dresses, minimalist coy humour, a set that looked like a clothes shop – sleight of hand, foot, and slight of content, it did not impress. As we were leaving the theatre the audience clapped while the musicians returned to get their sheet music – a girl behind me said, 'Don't encourage them. Showing their knickers for a laugh in 1989 – a bit like Benny Hill.'

HB arrived back full of anger about the Pets' edit. He said James failed to produce cards for the credits and arrived late in the afternoon with a roller caption. He had booked him on the earlier flight 'because it had better food' – though this meant he had to leave the edit incomplete. Later he calmed down.

Sunday 8
Inky black clouds looming over charcoal temples smudge china blue skies. Shafts of light on gaunt and distant hills – driving rain on taxi windows.

Monday 9
Woke feeling rotten – stomach destroyed again, and teeth on edge; at sixes and sevens. My centre is knocked sideways, I've fallen off the edge of hope. No story to tell. Nothing. Pointless pursuit. *The Garden* fades into the black. West pier at Brighton as a location? The pavilion as Herod's palace?

Fantasy of Danny Day Lewis and Matt Dillon with Tilda in a wild staging of *A Lover's Discourse*, spliced with *The Sonnets*. Just put the three of them on stage and let the audience watch them bicker, accompanied by a small string orchestra.

Unease.

Walked across to the west side of Glasgow and bought a large teapot while waiting for the second-hand TV shop to open. Then tarred and feathered the TV – and a skeleton holding *Leviticus* 20, 13.

~

The views of distant woodland and barren hills down the long straight classical streets are at their best as the light fades. Every day brings spectacular skies: low fast-moving clouds silvered by the setting sun, deep pools of blue and violet rushing in from the sea. Further down this street there is a cluster of terracotta buildings, lushly over-decorated from an ornamental handbook. With their sooty patina they hug the twilight shadows to themselves – cornices and cupolas of Mammon looming in the jungly dark. Many bars and shops have interiors unchanged since they were built, giving the city a lived-in feeling long since scrubbed away by profit in London.

Tuesday 10
The whole day putting up the show. One very angry middle-aged woman, fists clenched, said she had brought her children to the Eye. I pointed out that we had put a warning on the door. But it was too much for her – the two boys giving each other a blow job were pornography.

Another young man went round the room saying 'Great, great. You queer then?'

~

Exhausted and overcome by turpentine fumes scrubbing the tar off the floor with HB, as Gerard sat and watched. Back home by eight.

~

On TV an informative programme on AIDS and the arts in NYC by Simon Watney. It made me feel how far behind we are here.

R. Rosenbloom, Karl's old friend, who once came to my studio, was pontificating on high culture and bad political art. Shouted 'Goya!', but the TV did not hear me.

Wednesday 11

The exhibition opened at 12:00, and during the day 500 visitors walked through. No outspoken attacks, though one woman left raising her voice about the 'filth' in the centre, how she felt like a 'lesbian'. Some parents removed their children.

The reaction to HB and Gerard, who took up residence in their barbed wire four poster, was most interesting. People averted their gaze; others self-consciously walked round with their backs to the cage. A few, mostly women, entered into conversation. An American girl said, 'Come on boys, let's see some action.'

Thursday 12

HB and Gerard managed to fall asleep in their barbed wire cage. A hush fell over the gallery. Visitors tiptoed about, though some thought they were acting.

560 people came today, most very attentive; and some, particularly journalists, horrified at the accumulated anti-gay front pages of the yellow press:

Friends, Romans, Countrymen, lend me your rears. (The *Sun* on speculation concerning Shakespeare's sexuality)

A cartoon of Prince Edward as the tail end of a pantomime horse, with the Duke saying, 'There's a role at the bottom for you Edward.'

Some headlines raise a guilty smile, like *Sex Boys For Sale At Queen's Grocer's*, or *Beeb Man Sits On Lesbian.*

~

Today I had one or two uncertain responses from young men, sometimes verging on the aggressive. In the evening there was a packed house for *The Last Of England*. A party of first year art students, many quite at sea. My talk started arguments.

At nine in the evening the gallery was still packed. Some of the talented Glasgow painters were there, thoroughly enjoying themselves. Steven Campbell was very complimentary about my paintings for the Turner Prize – thought they were the best of the bunch at the Tate.

Friday 13

The attendance climbed to 600. At five we all drove to Edinburgh and I gave a talk at the de Marco Gallery.

~

No letters, but a telegram from New York.

Later in Bennet's bar a conversation with a catholic boy. Tight-arsed, restrictive upbringing, confessional. I cut a long stumbling conversation short by telling him he should let himself be fucked by his next lover – all the pain and hurt he felt was in the mind. He had admitted his only reason to be in the club was for 'a bit of cock', and then told me my chakra had slipped below the belt years ago. I admitted that I'd allowed my cock more than its fair share in ruling my head. As we left he said: 'What are you doing now?' 'Going home for a wank alone.'

Saturday 14

At 12:30, walking to Bennet's through cold damp streets, I passed a crowd six deep along the entire length of the Central Station. As I did so a voice rang out, 'There's Derek Jarman', and the whole crowd turned to look. I didn't know whether to run. Tilda said I should have shouted back 'Where?'

~

'At sixteen I crept into a cinema and saw *Sebastiane*. It changed my life although I didn't understand a word of it. My fingers were on the controls ready to change the channel if my parents appeared. I turned the sound right down so no-one would hear.'

Sunday 15

The talk at the gallery was difficult. Someone objected to the obviousness of the installation, and then complained it was bad art. Others sprang to its defence. I talked of the barbed wire that had hemmed me in, quite literally, in the RAF camps – the fenced-in boarding school, the proscribed sexuality, the virus. During the discussion those who did not like the show caused me great sadness. Could they not see beyond art?

Monday 16

Dreamt that ******* ****** sodomised ******* ******** in a new Greenaway film, with the critic of the *Guardian* writing columns of praise that were published in the *Sun*.

~

Neil Bartlett brilliant and witty at dinner, back in leather after a week in fishnet and pearls – while I sank exhausted next to him after three late nights in a row.

He told a story of Duggie Byng, the music hall entertainer who died recently in his late nineties: blind, he had bought bread rolls instead of cakes in a Brighton cake shop, then served them up with the Earl Grey to a group of young admirers, none of whom said a word until the old man took a bite himself.

Neil told me Judy Garland had occupied room 234 at the Central Hotel. I hope the place was a bit more on the ball then – the management sleeps through the day, and growls if wakened to do anything.

~

These two weeks have been the most intense of the year: I've hardly slept, swept off my feet in a torrent of conversation. Even if the installation is bad art it has lead to good ends, provoked but not trapped the audience. Two American women were the most vociferous in my defence; criticism mainly male.

~

Intense work has obliterated the garden at Dungeness from my mind. I can live in a hotel room with a change of blue overalls, toothpaste, a razor, and this diary.

~

The day ended with a twenty-one year old pouring out his heart – his lover had been diagnosed HIV+ and had shut the doors on him. I told him to batter them down.

~

Drove southwards for six hours – downhill all the way – to London. Black clouds and driving rain. Mists and sunlight over the hills and dales.

Tuesday 17
Met Genesis P. Orridge wheeling his daughter Jeunesse in a pram. Gen was dressed immaculately in a grey suit, grey shirt and dog collar, a gold Psychic TV cross on his lapel. He had bought the dog collar and shirt in Brighton from an earnest lady who asked him which parish he was from.

'I'm a missionary,' said Gen. 'I travel the world.'

'Oh, who do you work for?'

'Young people,' said Gen.

'I do a lot of that sort of thing, gays and the like,' she said.

Dressed as a bishop he gets put in first class carriages, people help him with the child, taxi drivers cross busy streets, and everywhere he goes people call him Sir.

'You should try it, Derek, it makes a world of difference.'

Thursday 19
Paul died this morning.

Spent the day at St. Mary's with Bishop Berkeley's *Siris* to while away the time.

Friday 20
Strong gusts of wind, rainstorms, fire sirens and flashing lights.

~

I am wandering aimlessly in this labyrinth of memories. Paul's death left me numb. Most registered zero on the Richter scale of emotion; others gave me the impression they were glad he was out of the way. A telephone call, barely a ripple.

Saturday 21
The gale continued to blow through a second night. At midday Gerard arrived and we drove with Dagmar Benke, commissioning editor of ZDF, down to Dungeness.

It is over three weeks since I left Prospect Cottage. All the way we drove in torrential rain. But the garden was still quite dry, much of the driftwood blown flat by the winds, and the plants scorched by salt.

In spite of the wind it is very warm. Late at night we walked to the tip of the Ness to watch a high sea under a starlit sky. A huge crescent moon, dull orange, hovered and set over the sea in the time it took to walk home.

~

We looked at the rushes – many thoughts, an impossible subject. Flashes of the most beautiful film, particularly when the subjects forget the camera or step out of the scene, forgetting to 'act'. Philip and the child washing – he gathers him up and walks into the light, which on automatic exposure turns to night. There is a shadowy kiss.

Other moments lack this mercurial quality; but the three days we spent filming have brought us some fine footage. How will I find my way? Why the life of Christ? Why the garden?

In this film the story is told somewhere else. The most evocative moments are those that are disintegrating: the debris, the camera faults, the act of pre-paration, the Barbie doll Eve being made up – all work better than the scene at the end, the Doubting Thomas who doubts.

Sunday 22
A hawk perched all day on top of the telephone wire, every now and then swooping into the broom. A flock of greenfinches twist and turn. There are large white *Fungi lactarius* under the trees.

The rain has brought green back into my view, though the water in the Long Pits is even lower. Walking over to them this morning I noticed the first yellow flowers out on the gorse.

In the garden fennel, sea kale, borage have germinated. I picked a head of evening primrose and scattered the seed. Planted daffodil bulbs and tidied up the front flower beds.

Monday 23
It rained through the night.

At five the dawn came, pallid and grey. The fishermen left the beach.

I'm always thankful for the dawn: the restless nights evaporate – deep sleep never comes, as it once did, to drown out the fluttering nightmares that hover at the edge of consciousness.

At breakfast the kestrel took up his perch on the power lines.

~

A warm sunny day. Dragonflies and a last painted lady butterfly dart across the Long Pits.

I brought back burdock and oxeye daisy, planting them in front of the house. Mark's white T-shirt with its message *May Peace Prevail On Earth* and my overalls kept me warm enough.

Tuesday 24
Deep red sun climbing from a still sea, the wet shingle ablaze with reflections. Walked into the garden floating on a sea of pearls. The garden casts mysterious shadows. Not a breath of wind.

~

David arrived at midday bringing a nineteenth-century copy of Burton's *Anatomy of Melancholy* – £45, much less than the £100 I was quoted in London. OUP have republished it at £140, so whichever way you look at it I did well.

~

We drove to New Romney, bought provisions, then walked along the beach. The sun stayed with us all day.

~

The windows I ordered two months ago arrived, and the first of them was in by four.

~

A dusty rose sunset under which float patches of pale grey cloud. As the light fades the pinks turn magenta, the clouds a pearlescent white, the sea turquoise, while the power station glitters under a scarlet and black sky, slashed with orange and vivid blue.

Wednesday 25
A crescent moon with a swarm of silver stars hung a hair's breadth over the sea. I shaved, had breakfast, and walked over the shingle in the dawn chill – filming the sunrise caught in the windows of the little wooden houses in blinding flashes.

The sun and cheerful clicking of the camera in timelapse dispelled the worst of my fears. Is the film as ugly and unhinged as I dreamt last night?

Thursday 26
At eight the six swans from the Long Pits flew over the house from the sand flats at Littlestone, white in the grey sky, very silent.

Warm weather. Waiting for a change – for rain or the first cold snap.

~

Returned to London. The phone was broken. Found no HB or message. Panicked.

Rushed to Lorraine's to phone James Whalley, who suggested a sequel to *Sebastiane*. St. Irene rescues him, pulls the arrows out. Then what? 'Well heterosexuality is big this year Derek. Didn't you know?'

~

All the way back on the train I was plagued with misgivings about *The Garden*. Looking at the rushes over the past six days, I discovered not one sequence that worked. Glaring faults everywhere: no close-ups, camera faults, out-of-focus shots, shots that fall like confetti. 16mm deadly, with no resonance. There is not a shot that is not ugly.

Why should this happen?

No more the coherence of shared projects – this has become too big to manage. Shackled with the dozens of hangers-on I cannot improvise. The shoot is a hydra – I cannot hear anything for all the voices asking questions.

We have no organisation. James, the producer, makes arbitrary decisions about cameras, accuses me of being 'absent', foists 16mm on me – a truly hideous experience.

The sun has gone, the idea is two years old, the design is haywire – a tin bath glows like the unused family silver in the frame. Actors arrive in 'costumes'.

And the landscape, so vital for my film, is bathed in a gloom. The summer sun lost while James shops at Fortnum's.

Friday 27
The phone is still dead.

The Last Of England went out at 11:00 last night; all the other films in the season were out at nine. Special rules for me again.

~

The silver sea turns to lead
The honey sours in the spoon

Saturday 28
Back through the Saturday crowds to Charing Cross Road from Rassell's with the last spring bulbs – daffodils, snowdrops, crocus; also a packet of chicory seed.

Stopped at Daquise for a Polish lunch – endless wait for service that turned from relaxing to aggravating.

25 minutes waiting for a bus.

The V&A is in scaffolding with polythene blowing about in the gale. Shut my eyes through Knightsbridge – all flimsy macs, suntans and sunglasses in the gathering twilight.

Sunday 29
Hampstead. Drunk on vodka, my eyes fix on my feet in the pale moonlight; they step across gnarled roots and sodden ground marbled with dead leaves. The wind roars through the groaning branches as the storm lashes the trees.

Hardly anyone here. Not surprising, though someone says: 'Fucking no-one here.' 'Afraid a tree will fall on them,' I reply to the stranger. That's what I'm hoping will happen.

By one my footsteps drag and I'm shivering with cold. Whatever keeps me here it's not the promise of blowing the boy in the baseball hat.

What is it? It can't be the danger, it's safer here than Soho on a weekend evening. The dark after years of gloomy warehouses certainly doesn't frighten me. I know all the paths and beaten tracks through the trees and bushes. The moon, stars, and distant airliners that roar through the night above the ancient beeches.

Ours is a separate and parallel world, under the stars. Here you can fade away into the dark.

OCTOBER

On any other night there must be two hundred others here, beside the good-looking jogger, who I've seen dancing alone on the street outside Comptons. Someone said he was a New Zealander – like my dad. He skirts round the few groups of men and disappears only to reappear again half an hour later. After ignoring me he suddenly passes by, and turning a corner I find him standing, facing me.

I knew before I touched him that this encounter was doomed. I was freezing cold and all he wanted was attention that he could reject. The fact that I had turned my back on him earlier was the reason for his provocative stance. He kissed me very reticently and said 'Suck it mate'; but before we made contact disappeared, this time for good.

NOVEMBER

Wednesday 1

Planted wallflowers, snowdrops and crocus early in the morning; then weeded the front bed. By lunch the rain had cleared.

A luminous grey sky, and a sea white as milk with a rim of indigo blue.

Simon Turner arrived and we sat down with the tapes and worked out a credible beginning to *The Garden*.

A brief squall and then a starry sky. Turned in early.

Thursday 2

Up with the dawn. A strong wind blowing, bright sunlight.

The tide was out and I brought back several large wooden planks, probably part of an old sea defence; also a dozen flints for the circular beds. Exhausting work. The shrimpers and the luggers on the sand flats must think I'm truly eccentric, turning over the flints at the shoreline.

~

After lunch I filmed the sea. I have no rough seas in all the hours of rushes, except one reel taken two years ago, covered with scratches and tram lines.

Dave, the handyman, arrived and completed the tiling of the kitchen floor. As he worked he told me the Magnox power station was a shambles of rusting piping and escaping steam, with little men running hither and thither with spanners and screwdrivers.

~

The army keeps us all awake practising into the small hours. After a particularly noisy night they bought large bouquets of flowers for the ladies of Lydd.

~

HB's 25th birthday. He says he's now a man. He celebrated it all alone with a five hour bath and a large microwaved M&S dinner. Simon says he's never seen HB except when he's smiling.

~

The rain came down in torrents as the weather closed in. Simon and I lit the candles in the wind lamps and made ourselves tea – the rebuilt kitchen transforms the house.

Later we went to the pub for whitebait and 'profitballs' as the landlady calls them. Then watched the film rushes and made phone calls round the world.

Before we turned in: a ravishing film by Joris Ivens, at 90 chasing the elusive wind in China. The most refined work, it made the Hitchcock season look dreadful.

Friday 3
Showers scudding past. Walked with Simon to the Long Pits – only a foot or two of water in them. The downpour hasn't made an impression: at a trowel's depth the ground is still bone dry.

~

At tea Andy arrived out of the dark. Only two weeks ago he was arrested on a murder charge and held for 24 hours, he had been in the States when the murder took place. His conversation is still caught in a whirlpool of theft and bravado; he was arrested, he said, for stealing a pint of milk when he was sixteen. He was sent down for 10 days.

Saturday 4
Derek Ball cooked one of his piping hot Dungeness fish stews. His friends Tim and Tod lit the guy they had built: a Minoan snake goddess in the image of Imelda Marcos carrying a pair of golden shoes – with a conical dress of driftwood and floral crimplene wired together with fireworks, high-waisted with a belt of gold streamers and breasts of bangers. A small face painted on a paper plate – delicate as the moon, with an enigmatic smile. Arms outstretched, she stood ten feet tall and burnt like a torch.

Derek's cat Spyder chased the sparks in the dark. The lighthouse flashed over the Channel and the twinkling lights of fishing boats. Sheet lightning illuminated distant thunder clouds. The stars shone bright and Maria Callas blasted out Puccini arias in the dark. Tod and Tim stoked the flames in long black highwaymen's coats.

Sunday 5
This morning very cold, with a hoar frost. Everyone round for breakfast – coffee, toast and home-made blackberry jam.

We sat and talked of the sixties – all those London restaurants run by Spanish waiters, refugees from Franco's regime, in tight trousers, mincing about. The doorman Amadio's oily welcome at the Sombrero.

Here Vicky de Lambray sat drunk on dropping names, propped up by empty champagne bottles. As the years passed he grew more and more androgyne, his voice becoming as high-pitched as a dog whistle. For a while he retired to Parkhurst 'for a little holiday with Her Majesty'.

Back in the early seventies he used to arrive in a white Rolls – reputed to be the property of a Labour peer, one of Harold's Gannex mobsters (no-one ever saw this peer). He looked like my grandmother's jade Buddha: pear-shaped, with long lank sugar hair. Without him the transparent colourwheel dancefloor below played to an empty gallery.

So many nights standing in the cramped aisles avoiding those Spanish waiters – José, Mañuel – balancing drinks above us on trays.

~

Brought back flints from the beach, and planted two more of the wild stock that I plucked out of the rubbish tip last night on my way home. Then stripped and painted the dormer window of the fishing loft.

Derek arrived and admired the fax that is hidden in a laundry basket. It is very ugly and called 'Brother'. Then he invited me to finish off the remains of supper.

It was scorching hot. We sat outside in the bright sun, which evaporated the hoar frost. A red admiral flew round the table in circles. Tim said I should put down more of the sixties as we seemed so happy then.

~

Time has softened the decade – made it seem less complicated. The sixties opened the floodgates of consumption; and as more – much more, became available we lost a sense of the New. By the eighties the excitement of the New had disappeared.

In the sixties the New was still ours, and the media was only just taking its first faltering steps to exploit it.

'Being in the know' meant the thrill of entering a secret world. In the colour supplements and media shows of the eighties everything withers – little survives publicity. A world is experienced through a filter of journalese. Exclusivity is in the hands of the doorman infantry of a popular nightclub, forbidding entry in an arbitrary way. In the sixties the doors were open.

Now the media rummage each morning through our discarded psyches to make a few bob.

In the junk yard we are all richer, have more opportunities, more information, but are dispossessed. The city no longer belongs to us, it is a Disneyland of shallow style – we are all tourists here, rootless.

NOVEMBER

~

In 1962 Ladbroke Grove was the end of the earth. My first student flat was in Coram Street near Russell Square. We lived in the city centre, within the inner circle – 'civilization' bounded by the Circle Line.

Now London's youth is fragmented: the luckiest live mortgaged to the hilt in refurbished wastelands, the poorer are unable to afford to leave their economic ghettoes – so many stops away you lose count.

One of the pluses of the sixties was a depressed inner city, where you could find a grand old Victorian room with dilapidated plumbing for a few bob a week. All this has gone in a tidal wave of mortgage that has throttled the life out of London. The same fate befell Manhattan. How can you describe what has been lost to those who've never known different?

As I approach fifty London is foreign – all the nooks and corners of my student days sanitised, scrubbed, like the buildings, and overwhelmed with rubbish from the convenience food industry. And everywhere *clothes* shops – as if everyone, knowing their time was ending had put on their best suit for the occasion.

Monday 6
A still, frosty morning – sun bright on the glittering shingle, not a cloud in the sky and very cold. Well wrapped I walked to the beach.

I love the mornings here – up with the sunshine, cups of coffee, steaming porridge and toast. The quiet is overwhelming after the snarling traffic of the Charing Cross Road. Only a year old, the garden looks as if it has been here as long as the house.

Now the flowers are dead; the multicoloured flints, and the bright red bricks ground by the waves give it a friendly appearance.

It isn't a gloomy garden, its circles and squares have humour – a fairy ring for troglodytic pixies – the stones a notation for long-forgotten music, an ancestral round to which I add a few new notes each morning.

Tuesday 7
By sundown yesterday a new window was opened up in the kitchen wall. I ate my supper facing the nuclear power station – ablaze with light under a star-filled sky and a mandarin moon. A twentieth century Babylon, great glittering liner beached in the wilderness.

A new ladder to the fishing loft is also in place, which has made the house asymmetrical. It has made the climb a leisurely affair: no more balancing on wobbly ladders. I painted it with sticky black tar varnish – tar itself is impossible to find since the coke fired gas plants closed down.

I don't know whether to laugh or cry for the unseasonable warmth and sunshine of the last four days. The thrift outside the front door is at sixes and sevens and has put out bright pink flowers. In spite of a weather forecast that foretold rain it is warm and sunny again. I walked along the beach gathering stones with holes and returned to thread them into a necklace.

~

The phone rings: yet another painting for charity – they go almost as quickly as I paint them. Aside from the generosity of Roger, who bought five last summer, I've not sold any this year. At least these charity auctions get them out of the house.

~

As the sun went down the rain set in. I am surprised how happy I have been with my own company these last few weeks – by now I should be itching to get back to London. But I'm happy here, brewing a scatterbrained mix of soups and porridge.

Friday 10

A storm blew up the Channel last night. I woke twice, once at 2:00 thinking dawn was round the corner, and again at 5:00.

HB said that since I was no longer in love with my work the only way I could drum up passion was to live on a knife edge of demands. I do feel trapped – no light anywhere – however hard I try to dispel the gloom both nurture and nature conspire to make me continually uneasy.

~

The philosopher wrote:

> *The fairest order in the world is a heap of random sweepings ... All we see asleep is sleep all we see awake is death*

~

Old friends died young

The virus attacks creation
Creativity withers
No consuming passions
Only these slow melancholy days

The garden is built for dear friends
Howard, Paul, Terence, David, Robert, and Ken,
And many others, each stone has a life to tell
I cannot invite you into this house

~

Thomas Knaupf phoned me from East Berlin to say thousands crossed over to celebrate in the Kurfurstendamm.

All day the rain drove down, no break in the clouds. Spent the morning rearranging rooms; in the afternoon stretched new canvases. David drove me to Rye and we got drenched shopping.

Saturday 11

Slept well. Bright and sunny morning. The wind died away in the night.

Dave dropped round to measure the new doors; afterwards Derek and I drove to New Romney.

We talked of the effect moving here has had on us – throwing our lives out of kilter. We needed to get away to find solitude. Yet when the weather sets in as it has in the last few days, the roof rattling and crashing on a windy night can make you long for the city.

It has also distanced us from our work, made it much more difficult. My futile attempt to bring everyone down to film this autumn floundered in the weather and logistical problems.

Yet in London I feel a stranger – the city has moved on.

~

What has happened to me under these awesome skies? Here the preoccupations of a film world bounded by Soho seem ridiculous. Walking into Working Title or Basilisk, the offices seem so cramped, so steeped in gloom all this glorious summer.

~

Derek Ball came here after his 'accident', I after the discovery of my seropositivity. Behind the façade my life is at sixes and sevens. I water the roses and wonder whether I will see them bloom. I plant my herbal garden as a panacea, read up on all the aches and pains that plants will cure – and know they are not going to help. The garden as pharmacopoeia has failed.

Yet there is a thrill in watching the plants spring up that gives me hope.

Even so, I find myself unable to record the disaster that has befallen some of my friends, particularly dear Howard, who I miss more than imagination. He wanders into my mind – as he wandered out of a stormy night eighteen months ago.

~

A full moon chalk white in the dying sunlight – Berlioz' *Damnation of Faust* fading as the shadows gather in.

I spent the whole afternoon waiting for visitors who never arrived. The sun has sunk behind the nuclear power station. I had hoped they would see the garden. Perhaps by moonlight?

Sunday 12

A cloudless sky turned a dusty rose in the sunrise.

The day turned out so warm I worked in the garden in shirtsleeves, raking in bone meal round the plants in the front bed. The dill seedlings are now six inches high. The fig cutting is thriving; parsley has germinated.

~

Derek came over in a daze at lunch time. The lady who owns the beautiful old lifeboat house out on the shingle offered to sell it to him. It would mean uprooting himself from London.

We walked over to the building. It is constructed like this house, would make a perfect studio.

~

At four Jon Savage arrived, very tired. I put the kettle on and the cooker blew up in my face. Jon said it was either the full moon or his psychic state, perhaps both.

We had a late lunch, then walked along the beach. Jon has written 55 thousand words in the past week for his punk book, burying his childhood. We talked of the Jubilee year, and of Vivienne Westwood appearing on Dame Edna's show – a cross between Margaret Thatcher and Miss Jean Brodie. She lacks humour. Perhaps it all went into the clothes – her fig leaf was very funny.

Drove back to London through autumn mists that blotted out the marshes. At the flat, cold and tired, I took an armful of the hated mail from the hall floor and sat in the corner of the British Museum Pizza Express – once a very beautiful tiled dairy. Then, as HB had gone to Newcastle, I took a taxi to the Heath, which was silent and mysterious, with the full moon refracted in the fog and the sound of water dripping on leaves.

~

Today brought another film crisis. Should I carry on? I decided not – but know I'll wake up tomorrow morning and change my mind. I'm being very silly playing little boy lost.

Monday 13
Tired, but happy to be back in London. The separation of my two lives – work here, sunsets and sunrises there.

Tuesday 14
HB caught in the fog arrived home late in the evening. Norman, Richard, Thomas, and Julian at dinner in the Rodos – one of those disconnected evenings when everyone wanted to see each other without the company of the others.

Ended up in Norman's house in Soho: wood-panelled gilded rooms, Joseph Beuys and the master of the mouse furniture; and a jolly tartan stair carpet – the whole place as eccentric as the twin washbasins in the bathroom. Why not twin toilets? What Thomas Knaupf from East Berlin thought . . .

Norman said 'How lucky that John and Volker had such good taste and I could move in without redecorating,' and thought we were smiling as our lips curled in disbelief.

Conversation ended with Vera Russell, whose shadow falls heavily across the insecurities of the secure. Of all the people I've met in the British art scene Vera Russell is the most talked of in her absence. Richard says that at a dinner he found his name on a little sticker next to D. Hockney; but before he had managed to sit down Vera loomed up and said 'There seems to have been a mistake,' and physically moved him down the table, before sitting in his place.

Everyone chips in with a Vera comment. On gay artists: 'They all seem to have something missing' – perhaps this accounts for her missionary work in this department. To me at the Tate: 'You can't take an artist as distinguished as Robert Medley dancing – he's much too important, he might drop dead!'

Norman says that many years ago she turned a directionless Picasso onto African art; and 'Voilà, my friends, the Demoiselles'. The Demoiselles is Pablo's tribute to Vera. Stravinsky trumped him – you can hear her dancing in The Rites Of Spring.

~

I was shocked to see Philip Core's obituary in the Independent. For a moment I thought it was an article on his painting, as it was illustrated by a self-portrait.

I met Philip quite regularly over the years on street corners. At first I was quite suspicious of his enthusiasm: he was another of the glitterati – his sensibility seemed out of joint. But I came to realise my mistake. He was much tougher than casual acquaintance might suggest. His writing on photography and the arts, even the obituaries he wrote for the *Independent*, were perceptive.

At the arts lobby against Section 28, Philip made a 'performance', smashing a plaster statue of Michelangelo's David in front of the large audience.

His uncompromising gay subject matter never allowed him to fit in. Last week, dying of AIDS, he fought a court case over some Tom Of Finland catalogues stolen from him by HM Customs and Excise.

~

A dicky bird flew into my dreams last night and said:

Do you know that ****** ******** is buggered by his caddies on the golf course?

Never! I said.

He flew off laughing.

Don't go! I said.

I have to, the Queen Mum's expecting me back. She saves my feathers for her hats.

Wednesday 15

A successful meeting for *The Garden*. Sarah Swords, back 'on board', gives me confidence. Whenever there's a crisis James reacts angrily or buries his head and takes down random jottings. Suggestions are countered with a *But you said* this or that – never taking into account that nearly two years and at least four schedules have been abandoned. Very selective memory.

Can't say I'm entirely blameless as the whole process is exquisitely aggravating and I can't for the life of me find much point in film, though I enjoy filming.

Thursday 16

A series of successful film meetings. If I remain in London everything should stay on an even keel.

I can enjoy London now I have something to (pre-)occupy me – walking to and from the bookshops as the winter draws in.

Sitting unfocused on the large bed being continually bombarded by phone calls for help is unnerving. I hide, try to push people off the line and then I feel guilty.

Richard Salmon threw a dinner party in his studio, the most elegant room in London. We sat on a table and talked ancient art scandal, hedged in by Gilbert and George's *Bloodsports and Bloodbaths*, and the life-size Van der Weyden crucifixion.

Paul Bartel was amused, and curious about the paintings on the walls – nearly all British: Sickert, Ben Nicholson. He and Gus Van Sant talked about their Warhol project. Paul, like a sea captain on leave – large and reassuring – gave us all a hug as he left.

Matt Dillon arrived with the drummer of The Clash, and a tall girl dressed in fashion black, pale as late nights. They stood in a corner of the room wrapped in a cocoon of self-absorption. It was as if we had been invaded by the little troupe of players on the hotel verandah in *Death In Venice*.

Matt was very friendly. I talked of Howard and asked him for his heartbeat for the soundtrack of *Blueprint*. He said he would let me have it, just to ring.

Matt and his friends went off to an all-night chess tournament, the rest of us to bed.

Friday 17

Meeting at Christopher Hobbs' to tie up the art direction – the room full of curios: incunabula, mirrored cabinets, Roman lamps, an old carpet – its colours washed away with age.

Drove with Sarah back through the city, where at the Lloyds' building we passed 50 acrobats, jugglers and fire-eaters performing on the pavement. We invited them all to the marriage of the two boys – a celebration in pink: pink suits, pink balloons, pink triangular flags.

Derek arrived and we drove down to Dungeness.

Saturday 18

A cold southeasterly has blown through Dungeness the past four days, frosting the windows with dried salt and burning my plants.

The sun shone today but I stayed inside, lit the fires and stretched canvases. The persistent croak in my throat enjoys the cold, and I don't want to encourage it. With both stoves roaring away the house is quite warm.

~

Mark phones from NYC to say he has seen photos of the house in *Interiors* magazine.

~

The nuclear power station has been in the news for breaking safety regulations: it was fined the ludicrous sum of £6,500 in Folkestone Magistrate's Court.

Derek's friend Janet showed me a series of old photographs of the Ness: the railway station out near the lighthouse; the original foghorn, whose foundations were used for the new lighthouse; and a group photo outside the pub, The Brick. It burnt to the ground when an oak beam in its chimney caught fire, nearly killing the occupants, who were dragged from the building unconscious.

Back in the 1930s the shoreline had not yet been destroyed by the dredging for shingle (to protect the nuclear power station) and had not been colonised by the grasses. The first of the railway carriage chalets, *Samoa*, was built for a retired civil servant.

After she had shown me the photos we went over to the old lifeboat building which I hope to buy from her. The tongue and groove interior is very similar to Prospect and must be about the same age. The building is on rollers so it can be pulled nearer the sea.

Sunday 19

The house is joyful, smells of oil paint – both pithers roaring away, almost too warm.

Monday 20

The whole day working on *The Garden*, with so little time: two weeks to prepare the film and eight days to shoot.

I'm not going to be unduly adventurous with casting. Sean Bean is free, so perhaps he could play Christ. The extras have all been alerted by Simon Turner, who has called them now on several films.

By lunch Jo, the secretary at Basilisk, had printed up the schedule; and Debbie McWilliams, who has given up her time for free, had taken me through *Spotlight*. She's leaving the 'business' and is off to France to teach. I confessed to her I hadn't a clue what I was up to, that the events of the last years have left me at sea.

At lunch we talked of humming and the orchestration of bells in Mussorgsky. Humming lament of Aunt Euphrosyne in *Ivan The Terrible* after the killing of the Czar's childlike cousin. Children seem to be creeping into every scene of the film – as wise men and shepherds. If Philip is Judas, Jody becomes his child, the Judas child.

Tuesday 21

As I drowsed news bulletins of a great march for reform in Prague wove through my dreams.

Worked with Derek Brown for an hour on the design for *The Garden*: a purely pink affair – balloons and banners.

~

In the gloom of the National Gallery I noticed that in three Italian paintings of the Renaissance, Christ wears a pink robe.

In the weak failing light of winter London, the gallery looked appallingly dowdy. In the process of 'restoration', much of it closed. Not one picture happy.

I left with a feeling of desperation – I had parted company with a dead inheritance, its spirit evaporated under the tedious explanations of the guides. One was describing *chiaroscuro* to a group of bemused middle-aged tourists. What were they thinking? What relevance did it have to them?

Paintings glimmered in the ashes: two Pietàs; Riberas; a very small Dossi; Poussin's mysterious landscapes in the Campagna; a bright portrait of a young Medici by Bronzino.

Western easel painting – knick-knacks on brocade.

Standing under the portico, over to the left, the Trafalgar Square Grand Buildings are being restored in tawdry reproduction. The original design was mediocre, what value the copy? While to the right the new extension is still disguised behind its polythene wrap.

When I got back to the office I found all the actors Debbie had pencilled in were available. Somehow I had hoped that fate would weed them out. No luck.

Wednesday 22
Quick trip to the Beeb to talk about 'art school in the sixties'; then to John's to get my hair cut.

John said Malcolm McClaren had come in to have his hair cut the other day, slapped a £50 note on the desk to pay, picked it up with his change and was off like greased lightning with a 'Thanks, see ya!' The girl at the desk was gobsmacked.

Back home to find HB leaning out of the window like Harold Lloyd, polishing. Dressed in his blue overalls he spent the next three quarters of an hour chasing me with hoover, duster and squeegee, humming little tunes.

Thursday 23
Nothing that Basilisk organises is as organised as it seems. Perhaps an office the size of a rat-trap leads to endless crossed lines. Conversations blur – you chat with the walls that hedge you in. No-one is exactly clear why they have been summoned.

~

Lunch. Set out from Working Title through Soho with Sarah Radclyffe. She is troubled by the lack of scripts, says as soon as directors make a film they are off to the States, leaving a vacuum.

The tedious minutiae of film swallow everything. To retain enthusiasm you have to stoop low. In the foyer Bernard Rose laments the lack of any decent screens. The Lumière is the only home for my films; and if that is impossible the openings are mismanaged, like *The Last Of England* and *War Requiem*. *Caravaggio* is the only film of mine to have been properly promoted.

Walked home through Berwick Street market and climbed straight into bed. Drako arrived, made ginseng tea and recited poems. HB typed. I fell asleep. Alexander Dubcek on TV. If you wait, the world turns in circles.

Friday 24

Read Ballard's *Running Wild* – a Red Brigade fantasy for kids. Sarah was interested in making it for Working Title: 35 murders in ninety minutes, the best moment of which would be the attack on a Prime Minister known as National Mother. It would make a very ugly film, would no doubt upset everyone. I doubt whether it would get over its sociological point – the stifling atmosphere of plenty in all the blood letting.

~

Spent the morning at Berman & Nathan's talking to Monty Berman; then through the building to choose a mismatched set of costumes. Found the pink robe from the Piero della Francesca resurrection.

~

Feeling much happier today having grown used to the cold. The first days of winter are always depressing – I'll take to my bed like a hedgehog, crawl under the sheets and sleep with my feet on the pillows.

~

Horrible queue of Alice Cooper fans outside the window chanting 'Give us an A, give us an L . . .' I wanted to shout 'Go away' so loud they would have been blasted down the Charing Cross Road like dead winter leaves.

~

In 1972 I was invited to stage Alice Cooper on Broadway.

I joined the band in Copenhagen. There were thirty or more of them, resembling a gang of Davy Crockett trappers. They travelled in a private jet, took over the floor of an hotel, and played a long-running table-tennis tournament as they downed an infinite supply of Budweisers. I arrived late and missed the concert, but was whisked away to see a 'live show' where Alice was to be photographed.

The seedy basement was piled supermarket-high with more mountains of Budweisers: Alice carried one around with him wherever he went. At the end of the basement was a double bed on which unattractive, sweaty men humped equally sweaty and unattractive girls. Alice, together with python and Budweiser, capered about like a praying mantis in bondage while the furry-looking band shouted obscenities to cover up their embarrassment.

Later a lesbian scene with organ music subdued them; this was followed by a girl in Alice bondage who wriggled on the bed inviting the band to join in the action. After a few remarks like 'she'll give you a dose' the girl switched to the offensive. 'Are you all gay?' she asked aggressively.

At that one of the band clambered on the bed to the cheers of the rest of them, and the girl started to give him a blow job – but to his embarrassment nothing happened. She gave up with a shrug, he hitched up his pants and climbed down scarlet-faced. The girl followed him down and sat on Alice's lap.

Alice jumped like a jack rabbit, sprung on to the bed, and laid about him with a whip. The photographers clicked away. The girl tangled with the whip as Alice lashed out and she started to cry.

Saturday 25
HB makes me laugh all the time. We dug holes in the shingle which filled in as fast as we made them and planted the twelve wild roses which had come in the post; they were very well packed though the cold winds had dried them out. We got them in as quickly as possible. HB said Prospect Cottage had become the palace of the sleeping princess.

Sunday 26
Excruciating and sleepless night, woke parched and drained of energy. Putting the kettle on was like climbing a mountain. Pulled my clothes on very slowly and could not face shaving.

There has been a very hard frost – the borage plants look as if they have been boiled, and the fig has lost all its leaves. Threw out scraps – starlings appeared out of the blue and squabbled until chased away by two magpies.

Walked around the house picking up props to take back to London for the shoot: a water jug, palms, a folding chair, gold jar and mirror glasses. I have done this so many times before.

~

Hallucinatory moments on some of the film we telecined on Friday evening – just when I had the answer I forgot the question.

It's a strange feeling to put in the roses and wonder if you will see them bloom. My aches and pains hurt. This is all too melodramatic, I've just got a bout of flu.

Monday 27

David drove me back from Dungeness, talked most of the way about the problems of the *Pink Paper*, the polarised approach to aesthetics, modern cookers, and computers in repro houses! Lost is the unified approach to design of the early modern movement – everything has been taken over by marketing. The agenda can be quite farcical: the wipe-clean cooker in a spotless empty kitchen where there is not so much as a dish to wash – the labour-saving device takes off into the realms of phantasy.

Tuesday 28

Sean unable to play Christ, his parents are Jehovah's Witnesses. This has left me with a gap at the centre – we'll have to develop the two lovers, make it *their* passion.

Viewed *Visions Of Ecstasy* with Colin McCabe in a video dungeon at the BFI: the film has been refused a certificate on account of blasphemy. I didn't find the film remotely titillating – if that was the intention then it's a failure; it should be called *The Kiss Of Life*, it's about as exciting.

~

This evening we went to see *Last Exit To Brooklyn*. Everyone loathed it, which is strange as I thought relentless action and violence in every conceivable form is what sold the movies these days. It had terminal settings with a millennial feel to them.

Very well cast and photographed, it chopped about to a score of trivial grandeur. From the moment of the first mugging it gave the feeling of being caught in a fairground octopus, every gentle emotion negated in a twilight world inhabited by cartoon stereotypes of thwarted sexuality. Quick violent and unfulfilling.

A parable for the wider exploitation in American life. This sorry corner of an ant-heap is the microcosm of a greater horror, far away in Korea, or coming shortly in Vietnam?

How, after 20 years of feminist lobbying, do you view the act of the girl who invites gang rape as a triumphal revenge?

I felt a horrible pit in my stomach all the way through the film, the same feeling I had driving through the slums of Chicago – unease, disgust, helplessness. I staggered out of the 20th Century Fox theatre as if I had been caught up in the fighting.

We went to Comptons where I asked a young man if he would be in my film, without hesitation he said, 'Not on your life.' I can't help thinking he was right, I was incapacitated by such an instantaneous response.

Later we drove to The Fridge in Brixton where Boy George tripped through an endlessly repetitive B side like a curio in an antique shop wearing the sequined dress of another era. I overheard someone say the evening was a benefit, and another answered, 'For Boy George.'

Wednesday 29

Lunch with Nico, he said G&G were crowing about their TV appearance with Jonathan Ross. I thought they were brilliant. The chat show seemed the perfect location for George's dry wit.

Nico met an Italian producer with two million to give to Peter Greenaway; got hold of his phone number, and rang him. Nico, who is an enthusiast, said it was like a straight line to Jack Frost. He said: I began by introducing myself as the producer of your *Caravaggio*. The silence echoed. I then said I had two million for him, and he replied, 'I'm a busy man I'm making my *Tempest*.'

Nico said he was taken aback. How often does someone genuinely phone you with two million? 'Well no-one ever offered me anything like that,' I said. 'Quite,' he replied.

If Gucci handbags were still in fashion Greenaway would carry his scripts in them. I thought it quite funny he asked Sir John to be in *Prospero's Books* – he turned *Caravaggio* down in a letter that said: *At my advanced age I cannot allow myself to be involved in projects of a semi-pornographic nature.* Now if I ask famous young fags in Equity to kiss each other in my films they run a mile. It's Wednesday and I've been turned down by a string of young actors for *The Garden*.

As he left Nico said, I rang the producer and suggested you knew far more about history than Greenaway and could do his series, they told me they wanted someone who had the reputation of being controversial but was safe. You I'm afraid they saw as just controversial. The problem, Derek, is I know that you're nothing of the sort!

Thursday 30

Frightful bust up with James on the corner of Old Compton Street and Charing Cross Road.

We're showing the films.

Which? *Imagining October*?

No, the Pet Shop Boys' concert film.

You mean the backdrops from the staging?

(I had told James that I didn't wish them to be shown.)

But they're like *The Queen Is Dead.*

That was a film, these weren't constructed like that, just ambient backgrounds with great big gaping holes. They looked great at Wembley with the boys singing and dancing. In any case there's only one good one, *Nothing Has Been Proved.*

That's a horrible mess, said James.

I decide to shut up.

And they're going to be on the video disk with the new film.

The elegiac garden film that has hung like an albatross – to be sold on the back of the video wallpaper made for the Pet Shop Boys. After a five minute slanging match I came home with Connie Giannarris, who had witnessed the outburst on Charing Cross Road. He made tea.

~

Slept not a wink – still no-one cast for the film. I'm praying that HB's friend Johnny will be able to get leave from his job with Islington Council.

The cold, pinched weather continues.

~

My father was determined I should go to university. We made a pact: If I got a university place, and also got into the Slade, where I dreamed of going, I would go to university and he would see me through art school afterwards.

I surprised my father by getting into King's College. Where I read a general degree in English, History and Art History. For two years I commuted to the Strand from Northwood.

I've often wondered what effect my mother's long illness had in keeping me from breaking out and rebelling at this time. I think I may have been saving it up for later. At the beginning of my third year I left home.

That autumn day in 1962 when I moved to our flat in Coram Street – round the corner from Russell Square and a short walk from King's College – I left the garden I had planted for my parents at Merryfield. It was not until I came here, to Dungeness, nearly thirty years later, that I could re-acquaint myself with the plants of my youth, jog a rusty memory, re-learn the names of annuals and perennials, the seasons for planting, pruning, and taking cuttings. During all those years I kept my gardening books and tools carefully locked in the shed, never imagining they would be resurrected.

My uncle Edward had a flat in Whitley Court – and when I was looking for somewhere to live in London in August '62, he found us an unfurnished flat there, with three rooms for £7 a week. The Court was a thirties' mansion with a uniformed doorman. Our flat was centrally heated and had hot water, all inclusive. The lease ran for a year.

Our rooms overlooked a nurses' home – which gave Michael and Dugald constant amusement as the nurses displayed themselves for us in the windows and invented candlelit ceremonies. Michael acquired a naval telescope, which he manned in the dark.

On Sunday mornings the Happy Wanderers would busk along Coram Street, playing wistful melodies like *Stranger On The Shore*. We would open the windows and throw pennies to them.

Round the corner, Marchmont Street, with its decayed Georgian terraces, had all the shops we needed, including a good second-hand bookshop, and a cheap Indian restaurant for special occasions.

~

Dugald, an old school pal, was an architectural student at the Middlesex Poly; and Michael was studying medicine at King's. We painted our new flat white and Dugald painted the tangle of pipes in the kitchen all the colours of the rainbow.

That November the last of the great London smogs descended – so thick you could see it hanging in the rooms.

~

Of the three of us Michael was the most adventurous. He was off playing the pinball machines while I swotted for my finals with Gregorian plainchant on the radiogram. Michael knew London well as he had been to Westminster, and had explored Soho as a schoolboy truant.

Perhaps because of this, Michael's parents were the most concerned; and in the first few days of the new home arrived to talk frankly with Dugald and myself to make certain he came to no mischief – much to his embarrassment.

~

My own parents' fears at the loss of a son were allayed by the proximity of my mother's brother Edward – who couldn't have cared less what we got up to. He probably thought of me as a milksop, mother's boy, and lost no opportunity to criticise her before me as both bossy and batty.

Edward had a deep dislike of suburban life, which he never managed to articulate. He was always in revolt – leaving Sunday lunch to make an impromptu salad of dandelion leaves and nasturtium flowers, which he insisted we all ate.

Edward had returned from the Japanese POW camp as from the dead. Tall and handsome, he remained a semi-invalid. He shared my interest in the garden, nothing else.

He popped into the flat once, shrugged his shoulders and never appeared again. None of the parents had much to worry about, as London in those days had few distractions.

~

At Whitley Court, London could hardly be said to 'swing'. John Stevens had opened his shop in Carnaby Street, but only one student at college had discovered it: Stuart's sartorial extravagance – a pair of trousers without turn-ups – rocked the college refectory.

At Whitley Court the music was classical, though Peter Asher and his friend Gordon had befriended the Beatles and had taken to twanging guitars in Michael's room. Peter was a philosophy student at King's.

At school I had sung in the choir – the *Creation* and *Messiah*; and had been taken to Bournemouth at the age of fifteen to hear Dame Myra Hess thumping out a Beethoven piano concerto – a cross between a Valkyrie and Gertrude Stein.

At King's we often crossed the river to the Festival Hall or took ourselves off to the Proms – where once a friend of Michael's mysteriously disappeared for ever in the interval.

When I wasn't attending lectures I was designing covers for Dennis Brown, the editor of the magazine *Lucifer*. Or painting the scenery for the drama society.

It was on our tour round the industrial towns of North Germany that I met Michael and his future wife Robby. They, more than anyone, opened up my life at college. In the year we prepared ourselves for our finals we found ourselves free of parental guidance for the first time.

~

That winter the weather set in. After the November fog it snowed over Christmas and on into January. One weekend the fall was so heavy that Kingsway was impassable. An eerie silence descended on the city – the only time in my life when you could hear a pin drop in the West End.

~

A suburban child, I was inexperienced and insecure, my upbringing designed to protect me from life. It was not that my parents neglected me – they were enthusiastic, though cautious. But the mores of middle-class life meant that no problems – unless financial – were ever discussed. They had no language for the emotions. What could this introspective and nervous son have in common with the director general of the Engineering Industries Association (the job my father had taken after leaving the RAF)?

We travelled to London together in silence, he with his bowler and furled umbrella, I in a duffle coat and black polo-necked sweater; he reading the Annual Report and I immersed in Joyce's *Ulysses* – which I read from end to end with little comprehension. On holiday, he sailed – I pruned the apple trees.

~

Meanwhile Michael arrived with new books: Klee and Pound's *Cantos*.

After a month or two he started to paint, unleashing a flood of bottled-up creativity in the little room at the end of the corridor. His medical degree doomed.

At King's my tutor Eric Mottram introduced me to Ginsberg and the Beats, and the ubiquitous WSB – everyone's literary big daddy. These writers were pretty well unobtainable, and consumed when the parents were not looking. At 21 – though I had read *The Naked Lunch* – I had never been to a nightclub, had hardly had a pint in a pub.

~

Angels do not wish to dispirit you with the primal black of the void. They are the light in that dark, the star swarm, singing the music of the spheres. Every angel bears a true thought. They are the bees of infinity, the messengers of Lady Wisdom. Their thoughts are honeyed sweet. 'Dead souls,' they whisper. Wisdom is opaque, indistinct, only discovered by an archeology of soul.

~

What was London like in the early sixties? It was still a city that worked in distinct areas.

Covent Garden vegetable market came to life as the theatres closed – its buildings dilapidated, their ground floors open to the street. In the daytime the iron shutters came down as the rubbish was swept up. But at night it was alive, and cafés served bacon, eggs, chips and peas with brown sauce till dawn.

We ate here early in the morning after watching Churchill's funeral procession being rehearsed, from Westminster to St. Paul's through coal-black streets. Muffled drums, soot-covered churches like Mary le Strand. Building sites in the bombed ruins around St. Paul's.

There was no love of Victoriana – Betjeman was a cosy voice on the Third Programme. None of us could have cared less as the Euston Arch fell; or as Birkbeck's Penny Bank and Josiah Doll's Imperial Hotel bit the dust in showers of terracotta. There was hunger for the new – these old buildings seemed as dated as the class system which was still firmly in place.

Plans were afoot to raze old London to the ground – all of Covent Garden, Piccadilly, Soho, Whitehall. Nothing to be left standing except the monuments – Inigo Jones' Banqueting Hall, Adams's Scottish Office, 10 Downing Street, to be retained for nostalgia. At Church House new buildings would bisect Victoria Gardens by Rodin's *Burghers of Calais*.

As yet there were very few twentieth century buildings. Castrol House in Marylebone, and Sir Basil Spence's Thorn EMI in St. Martin's Lane (now demolished) were exceptional. New buildings like the Bethnal Green tower block demanded pilgrimages. Everyone agreed that they were a breath of fresh air.

On streets like the King's Road there were family-run shops, no supermarkets, very few clothes shops – Moss Bros, Cecil Gee for the teds. The King's Road was still a typical high street: bread shops, newsagents, a tailor's, cafés and a couple of art stores. Ossie Clarke's Quorum, which opened in the middle of the decade in Radnor Walk, was the beginning of the fashion invasion which destroyed all this.

Camden Town was a pocket of poverty to the north. Between the station and Chalk Farm was a string of shops that sold old electrical equipment and cheap second-hand furniture stacked in unloved piles and spilling on to the street. The last train had just left the Roundhouse.

~

When I try to recapture our student life in Whitley Court I think in black and white. Lindsey Anderson's film of Covent Garden in the late fifties gives you a good idea: this was the world through which we passed every day to college.

We took no photos of ourselves that year – no-one did in those days. The Super 8 camera had yet to be invented. We did not record our lives. Andy Warhol was to do that in New York; no-one had yet heard of him, and wouldn't for a while.

Our world was one in which Britain caught up suddenly with the twentieth century. The postwar austerity was a thing of the past. European and American influences flooded in – not Elvis, but Miller, Pound, Genet, Cocteau. The plays we performed at college were Lorca's *Blood Wedding*, Miller's *Crucible* and Genet's *The Maids*. It was a heterogeneous mix, all of it quite new to me – no twentieth century book had been on the 'A' level syllabus except Hardy's *Return of the Native*. *Lady Chatterley's Lover* was still banned, Bloomsbury not yet canonised. We stumbled across this cornucopia in a jumble – editions by the Olympia Press and City Lights excitedly exchanged.

It was the same in painting and architecture. For us the Bauhaus designs of Braun were contemporary, the small black fan heaters treasured possessions. We were not into the past, or the junk markets. No-one had heard of chi-chi Deco; but Mies and Corb, the modular, and curtain wall.

That summer Ron Kitaj's exhibition at the Marlborough seemed like a break with the old world – we spent hours studying the paintings.

On Wednesday evenings I would walk round Victorian London with my tutor Nicholas Pevsner – author of *The Buildings Of England*. He passed before the *Daily Mirror* building in High Holborn and praised the great blank wall at its end as if he had stumbled on Rheims. Nik was for the

Moderns – as was Eric Mottram, who said the only place you could receive an education in this country was the Royal College.

There was no way he could have known that a particularly gifted generation, including David Hockney, was about to graduate. It would be another year before I met David – though two years before I had won the university art prize in the amateur section, and stood on the platform with him as he received his prize as David the Professional.

~

King's was a strange mixture of rugger, theologians and the rest of us. A compulsory college lecture on Monday morning might bring us Monty, complete with cap, telling us about his 'friendship' with Mao, and the dangers of communism. Another day Stanley Spencer's eccentric brother Gilbert described how the whole family had been brought up in one large bed.

I had never shared my bed with anyone – except for that disastrous infatuation at prep school, and, one Christmas night in Grantham at the age of eleven, a mutual masturbation session with my cousin John and a crumpled photo of Debbie Reynolds.

Both Michael and Dugald had girlfriends, and Michael frequently went absent for a day or two. Homosexuality was taboo. I closed my horizons, cranked up an old studio easel and painted with dedication, to the admiration of the others – distracted, but with no distractions.

I fell in love with a particularly charming theologian, Roger, and walked from Russell Square to Bethnal Green on several Sundays to see him. I eventually blurted out my dilemma over a cup of tea, didn't tell him he was the object of my desire – so our friendship continued. He was sympathetic but knew nothing. Few did then. The *Livre Blanc* hardly told you how to conduct your life. Frightened and confused, I still felt that I was the only queer in the world.

Then I ran into an old school friend, Roger Ford, who was living with a young designer, Brenda, and an older man, Michael. On an old piano Michael would thump out lewd songs from unperformable musicals. I started to spend evenings away. Michael ragged me about my sexuality. But I kept quiet – while he carried on singing cheerful songs of buggery.

~

Everyone who experienced the night of Kennedy's assassination will remember exactly where they were as the first incredulous bulletins were flashed across the world. I was in the Piccadilly Hotel at my friend Caroline's twenty first. The news ended the party – assassination was not part of modern life, seemed aberrant, out of date; it struck down 19th century

Czars and Emperors – not the bright young president of a new era.

Politics at Whitley Court was a secondary preoccupation. I never voted in the sixties: my sympathies lay generally to the left of the Labour Party.

During the Cuba crisis we shivered the nights away, felt our time was up, discussed our last moments. But none of us went to demonstrate outside the US embassy – though the march was only minutes away, and we knew it was taking place.

We had other priorities; and politics, we naïvely thought, was a thing of the past. They sucked you into their merry-go-round. CND marches from Aldermaston seemed outdated – though we attended the rallies in Trafalgar Square to hear Bertrand Russell. He seemed nearer to us than the angry young men who were not of our generation.

We were not apolitical: our agenda was personal – how we were 'to lead our lives'. We had no enthusiasm for marches, lacked an earnest view, the black and white of a Pat Arrowsmith.

At the theatre, Stratford East, with its conscious attempt to green the East End, seemed an embarrassment. The Arts Labs were to carve a place for our generation; the bricks and mortar of institutions had not yet embalmed the new in concrete.

~

At Whitley Court we began to redefine our living space. We hadn't started to throw out furniture – none of us slept on the floor; but we were very aware of the look of our rooms, after those of our suburban parents. The architects bought white lino paint to slap across floorboards – like the room in *The Knack* that Rita Tushingham paints a blinding white.

White paint blotted out the past. The fifties fad of painting every wall a different colour was obliterated in these rooms. The black Braun fan heaters whirred away.

We had a few objects – picked up early in Bermondsey Market or from the far end of the Portobello. Both were street markets, busy redefining junk as antiques.

In the late fifties the large antique shop at which I bought a reading chair of the 1830s – heavy mahogany, wicker and brass – burnt all its post-Regency furniture on a bonfire. My chair cost 25/- and another £1 to bring it to London. My parents were very unhappy about it.

The junk that fills the markets now would never have made it to the Portobello then – the twenties and thirties were not yet discovered. *Fin de siècle* barely made it; large Victorian canvases by Leighton or Watts changed hands for two or three hundred pounds.

~

London was an austere city for the young – there were no discos or pubs with music, the clubs were for the well-heeled. There were a handful of coffee bars, like the Macabre in Soho – with its black and silver interior and skull-shaped ashtrays, and candles stuck in old Chianti bottles dripping wax. Some of these had jukeboxes.

In 1963 none of us went out. We met in each others' flats, at parties, or at college – college balls were looked forward to.

There were no drugs at Whitley Court, though one of Michael's friends in the medical department was experimenting – making mescaline in Hampstead; another bought a packet of Morning Glory seeds, swallowed them before a Prom and was sick all night. None of us smoked cigarettes, let alone marijuana.

Restaurants were a new experience – we had our first Indian in the Madras in Marchmont Street. Our parents' generation had never eaten out except at hotels, on holidays, or at some convention, where they were trapped in a photographer's flashbulb. The men in dinner jackets, and the women in very unflattering evening dress – which would never be worn again.

The food we take for granted these days had not appeared in the shops – mushrooms were still a luxury; the first delicatessens had only just opened. Few had seen an avocado.

Life was much simpler, pleasures fewer and perhaps for that more intense. There wasn't the competition for our attention – it was easier to bring your life into focus. Unsophisticated as we were, we were to be part of the change that was to revolutionise life in the next few years.

~

1963. I took finals during a heatwave in late May – we sat sweating it out in our shirtsleeves. A week before we had given up the endless revision and taken off in a gang to sunbathe with our books on the beach at Southend.

After finals, there was a great feeling of anticlimax – three years of relationships evaporated.

After a few brief weeks working in a betting shop in Ashford I returned to Northwood and got a job cleaning up an overgrown garden.

Digging flower beds in the pouring rain I became ill, gave up the work and took the train down to the Isle of Wight for the last of our family holidays, in Seaview. There I spent most of the time keeping my invalid mother company as she recovered from the first of many operations for cancer.

Whitley Court was given back to the landlords. About to start the first of four years of Fine Art at the Slade, I returned in September to search for digs in North London.

DECEMBER

Friday 1

Dreamt last night I held a bowl of the rarest jade, the colour of honey with a sage green iridescence. The bowl of precious stones was threatened by a thief. I preserved it through terrible trials, assailed by the demon thug intent on stealing it. He curled round me ceaselessly, like a crab, with switchblade claws; then suddenly it was over. He deflated like a balloon, disappeared like a little Michelin man with a gasp of rushing air.

~

Spent the evening with Johnny Mills and HB doing a little audition on video. It all went well and the film is cast. My fury with James gradually abated during the day. Next year *Edward II*.

At eleven this morning this room was a maelstrom: a student from Birmingham with a recorder; a lawyer with my statement for *Visions Of Ecstasy*; a journalist with a recorder; a young man desperate to escape Jobfit; an actor reading my notebooks. Poor HB brewing tea. The day rocketed past.

Saturday 2

Drove to Dungeness with Toby, HB and Johnny in thick fog. It cleared during the afternoon and the sun came out. We lit the fire and huddled around it in the cold.

~

Spent over an hour talking into Toby Kaliatovsky's video camera – guilt, fear, childhood sexuality, bullying, parents. At five we packed up the house and started back across the marsh. The skies at Dungeness were clear, but at Lydd a dense fog closed in around us so we could barely see the road. Crawled to the Little Chef where we had 'breakfast'; and by six, when we started back on the road, the fog had thinned out.

~

FILMING THE GARDEN

Day 1

7 o'clock on a cold, dark, winter morning. Len James's studio off the Old Kent Road is ablaze with summer light and bustle: against a blue sky, a shingle and rock garden with a white tiled sauna half-buried by time.

Dressed in cast-offs from old movies – a huge fur-lined magenta robe for Jack (Pontius Pilate), a primrose dressing gown for Michael Gough – assorted patriarchs, viziers and petty princes wash their hands of the two lovers. Venomous laughter.

HB and his friend Johnny stand impassive as the scene unfolds – a sharp-eyed child's memory of a Hollywood epic. Ambience of make-believe, oil and vanilla.

The gang of old reprobates leer through to lunchtime. Zoran Vidnic kneads Spud's tattoos, HB glances at Johnny. The extras have become the leads, the leads, extras. Soon it is all over.

As we break for lunch Jack takes hold of his foot and brings it up to his face, pushes an imaginary nail through it. Milo Bell, the bath attendant, stands in the corner biting his nails.

Now a series of emblemata (improvised): Tilda holds a sword and lilies; Pete, as a haughty princeling, crowns himself; Jack does a Can-Can in a scarlet judge's robe.

The hours pass. A huge column is brought on to the set and lifted into place. HB and Johnny, bound and bloodied, are lashed to it, then thrashed by a group of skinheads dressed in Father Christmas robes. After that's done HB and Johnny vanish into the shower for a very long time. I stumble off the set and home.

I leave a half-eaten main course in the Greek restaurant and fall asleep as the ice cream melts.

Day 2

HB says Johnny is gifted in bed. He has the baby-face of a Cocteau sailor. I'm glad I chose the two of them to do this film; as they sit on the sofa between takes wrapped in each others arms, quite unselfconscious, no-one on the set so much as looks at them.

~

Today the extras from the Greek and Italian communities that Simon originally found for *Caravaggio* come for the first of several scenes around a fine old refectory table.

We film a sequence of a glass harmonium. As hands circle over glasses and the studio fills with the unearthly sound, we watch mesmerised. What spirits are they conjuring? Tilda asks to be put into the scene.

We film a Pentecostal fire ceremony with the boys carrying the sacred flame. We end the day with Jody as a schoolboy menaced by the canes of schoolmasters, which move like a spiky sea-urchin as he writes the lines *I must work harder.*

~

Matthew (the assistant director) works wonders: everything is kept in order and everyone is in a good mood. He throws very good suggestions my way.

Jessica (one of the extras) brings bunches of mimosa at the betrothal of the two boys – making a film with no script you have to be on your toes: visual ideas develop as they run.

~

Improvising sets and costumes we work to music: Mozart, flamenco, or dervish flutes. At moments the whole set is cast in a spell – such laughter and applause on a set.

~

The filming, not the film.

~

David Lewis asked me on the way home if I had an image which I worked to. The answer is No. I have no idea how the scenes will look, and no wish to.

~

Do I have sufficient confidence to let anything happen? As you light the Amaretti papers they flare up and disappear into the dark.

Day 3
Mirabelle dances the flamenco with Jody on the table.

Jody feeds a burnished turkey, which gives him a nip. There are a few tears and a lot of cosmetic bandaging.

Day 4
In a panic last night – how I could bring Johnny and HB to life on the screen? So far they have been very good – exchanging glances, and smiles; but all in a very static manner. Sudden mad thought to put HB in the bath – his favourite place. He'll spend up to three hours ducking about in a bath, praying with his head under the water, reading the newspaper, balancing bowls of cornflakes.

There are a lot of second hand shops on the Old Kent Road with baths and fireplaces. Rang Derek Brown (the designer) and suggested we try and get a cast iron bath first thing in the morning.

Roger dressed in his fine white robe against the blue-screen, Jody in a golden jump-suit climbing a gilded ladder to heaven, Annie Lapaz in the finest sari materials, as a water bearer, passes Christ on the road.

~

At eleven the bath arrives, is shipwrecked on the rocks and the boys climb in. We all shut our eyes.

Johnny looks like an extra from *South Pacific* without the sailor's hat.

In the bath, they look sexy and natural. I'm so glad I didn't get Equity thesps as none of them would have done this – you cannot fake this.

After lunch they nearly drowned Jody in the bath – something they had both wanted to do all week. He had asked 'Why are you cuddling?' 'Because we love each other.' they replied. The next day he came up to them and said 'I know why you're cuddling, it's because you're poofs!' – so much for the age of consent and protecting the young!

At nine years old – as we all know from our own lives – we know it all, however hazy and jumbled.

HB threw Jody in the air and dangled him over the bath.

~

Then we all went into B stage and filmed the Mocking – Guildford Four style. Off-duty policemen – the boys tied to the canteen chairs and gagged.

The day before, Sarah Swords, who had the thankless task of holding this shoot together, found an actor with a penchant for opera who played a policeman. At the last moment Dawn Archibald put on a waitress outfit and produced the black treacle for the tarring and feathering.

~

Everyone has the magma of violence bubbling – as if we were all semi-extinct volcanoes waiting, like Krakatoa, to explode one last time. Pete ripped his jacket in a cloud of feathers and the 'opera' singer, Martin, turned the scene into something frightening. A grand aria.

When it was all over HB was cut out of his handcuffed position on the chair – he turned round and hugged me in an angry treacly embrace. Then he disappeared into the shower leaving us all shaking.

~

Back on A stage Philip dangled from a noose above his shining red motor-cycle holding a sheaf of credit cards instead of the thirty pieces of silver. I had a fit of uncontrolled laughter, I couldn't stop. How rarely I laugh nowadays.

Pete Lee Wilson gave a good approximation of a quiz master – the Judas scene as farce. Philip pulled out his fake tongue.

~

David asked me on the way back how I thought of all this. The truth is I didn't – you start with one thing and end with another.

~

Home at 8:30, much happier – HB said I looked years younger. My clamped-down energy is getting released.

Saturday 9
Dungeness. The house was very cold when we arrived last night, the drive here endless. I lit the fires, made a cup of tea and watched snatches of the news.

~

This morning was cold and damp. The persistent easterlies of the last few weeks have left a strand of plastic detritus at the tide line for me to pick over.

With the exception of a few lavenders, which have dried up and withered, the garden has survived.

~

Gerard rang me in a panic about another houseboat in Amsterdam. I threw caution to the winds and bought it – if he doesn't use it it can be sold next year.

The sun came out; Derek and I walked to the Long Pits. Derek said a young man shot himself there last week. I had a premonition I might find a body in these sallow copses.

~

Wrote letters. After a walk on the sand flats, the light went.

~

Slept well last night, with two strange and vivid dreams. A boulder rolled across the desert a vision of Simon Stylites in the Buñuel film. But the strange part was that it was a waking dream. I was quite conscious when I saw it pass by. Then I was in a large jet which crashed mid-Atlantic like a swan; the doors opened and we found ourselves surrounded by lifeboats and happy faces who helped us aboard without the slightest panic.

Sunday 10

HB rang early to say it was a grey misty day in London. Here the sun was out and it was much warmer than it had been in the last few weeks.

Walked along the shore to the fishing boats.

~

Takashi, who has organised the Japanese funds for the film and the exhibition of paintings at Fuji, has said he could bring in the first of the cash for *Blueprint*.

~

It's so quiet this morning. I slept well – no disturbing dreams. Inspected myself in the mirror for any telltale signs; found none, felt better. HB happier on the phone – made my morning.

~

My rosemary, which died back during the summer – only one branch dodging the creeping death that has claimed most of the plant – has come into bloom, along with the first bright yellow gorse flowers. The Californian poppy are growing everywhere: they have colonised the garden. In every nook and cranny the scarlet field poppies have germinated: if they survive the winter they are going to cover the garden in a field of scarlet.

Day 5

Christopher Hobbs in his element, swathing large lengths of silk round columns, others blowing up pink balloons. Thirty or so jugglers all of whom have jobs as teachers, shop assistants, or the full-time preoccupation of unemployment. We gradually shuttled them through make-up and by lunch they were a riot of colour. HB and Johnny appeared in splendid pink suits and we let the whole thing run its chaotic course.

Ian's friend Jessica (he told me about her yesterday) performed *Think Pink* from *Funny Face*, at 10:00 we were still trying to find the song – it arrived at 11:00 by bike and she learnt the lyrics in minutes. We put in HB and Johnny; Annie dolled up her baby and the four of them played a great musical number, 'Banish the blues'.

Day 6
Today we filmed the crucifixion.

~

Dawn danced in a primrose yellow sari with two bunches of red berries. This was beautiful.

Day 7
The day's filming went well – the old men rolling the devil's stone, and the cardinals pulling the great gold rock in a howling gale. Spencer danced to Madonna as an unregenerate Magdalen – blue-screened Roger in a golden space suit. Stephen said he looked like the Sutherland tapestry in Coventry Cathedral.

Day 8
Crawled across the morning in a state of exhaustion. We wrapped at 1:00, so I returned home and dozed till I fell asleep at nine.

Without the good will and concentration of the old gang around the camera I would not have survived the eight days. I was continually on my toes, as so many of the scenes were improvised.

I climbed into bed as HB packed to go to Paris – he left me many little messages, and one hundred instructions. At 12:30 he disappeared through the door.

Friday 15
Plans afloat for another boat on an Amsterdam canal. Gerard flies off this weekend – money runs through my fingers in a torrent.

~

Back home tidying up. I carefully packed several dozen photos of a young policeman from Terni called Massimo: some in his uniform, some in semi-Renaissance undress; and dozens of slides of the work of an American painter who had fallen in love with *Caravaggio*.

~

At five I walked over to Comptons. An unshaven boy with a fifties hairstyle, crashed in the corner between the fruit machine and the bar, kept glancing over. I thought he was probably on the game – he came over and asked if he could speak to me.

'My name's Torpedo, and I've written a film. Only you can make it.'
My mind detached itself and floated to the other end of the bar.
'It's a love story, that turns into a thriller, and then a ghost story. I've got

the end down.'

I found myself asking Torpedo where he got the inspiration – a terrible relationship, in which he left spraying the walls with fluorescent graffiti.

'I fucked the bastard every night under one of your paintings.'

Before he left he invited me to an orgy in Earl's Court. I declined and invited him to our end-of-shoot party.

~

David Butler came for supper. At the table opposite, Kevin Witney was having dinner with a young man he introduced as 'this one'. He was laughing his head off about the gigantic scale of Andrew Logan's new studio – said it looked like the entrance to the Nat West tower. Andrew is raising the money for a marble floor. Perhaps, I suggested, we could all have a slab inscribed with our names – like the seats at BAFTA.

Kevin, his white bow tie slightly crooked, was off with 'this one' to the Colony Club. As he left he said, 'She's gone quite mad, my dear.'

~

The end-of-shoot party at a club in the Old Kent Road called Paris Metro.

Drew, who puts up scaffolding with the grace of a tightrope walker, said, 'You're an outsider, even at your own party, Derek.'

Outside the rain poured down.

Torpedo never materialised – so the mad adventures that I had hoped for were dashed. At 2:30 Julian Cole gave me a lift home.

Sunday 17

Matthew here at eleven. We walked round Camden Lock in the rain – too many people for comfort. Went for a drink at the Cap, where a drag queen in vivid yellow was belting out *Blue Moon*.

Retired with a hangover to the BM where we spent the afternoon looking at the Celtic metalwork. Blindness-inducing patterned gold displayed in reverential gloom. Meandered round endless buckles with sniffing influenza-ed crowd.

Matthew told me the London Lighthouse was nearly empty – who wanted to be confronted with a twenty-two year old counsellor fresh from a degree in sociology? Much better to fade away with the ruins at the Mildmay.

From what I gathered, those who had come together in the eighties were going to spend the nineties dissecting each other. I suppose in the end it boils down to which chemicals attract you. An open landscape for caring careers . . .

~

The queue for tonight's concert at the Marquee were already smashing bottles underneath my window. The debris along the Charing Cross Road this morning, after the night's high winds, was indescribable. I don't need to have nightmares here any longer, sleep is so disrupted.

Monday 18

Starlit sky washed out by the early morning rain. Breakfast alone at Bertaux'. Then walked to Covent Garden, stopping at second-hand bookshops in my quest for information on Edward II and Gaveston. The entries in various compendia of the fourteenth century are so depressing: the failed King's unfulfilled promise, the evil counsellors.

In the market I hovered around a stall selling second-hand pens, the proprietor annoyed by my detached interest. Ran a gauntlet of earnest young men with collecting boxes – dutifully put in a fiver for a cause I had not the time to fathom; signed a petition and was propositioned five more times before reaching the safety of the flat. The deadly hand of Christmas stretches out.

~

Waiting for the bus in the grey drizzle I daydream. The Abbey is gloomy. I pass the tomb of Aylmer de Valence, its decorative ogees the subject of a long lecture by Nik Pevsner in the winter of 1963.

I owe so much to Nik. Here on the top of the bus I carry in my mind an encyclopaedia of architectural detail. With this I can while away the time – ogee, architrave, crazy vault, flying buttress.

~

The verger taking the party round the royal tombs described Henry VII as a miserly man, Edward I Longshanks as a tall man plain and correct as his Purbeck marble tomb. He omitted to say he killed the entire population of Berwick in an afternoon, expelled the Jews, and ruined the nation in his wars north of the border.

Later on, in the street, I remembered the fossilised shells polished by time on Longshanks's marble tomb with greater clarity than the crumbling cosmati on the grander tombs, or the elegant gilt bronze statue of Eleanor – the most beautiful of the effigies. Their grandson Edward III looks like a troll; his wife Phillippa wears the silliest headdress.

~

My eyes fixed on the patterns in the wet York stone paving, I walked through Smith Square to the Tate, which is being re-hung.

The collection no longer looks like a jumble sale of leftovers from the twentieth century – for the first time it seems coherent, pictures and painters have space. Quirky Stanley Spencer makes the pre-Raphaelites look maudlin. Where is Sickert going to fit in?

Now the battle for modernism lies firmly in the past and 'advanced' art is no longer the only art. The British school, which seemed so hopelessly out of touch in my youth, has come into its own. Could you have imagined hanging Naum Gabo and Spencer in adjacent rooms?

At two I found myself with Julian Clary in a dark corner of a subterranean club under the Trocadero. Without his glad-rags nothing but his voice would have given him away. I'm certain he could have walked across the dance floor without anyone turning a head – adept chameleon.

Tuesday 19
Protected by HB's impregnable phone system, I let the calls on my time fall into the void, remove myself from the student curriculum – fade into the past, a half-forgotten author of criminally cluttered celluloid.

The phone has a new button. It belongs to Mercury.

~

Read Julian of Norwich's *Revelation of Love* to the gentle whirr of the washing machine, which HB says puts his mind at rest.

Christmas cards fall in an avalanche through the door, along with unsolicited mail, advertising. Hobgoblins, fays and snowbound fairies – a rude calendar would be more welcome. I have to muster my strength to open them.

~

Julian says *It is today domysday with me, oh dereworthy moder.* I sing myself to the bookshops, mind full of the Middle Ages – Breughel's hunter returning home late in a snowbound afternoon, black crows tumbling across a darkening sky.

Everything I perceive makes a song, everything I see saddens the eye. Behind these everyday jottings – the sweetness of a boy's smile. Into my mind comes the picture of a blood red camellia displaced in the February twilight.

Grete dropis of blode, in this shewing countless raindrops fall so thick no man may number them with bodily witte.

For years the Middle Ages have formed the paradise of my imagination, the archaic half-smile on the Apostles' lips at Chartres, the blisse that unlocks.

It is not William Morris' Journeyman Eden, but something subterranean, like the seaweed and coral that floats in the arcades of a jewelled reliquary.

~

In his bookshop Ian Shipley said his father 'knew' Jeremy Thorpe was riding for a fall because of his florid waistcoats. 'And you,' he said, 'are wearing brown shoes.'

I've always worn brown shoes, since my father warned me off them in the fifties. Spivs, lounge lizards, interesting 'uncles' wore brown shoes. As soon as I was able I bought my first pair in Carnaby Street – some brown Italian hunting boots with pockets for powder and shot.

I polish my dozen pairs of second-hand shoes. HB calls them 'Dead men's shoes'.

Lunch time, Comptons, Greek Andy breezes past 'Looking for knob' he says, thinks better of it and leaves to continue his Christmas shopping.

Wednesday 20
Comptons lurched into the season of goodwill last night as a gang of drunken rent boys, led by a portly middle-aged accountant in a grey suit, harassed the clientele for CHART. The AIDS raffle was conducted across music so loud it had already drowned any conversation; people who refused the tickets or the rattling buckets were shouted at: 'You're a disgrace,' 'Disgusting.' By 9:00, under the bombardment, the crowd had visibly thinned out, leaving only the blind drunk and the raffle-boys, who blocked off the exit so they could throw their arms round passing punters. I hovered till I saw a gap and passed through the gauntlet of brick red drunken faces – £30 the poorer in raffle tickets.

~

The city is awash this morning. Under these grey skies day has barely dawned – it pours without a break, leaving the shops empty.

From 1:00 to 11:00 transferred the film to video.

Thursday 21
The Solstice. On the Heath saw a naked boy marble white in the moonlight lying in the cleft of an oak tree, motionless in the freezing cold.

Friday 22
Third anniversary of my HIV test. The 22nd has become a second New Year for me.

Still alive and hung-over I started the Christmas shopping and ended up buying a selection of soups. I become anorexic in food shops – waves of nausea in M&S.

~

Bought more medieval texts from the bookshop in Cecil Court.

~

Everyone talks about leaving for Home. Without any family Christmas is the time when I don't miss having them.

Saturday 23

David collected me during a violent thunderstorm. Headed south. The skies cleared over Romney Marsh – bright green with winter wheat, hedgerows scarlet with haws. Stripped bright yellow willows.

Prospect Cottage dark and deserted. Soon the stoves were lit and we cooked an enormous smoked cod.

As the sun set walked along the beach, where I found an antler, coal black with age. At six David left and I settled down with the rushes of the film for a couple of hours before turning in.

Christmas Eve

Derek Ball here for breakfast. Later we drove to Greatstone to collect the Sunday papers. He says the project to buy the old lifeboat station is ticking over and it should be mine by spring.

Did numerous odd jobs. Tended the fires, walked round the garden – it's coping with the winds and wet; crocuses are showing through the peat in the front bed.

~

The crocus produced the best yellow for the illuminated manuscripts of the Middle Ages – many of the plants that grow on the Ness once produced dyes. The finest blue 'turnsole' was made from the juice of elderberries – sap green from the berries of the buckthorn, and a bright green from the juice of the flag iris.

Other colours – vermillion, cobalt, and bright lapis blue – were mineral. Antonello da Messina's little study of St. Jerome in a monastery scriptorum – with a dazzling postage stamp sized landscape through an open window – shows the calm and tranquil rooms in which these manuscripts were prepared.

The crocus that was used as a dye was the saffron crocus – Arabic Z à Faran, the yellow one. Thomas Smith, Edward III's counsellor, brought it secretly from the Holy Land in 1330. The dye was exquisitely expensive: 4,320 flowers were required to produce one ounce of saffron. John the Gardener wrote:

They should be set in the month of September, three days before St.

Mary Day, Nativity, or the next week thereafter; so must it be with a
dibble you shall set him, that the dibble before be blunt and great.
Three hands deep they must set be.

Petals of the saffron crocus were strewn across Jupiter's marriage bed; it
dyed wedding robes and the robes of monks. Gerard says saffron brought
those dying of the plague back from the deathbed.

Christmas Day
Morte saison, only the gorse blooms. Woodsage and bracken rustle rust
dead and the brambles are bleached as fish bones in the shingle. Broom
burnt black by the wind. A seagull scooped up in a gust is blown across the
Ness. Breakers roll along the deserted shore.

Tuesday 26
The rosemary cuttings are flowering in the kitchen.

~

Watched another hour of the film rushes last night. They depress me. So
many fleeting moments lost to the camera, which seems destined to point in
the wrong direction. The spirit slips past the fingers – a sadness I try to dispel by watching Olivier's *Richard III*. Thirty years on it looks like a mincing
fairy tale for kids, full of posturing and sidelong glances. Wet pastels of
fifties' interior décor.

The fighting carried on in Romania. After a video of the execution of
Ceaucescu the newscaster wished us a peaceful Christmas, without much
conviction.

Pottered around the garden, but the rain blew so hard I was forced back
inside. The silence broken by rain on the windows.

Wednesday 27
Drove with Derek to Hastings. The town was shuttered and deserted – except for sad old men staring at us from cracked pink paving: the esplanade,
a jumble of architectural style washed by a grey December sea. Iceterias,
spaghetterias, one pizzeria – full of sad families in winter coats, half-
glimpsed through condensation on the windows. War On Want shops
manned against seasonal loneliness by elderly ladies in discarded furs.

We turned home at three. Behind us the setting sun brought some
warmth.

Glad to be home I walked to the beach. Then warmed myself up with a
bowl of soup and finished my book, before closing my ghostly eyes at ten.

Thursday 28

Sleepless night, tossed on the edge of oblivion. Woke shivering and damp with sweat, my eyes glued together.

I tried to warm myself, bustled around, tended the fires; but sadness hangs around me like these short and sunless days. The virus has displaced me – a refugee in my own conscience. I wander aimlessly. A picture, a note to myself, a chapter of a book half-understood, a song. The news – forgotten before the weather forecast.

Today it is too cold to walk in the garden – even the birds fail to turn up at their table, with the exception of one jittery magpie. The day passes in perpetual twilight, the shore as pale as bone under a frowning sky.

Friday 29

Jon Savage stopped off late in the afternoon on his way to Neil Tennant's. He was wearing one of his drape jackets the colour of Campbell's soup. We had a smudged conversation. Of *The Garden* he said, 'Oh Derek, more of your martyr complex.'

Left alone, I struggled on with the rushes until night overwhelmed me.

~

A very cold day, chalky white and drawn sky. Stood gazing at the chevrons on the Norman door of New Romney church, and the beaky demons like cartoon crows with rolling scroll-like eyes.

~

Finished reading the tedious life of Edward I. His virtues are all negative – a stubborn bore. No wonder his son clapped him in that unmarked Purbeck marble tomb. He threw his daughter's golden wedding crown into the fire during a family row. His campaign against the Scots was misjudged, his expulsion of the Jews bigoted. He murdered all 7,000 inhabitants of Berwick one afternoon. He invented hanging, drawing and quartering. His wife so neglected their children most of them died in infancy.

Edward II was the last of thirteen. Longshanks had left his son a bankrupt land – bankrupted by wars in which he had employed the largest standing army of the Middle Ages. For all this he is credited with being one of our greatest kings.

Saturday 30

We drove across the marsh under a pinched and sunless sky. Sombre houses neglected in dark trees. In an hour's drive we did not pass another car. No-one in the fields, the sheep with their bright blue markings motionless as we passed by.

~

Talked to my next door neighbour Brian about the disastrous influence Shakespeare had on medieval history. So difficult to see the past except through his plays.

I had another sleepless night – thrown on a treadmill of unease, hour after hour of tossing and turning until I was weeping for rest. Something terrible has overtaken my nights – shaken about like a limp rag doll. I got up to try and settle myself, without success.

By morning the fire had died in the grate. Brewed myself a bowl of porridge and slowly pulled myself out of the night.

A distressed letter from Ron Peck, who has more difficulties with his films than I thought. Film has brought nothing but sadness into our lives. The moments when the sun came out were brief, and the further we tried to wander from the straight and narrow of British Cinema the less we received.

Walked with Tod and Tim to the sea where I threw a plaster figurine of Christ into the waves. On the way back Derek found a human femur on the beach, which we buried with a makeshift cross.

~

My cold has overwhelmed me and I sit croaking into the diary. Another indecisive day: more rushes and a small painting completed by my ghostly eye.

Ideas are running out on me. If only I could recapture the dawn, the Wordsworthian 'bliss to be alive'.

~

My childhood garden, the pinks bowed by a heavy dew scattered along paths – all the flowers that bloomed so brightly then. The shiny poppies crumpled like party hats. Peonies, purple iris, a vase of tulips scattering blown petals across my grandmother's table. A butter yellow brimstone flying across the wide green lawn. All the summer ahead.

~

The night has closed in. After a summer's day, when it has been hot and the lawn has been cut and the sun has well baked the earth, if there should come rain in the evening, a soft warm rain, pottering at first so that it seems each leaf of flower and tree becomes a drum sounding with drum beats; then it seems the garden breathes deep and draws in great draughts of the delicious coolness. Then, after the rain, the night comes warm again, and all the warm earth smells, and the new cut grass smells also and every tree and flower joins force upon force, until the air is filled with a perfume which for want of a better name I would call the odour of gratitude. Bacon.

~

This year I've lost so many friends, none missed more than Howard. Without him I have no-one to confide in, no-one can replace his sound encouragement. His death in April overshadowed the summer. Paul died without fuss one October morning.

New Year's Eve
A dull thud brought me into the kitchen this morning. Looking out the window – a kestrel underneath the dog rose only four feet away. At first I thought it had stunned itself flying into the window; but after a minute it took off, and I noticed it had a sparrow in its talons.

The nuclear power station roared out the old year in a cloud of steam. They say there are plans to build a huge concrete dam around it.

At eight I walked over to Derek's. He conjured up a dish of spaghetti, then sat with an array of little bottles like a child's chemistry set – mixing Bach Flower Remedies.

I left before midnight clutching three little bottles, and before turning in swallowed a few drops against melancholy. I did not bang my head three times on the pillow to make a New Year's Wish.

1990

JANUARY

Monday 1

Derek Ball arrived for breakfast with his friends Tod and Tim before I was awake. He said the flower remedy was working. Pink pansies are good for you.

Read from the *Penguin Book Of Homosexual Verse* over the Earl Grey.

Breakfast was interrupted by the kestrel pursuing sparrows around my bird table, which has become a sacrificial altar.

I told Tim, who loves gossip, of my first meeting with Robert Mapplethorpe. I was set up with him one summer's afternoon on the King's Road by my friend Ulla. He took me back to a studio where he was staying and showed me endless snapshots of boys chained Prometheus-like to rocks in the Pacific surf. We spent three days in bed.

Robert was shamelessly ambitious. Years later, when he had become the famous photographer, he passed me in a nightclub in the small hours and barely pausing said, 'I've got everything I ever wanted, Derek. What have you got?' He didn't stay for an answer.

That was the last I saw of him.

Robert the sharp art-hustler. His first grown-up camera given him by Sam Wagstaff over a dinner. Sam had one of the finest collections of photos in the world. Robert became his dependant.

Robert retired behind this camera and fame, growing ever more reptilian. His blood turned cold. His photos deathly well-mannered – nothing to make you laugh or cry. The life and death of the disco. Pale, silvery, no blacks or dark spots. A little fun with a bull whip up his arse to tickle the prostate. I never understood his fame.

But when I met him that was still future, he was full of curiosity. We spent hours together combing junk markets looking for things he could string together for his fetishistic jewels – skulls and red glass dice. Bones. We made a ring with two skulls with diamond eyes, which I wore for years.

Two boys out on a jewellery expedition, all sex and glitter. Sadly I wear no jewellery now, though a sharp grey suit and three strands of mother's pearls would suit me.

~

The New Year's landscape deadly cold, the silence broken by the mewing gulls.

Rang Alasdair and Christopher to wish them a happy new year. Christopher spent a stately Christmas at a country house in Northampton. Alasdair fought with his boyfriend Barry into the small hours.

Derek passes on his way back to London. I'm alone again.

~

I view another hour (lifetime) of the rushes of the new film. They are so appallingly inept no wonder I am ill. How can I haul myself out of this slough?

Tuesday 2
Another ugly night dissolved in a sunny day – the sun rose blood red out of the sea. A white mist hung a few feet above the shingle, which after a night's rain sparkled like diamonds.

A very slow start – hardly slept. Brewed myself porridge, so painful to swallow I had to talk to myself as a diversion. I have never had such an unpleasant cold, it's fastened on to my eyes, nose, ears – everything has been gummed up and aches. It has made this Christmas, never a good time for me, the most depressed I can remember. The only consolation is I've given it to no-one, just spluttered it into this diary.

The fishing boats are returning home late on this sunny afternoon with innumerable seagulls milling around them.

Wednesday 3
The rabbits eat everything to the ground – poppies are particular favourites. The wild fig has been torn to shreds: large branches have been felled and stripped a ghostly white. I wonder if the bark of the fig is sweet and sugary.

The remains of the bush lie around half-chewed like cane and by the end of the winter there will be little left. It'll sprout again from the bole; but no wonder it has grown only three feet high.

Finished rereading Marlowe's *Edward II*. My flu slightly improved.

Thursday 4
It's very cold. I had another sleepless night: the flu gave up on my throat and drove into my chest. Sweated it out and rose very late – eleven.

Thought about buying a new sound system. I've never been very interested in them, treat cassettes like books – very few are replayed. The best gift is someone's compilation. I hardly ever buy them, unless it's for work.

~

Back in the fifties my father brought an LP from the States, the first I had ever seen — *My Fair Lady*, then the rage. I put it on my old wind up and watched the needle gouge up the plastic.

After a violent family row I went out and bought one of the large boxy Hi-fi sets with its working parts in cream plastic. It did me through the sixties.

~

There was very little music in my childhood. We juggled with battered sets of the classics in 78, Sibelius symphonies in a scrambled set; so by the time I came to own my Hi-fi I wasn't particularly impressed. I still find people tinkering with their sound systems faintly ridiculous. Though on film, of course, it's another matter.

~

At four we packed up the house and left for London.

Friday 5

Doctor's appointment at 5:00, the first for two years. I haven't had a GP since Arnold Linken left the University Health Centre.

Efficient, friendly health centre in Shorts Gardens, and a new GP I liked instantly. He said there was nothing structurally wrong, just bronchitis.

At lunchtime we met Colin McCabe on the street and he invited HB and myself for coffee at the BFI, where we talked about Edward II. He said he was interested in the secret service, the state within the state that has so efficiently monitored and removed dissenting voices — even in the seventies with the fall of Harold and the downfall of Jeremy.

Agents operated in a world of sexual ambivalence. A world in which an aristocrat learning her son was gay exclaimed, 'He's succumbed.'

I once met Jeremy moving like a shadow in the foyer of the Teatro Communale for the launch of Britten's *Peter Grimes*!

For his infidelities Marlowe, the secret agent, died with a fatal dagger in the eye.

~

What interests me about Edward is that his behaviour is no more eratic than that of Mark Antony. Edward and Gaveston are lovers who lose the world. Yet even now it is not possible to convey this, the parameters of love are so limited, like Dido, or Cleopatra, or Helen.

Saturday, Sunday

A long walk with HB, stopping off at the New Contemporaries exhibition at the ICA. All much too well mannered. Nothing like the Young Contemporaries of my student days, where the work was stacked above itself in a jumble jungle – ambitious and loud. This was cool to the point of indifference.

In St. James's Park the first white camellias are in flower.

The Abbey was closed for a service, so we visited the Chapter House and spent some time looking at the censing angels. Then across Westminster Bridge to the South Bank, where we were stopped by a painted middle-aged lady who said, 'I'm glad you're not dead Derek, the papers say you are terribly ill.' This uncompromising greeting was the start of an incoherent ten minute conversation which ended with my being handed a Xerox headed 'Countess Veronica'. Meanwhile the Countess had recounted the four hundred years of her genius that had been lost, found and pirated and purloined by popes, politicians and Toyah Wilcox. It was with relief we got away.

Back at Phoenix House I watered the potted plants along the railings. The winter jasmine is bright with yellow flowers.

Monday 8

What effect has being open about your sexuality and making gay films had on the opportunities presented to you?

Asked this by nearly every interviewer. Today in the middle of the question the telephone rings and Alasdair says Ian Charleson has just died of septicaemia. It's odd that this should occur at this moment.

~

In the sixties and seventies, before the political backlash of the eighties and the advent of AIDS, coming out was positive and helped the community. Crowds formed round the Gate Cinema in October '76 for the first screenings of *Sebastiane*. The reviews were all affirmative. My group of friends had all been out of the closet since the early '60s, when David Hockney caught the public eye. It wasn't a big step for me. *Sebastiane* just acknowledged something that already existed.

In 1977 I asked Ian to be in my second film, *Jubilee* – his first film rôle, a gay one. And we remained close friends throughout the decade. Then everything changed. David Puttnam, who has written an obituary in today's *Independent* lauding Ian's courage in coming clean in death, told him to have his association with me struck off his CV. And that from henceforth *Chariots Of Fire* was his first film.

Ian apologised to me for doing this, but complied. Until two years ago he was denying his sexuality and his friendship with me in the yellow press to protect his reputation. Unwittingly Ian ran for the opposition that brought us the British Film Renaissance and Mrs. Thatcher.

Today everyone praises his strength and honesty. I'm the only dissenting voice. Even Alasdair last night said 'Derek, let sleeping dogs lie, he died a good death.' I'm afraid I cannot. Unable to work for five years because my projects were 'gay' projects, marginalised by Ian's keepers. A change of heart would have cheered mine.

Instead he would cross rooms to avoid me, he was so embarrassed. It was indeed brave of Ian's family to allow the cause of his death to be published; but how much braver it would have been if he had come clean, but filled with fear he ran to win.

I'm not going to write Ian's obituary for the *Pink Paper* because few will understand my point of view. For them it is just an old film battle. But to see the world in a grain of sand . . . film was the grit in my life which enabled me to interpret what I saw on and off stage. This makes it for me the microcosm. Ian's silence brought no good. A clean-limbed 'hetero' boy erasing his past and present in case there was the slightest wobble as he ran the road to the Oscars and the Royal Command Performance.

After *Chariots Of Fire* Ian sat waiting for Hollywood to telephone. But he was no Matt Dillon, and sat waiting through the rest of the decade, sinking deeper and deeper into narcotic abuse. How true to spirit that all the actors are clubbing together to organise an Ian Charleson Memorial Scholarship.

Wednesday 10

An anonymous letter with a quote from the Gautama Buddha:

> *Above all do not lose your desire to walk. Everyday I walk myself into a state of wellbeing and walk away from every illness. I have walked myself into my best thoughts, and know of no thought so burdensome that one cannot walk away from it . . . by sitting still. And the more one sits still, the closer one comes to feeling ill. Thus if one just keeps on walking, everything will be all right; you cannot travel on the path before you have become the path itself.*

~

Ron Peck came to dinner. We talked over the past fifteen years at Jimmy's. He's re-looking at the rushes of his film *Nighthawks*. In those days he would walk across London to dinners with investors, he had so little money.

Ron has written a script loosely based on the Nilsen murders. He said he had gone through the extras' names of *Nighthawks* to see if Nilsen had been among them. I told him of my friendship with the mass murderer Michele Lupo. This horrified him as he has seen all the forensic photos, and they are most gruesome. When I knew Michele he was bright and easy going.

The manager of the Yves St. Laurent shop at Hyde Park Corner, he had a filofax full of the names and addresses of the rich and famous. He used to come and spend the night with me. Nothing he did in or out of bed suggested anything was awry. There must have been a tripwire – someone told me he discovered he was HIV positive, and took his 'revenge'.

One day I woke up and his picture was in the newspaper, he was accused of committing several murders. The young man whom he had lived with – and with whom I had also had an affair – didn't know anything about it either, until the police arrived in the middle of the night, pulled him in, and spent three days interrogating him.

~

Yesterday we had the first publicity meeting for *The Garden*. On my way back to the edit suite, where Peter and HB are poring over the rushes, I bumped into Gene October from *Jubilee* days. Gene's smile could swallow a Soho street.

Thursday 11
To the Royal Academy for the Franz Hals exhibition. Met Peter Blake and Tom Phillips.

Friday 12
British Screen gave a reception this evening. I felt like the ghost at the banquet – too many people enquiring after my health. However much I insisted I was OK, I convinced no-one. My hacking cough was noted.

The dinner in the gallery of the Central Art School – a room of granitic and Byzantine gloom. Mike Leigh was the cheeriest; and also Amanda Donahoe, who told me she clambered over the roof tops of Marchmont Street as a sixteen year old to infiltrate the first night of *Jubilee*.

I struggled to look happy and alive all evening – Ian Charleson's death hung heavy over the conversation. Left with James at midnight in pouring rain. Without James' patience none of my films of the eighties would have been made.

Saturday 13
Visited the food hall at M&S, it has all the English puddings: gooseberry fool, summer pudding, bread and butter, but no queen's pudding which HB said would be the most popular. Check-out like the check-in at a gay disco.

Sunday 14

Walked to the Tate – the whole place infuriatingly CLOSED. Joined the stampede for the Turners in James Stirling's discordant annex – painted the colours of a municipal crêche. Beat a hasty path back home.

Spud and his boyfriend Johnny came for a pizza, all glittery in studded leathers. I tried Spud's jacket on, which made HB laugh.

Tuesday 16

Julian Cole here. We had an indigestible supper that came off the stove in fragments. By midnight my bronchial chest had winded me. I retired to bed breathless.

Wednesday 17

A warm sunny day. The gardens in Edwardes Square bright with forsythia, japonica, and camellias. Lunch in Richard's studio.

When I returned to Phoenix House I found HB hanging perilously from the windows high above Charing Cross Road conducting an intensive spring cleaning operation in every dusty nook and cranny.

I beat a retreat to Rowney's where I bought oil paint – there was a particularly fine Auerbach on Richard's wall, of the Shell building site. It gave me the urge to pick up a paint brush and stop collaging.

I thought of painting the nuclear power station across the garden, and also HB's portrait. He seemed willing and asked me if I could draw. I'm not certain I can any longer. I got a First for draughtsmanship at the Slade, but I think that was sleight of hand. It surprised me at the time, as I didn't believe I could draw, just fudge and smudge.

~

My bronchial lung is extremely susceptible to cigarette smoke; Simon Turner lighting up his Gitane this morning as we mulled over the sound-track nearly asphyxiated me. We made an outline for *The Garden*, which we can dispose of if need be.

Today my dear friend Joany Hunt died, and sweet Paul.

As I left the flat this evening I was accosted by a middle-aged man who stared at me intensely and said 'You've lost weight, you've definitely lost weight' and then disappeared down the alley clutching a sheaf of papers. I walked down to Comptons and drank two glasses of water.

Thursday 18

The New York publicist of *War Requiem* in tears on the phone – everything has been mismanaged. He says he has been given two black and white photos for the press! And has consequently lost articles and leading reviews.

I spent the evening making phone calls to help him.

The *Guardian* rang concerning the witch hunt of the Scottish judge who has resigned over the revelation of his homosexuality. Why should sexuality impinge judgement? No-one would suggest Michelangelo's judgement was faulty.

~

Still dithering about having a second opinion on my chest – decided to wait till after the weekend. Off the penicillin and expectorant I feel better, though I'm still breathless.

~

Walked to the bank, and on the way back met my dear friend and doctor for many years, Arnold Linken. He was walking in the opposite direction so I changed course and walked with him.

We stopped off and had a coffee. He talked of the painter Keith Vaughan, who he had cared for. So intellectual and retiring it was almost impossible to communicate with him.

I missed Arnold's sharp eye and reassuring voice after he retired from practice two years ago.

~

Jenny Howarth and Terence Davies came for tea, HB bought lush cakes at Maison Bertaux. Terence, clinking his immaculate brown brogues together, filled the flat with fizzy conversation, dazzling montages, big close-ups. He described one famous thesp introducing himself: 'Teak from the knees up,' says Terence.

He was scathing about Dennis Potter's *Blackeyes:* he should see more cinema before claiming he was an innovator.

He acted out a meeting with Patricia Hayes in which she pinches him black and blue like a Walt Disney crone. He fizzes with anger at the mention of Janet Street-Porter who, showing off her truly awful home on TV last night, said she had based it on 'the crappy films of Orson Welles'. A genius, says Terence, a genius. How dare she – and Muriel Gray, who dismissed *Distant Voices* with the one-liner: 'Another British film with a lot of people who sing their way through the war.'

Friday 19
Caught the train at Charing Cross for Ashford. Grey pinched day. David met me and we drove across the marsh – a vivid emerald green under the dark sky.

Prospect Cottage was as I left it two weeks ago, buffeted by a gale which blew up and as quickly disappeared before nightfall. Lit the fires and took out my new paints blocking in three canvases of the nuclear power station across the garden at dusk. The phone rang ceaselessly.

Saturday 20

Dawn came magnificent in bands of violet and dark rose. The blaze of iridescent colours in the clouds over the sea soon disappeared as the sun came through, pale and wintry. But the garden looked magnificent, all the stones sharply etched in the low light.

At the sea's edge the winter storms have cut deep coves into the shingle, which undulate along the Ness like a dragon's back.

After breakfast the two lost pigeons that have made the cottage their home flew on to the roof and marched up and down making a great noise.

In the garden the plants quicken. The first crocuses are out, though battered by the gales. The daffodils are peeping through, and the sea kale seeds are germinating; the purple buds of the old plants are more pronounced.

The elder has broken cautiously into leaf, and the rosemary next to it is bright with blue flowers.

The poppies have germinated – but the rabbits have cropped them back to the ground. The periwinkle has sent up its first bottle green shoots.

A ladybird suns itself, a jewel on the purple sage.

The winter has taken its toll: the fennel has died, and the camomile; several lavenders have withered away. But for every plant lost, others have taken hold. The seeds of the alexanders that I broadcast have germinated; the mullein is growing strongly.

I search in vain for signs of burdock, knapweed and the oxeye daisy, but find the red valerian.

By three the rain sets in bringing down the dark.

Sunday 21

A pale white sun floats like an apparition in the flying grey clouds until swallowed and lost in a squall.

The wind is up roaring across Gesualdo's madrigals – those strange products of a Counter Reformation psychosis working through a late medieval art form.

And yet it does not matter that he's all in bits. The whole is disorganised, but each individual fragment is in order, representative of a higher order. The higher order prevails even in disintegration. The totality is present even in the broken pieces, more clearly present, perhaps, than in a completely coherent work lulled into a sense of false security by some human, merely fabricated order. You have to rely on

*your immediate perception of the legitimate order. So in a sense
disintegration may have its advantages.*   Huxley.

~

Walked along the beach bringing back flints for the garden. Derek flew a
kite. Walking through the broom I spotted a large drinker caterpillar curled
round a twig – looking a little worse for wear but quite alive.

Drove back to London as the sun set fiery red across the Ness.

Monday 22
Into the edit suite to view the last of the rushes before we start to cut the
film.

Tuesday 23
Broadcast at ten from Bridge House, Paddington – to the British Forces, on
'hiding homosexuality'. On the way back I got soaked in torrential rain.

Entered Tottenham Court Road tube this morning down the degrading
piss stink passage beneath Centre Point to the besieged ticket machines.

Cash in the pocket, loose change adrift – I've never had a wallet or plastic.
Unable to fill in forms. I cannot use a public phone without anxiety.

I fuse in front of the bank of station names, then cross to the kiosk, buy a
ticket from the sullen attendant, insert it in the automatic gate that throws it
back in my face. There are no escalators any longer, so you spiral giddily
down the rotting emergency stairs avoiding the pools of vomit and fungoid
walls blistered with putrescence, past the mental decay of Paolozzi's pitiful
attempt at mosaic, on to the central platform – to the strains of some faded
Utopian song of the sixties echoing in the corridors. A little death overtakes
me as I reel breathless into the final carriage, where the patterned upholstery
has disappeared in a slurry of grey dirt – until liberated on to the streets of
Lancaster Gate.

What has happened to the underground? Crawling with rodent passengers, malevolent dead eyes, stench of damp winter clothes, limp papers,
smudged tired fingers black with the world's problems.

~

On the phone to my art master Robin Noscoe, who said my obituary had
appeared in the school magazine.

~

Deep in the night HB had a boxing dream and punched the pillow next to
my face so hard I felt it coming in my sleep. He missed me by a hair's
breadth. I found myself shouting 'What the fuck did you do that for?' and

woke him up.

~

Robin's house on Cole Hill informed a whole generation of schoolchildren. This is where we learnt our architectural vocabulary. Asked to present a twentieth century building on BBC2, it suddenly flashed in my mind: Garden House, built by my art master in the fifties, set deep in its grove of camellias.

~

In the afternoon walked to Bush House to do a radio interview for the American opening of *War Requiem*. Spent the rest of the day reading another biography of Edward I.

Wednesday 24
Violent storm which blew parts of the roof away. Ventured out onto the street looking skywards for flying missiles. Soaking rain funnelled by twisters thrown up by Centre Point. Back late from Richard Salmon's – I had a glass of wine, my first alcohol for two months.

Derek rang in a panic: there are gusts of 112 mph down at Dungeness. Roofs are off and debris flying. His extension has blown down; and as he speaks the lights have gone.

At three, despite Derek's warning, we set off to Cambridge to see Paul Reynold's painting show. It took us three hours to get to the M11 from the centre of town and then almost immediately we were trapped for another three in a traffic jam the length of the motorway. Finally, at ten o'clock, we drove off at Exit Eight along with hundreds of other confused and lost drivers turning back along the A roads to London. Everywhere overturned lorries.

Beethoven's second piano concerto and a Brahms symphony passed some of the time. At hour six Rick grew despondent and said, 'This is taking longer than the *Mahabharata*.'

Sitting in the car we all caught up on the last four years. Paul told us a string of sailor stories from Cartagena, where he has been completing his studies of Roman pottery in a flat with a view into a notorious brothel. We arrived back home at midnight very tired.

Friday 26
The storm has taken its toll at Dungeness. The telephone pole outside my window has snapped and swings back and forth in the wind supported only by the wires. The new greenhouse has been stripped of its glass; and the garage that took such a battering in the hurricane has collapsed and is being

burnt at the side of the road. The army base measured gusts of 120 mph.

My garden was flattened. At least half of the driftwood poles were down and one of the metal buoys had entirely vanished. The house itself was undamaged; but the heavy chimney cowl had flown off like a discus and landed in the shingle unbroken.

Many of the stones in the circles were overturned. But the greatest loss is among the plants, which have been burnt by the salt wind and look very sad.

I view my world through windows thick with salt.

~

At three this afternoon the nuclear power station exploded in a roar of steam, which drifted over the Ness – a death rattle like a hundred jet planes taking off. Within seconds the enormous building vanished from view; sparks flashed in dark clouds.

'My God it's blown, what shall we take?' said David, rushing around the house. My suitcases packed in a second.

I'll ring HB, I shouted. Meanwhile David seized the camera and started to film. I rang HB – 'Get out immediately,' he said. Another great spark crackled between the towers. I dialled 999; the operator was infuriatingly calm. She asked:

Where do you say the accident has occurred?

Dungeness. The nuclear power station has exploded!

Can I have the address?

Dungeness!

I mean the exact address.

The world is falling apart, the lives of people from here to Amsterdam, even to the end of the earth at Chernobyl are at risk.

Can't you be more exact?

The nuclear power station, Dungeness.

The whole house is shaking. In a fury I slam the phone down. HB rings; always practical, he has phoned the station.

'They said they've had a controlled emergency shut down, the power lines were hit by lightning in a sudden squall.'

The panic subsides slowly. David and I sit shaking at the kitchen table. From here the lightning flashes looked as if they were a series of explosions, the rolls of thunder amplifying the roar of the steam: an extraordinary illusion, which perhaps only we witnessed. Ten minutes later the lights went out, leaving us in the dark with a congealed half-cooked dinner.

Saturday 27

A grey windy day. Scrubbed the floors and dusted – the wind has blown dust from every crack. Carried on painting oils of the power station, and gilded a notebook for *Edward II*.

In the afternoon I finished the biography of Edward I and worked in the garden, replacing the stakes blown flat by the storm.

On the beach I found the blackened timbers of an old boat – too heavy to remove.

At dusk Peter arrived and set up his video camera, and taped for an hour.

The weather set in, and gales blew through the night, so the house trembled.

Sunday 28

Bright sunlight with a strong gale blowing. I repaired the garden for the third day running. All the plants dreadfully damaged: the wallflowers look as if they have been boiled; even the lavender has wilted; and the crocuses have shrivelled in the bud. Feeling sorry for the lavender cuttings I brought them in.

Beneath the willows at the Long Pits I found the first primrose of the year.

Monday 29

The rain poured down all day. Damp and without much to do, I bought the [Allen] Ginsberg biography, then lay on the bed and read it for the rest of the afternoon.

Tuesday 30

At 8:30 walked against the rush hour crowds, crossing Hungerford Bridge and the Waterloo Viaduct to catch the train to Poole. Almost the only person going in that direction, I was pushed and shoved by the human tide; this way and that I bumped along narrow walkways as London commuters – slit-eyed, malevolent, ratlike – splashed through the puddles to work.

~

Robin and Phil Noscoe welcomed Ruth Rosenthal and myself into Garden House. Delicious smell of oil paint and wood ash. Outside, the rain poured down; and Robin mused over the many pine trees, including a wellingtonia, that had been brought down in the gale. Smell of damp bonfires, flames flickering in the gloom at Canford. Most of the old cedars had fallen, or had branches severed by the winds.

Robin's art school full of very grown up kids. We drove back to Bournemouth in torrential rain, discussing plans for the ten minute film of the house.

Wednesday 31

A long and charming letter from my Aunt Moyra. More family history: she thought the portrait of my father accurate, but said he should be credited with the selfless way he looked after my mother when she was dying of cancer. My uncle Edward was born at the height of the first German blitz on London in 1915 and, chased by submarines, was taken on a ship back to my grandfather in Calcutta. The passengers dropped like flies from influenza on the long journey.

~

Spent three hours at St. Mary's – had my lungs inspected. Merry atmosphere, though I was worried. The outcome – everything fine. The doctor said they were functioning remarkably well for my age.

Peter and HB, heads down in the edit. I haven't a clue what they are up to.

My birthday.

FEBRUARY

Thursday 1
The phone rings. I'm told old friends have been spreading rumours that I'm very ill. I celebrate by having a tooth pulled. I wonder how this is affecting me, do you think it makes it any easier to get a film financed, when people you know quite well talk like this?

~

There is a natural impulse to wish those who reproach our good health with illness quite dead: a great building burnt to ashes, a painting slashed, a tree fallen, the past cleared away for the future. Little deaths. All of us feel satisfaction in a dark corner.

My friend Alan died today.

Friday 2
I feel a strong urge to start painting again.

Jon Savage arrived at midnight last night and we went on one of our drives East, through the deserted Docklands – mile after mile of pinched houses with not a soul. The brave new world of the eighties.

Here and there we passed the location of one of my films: the *Mad Max* mercenary garden of *Jubilee* is still there, the gnomes looking a little sorry for themselves.

The rain poured down so we saw little, just the hypnotic lights reflected in every puddle.

We climbed out of the car and walked round the Cutty Sark to the Royal Naval Hospital. No-one about. Then to the Isle of Dogs – Legoland of lost causes: tinsel-town architecture over which the silent cranes hang like gallows.

~

My paintings scramble the initials IHS HIV.

~

Today the film took off – a pattern began to emerge out of the chaos.

~

Jon said he had given Julie Burchill's address to ACTUP – JB, the po-faced, ugly journalist who posed as a punkette to clamber up the column inches. She said she preferred homosexuals limp-wristed and dragged up in velveteen like Oscar Wilde, and hated the new faggots with their political agendas and macho styles. Jon said we must put an end to homophobia amongst the pea-brained fashion victims.

~

At a talk I gave at the gaysoc in London University on Wednesday evening, a lecturer at the University said that open homosexuals amongst the teaching staff were under considerable pressure. To give a good crit to a gay student caused the common room to bubble with innuendo. He felt he had to guard every word he said and hide every aspect of his private life.

While I was waiting for my doctor to see me at St. Mary's, a doctor – who is also a patient – came over and introduced himself. We talked for some time about the difficulties he had experienced. He wanted to know what effect my public statement that I was HIV+ had had. What is certain is strangers I meet in the street all look on me as 'dead'. I have to underline the fact that I'm OK; but doing this doesn't convince them.

On the other hand it makes me twice as determined to survive, to find a gap in the prison wall that society has created and jump through it. I told him I had no choice but to be open, I'm not a secretive person. Anyone who tells me a secret does so at their peril.

I was advised to keep quiet, but knew I couldn't; I was privileged enough to be able to break the silence. If not insurable as a film-maker, I could always paint.

Everyone close to me has been supportive. They don't, thank God, ask me if I'm well each time they see me.

The press was uninterested, I'm not a public figure or pop star.

Though when I worked with the Pet Shop Boys last year that changed: *AIDS Victim Stages Pets*. The openness brought relief and has strengthened my defences. I'm not defeated by enquiries about my health; but in the circumstances the question would be better off addressed to the skies.

Saturday 3

Took the pinstripe suit I've been wearing all week to the cleaners and stole HB's blue overalls. They are much more comfortable. HB says as soon as he turns his back I'm rifling through his clothes. Wearing someone else's clothes is so much easier, you don't have to make decisions. HB looks immaculate, feels I've stolen his look. It suits me, black and blue.

~

Rain pouring down, the empty streets awash. Even the stallholders in Berwick Street market have put up the shutters, and stand disconsolate in doorways.

I returned home clutching a soggy *Independent* and a bread roll. Wrote letters, then picked up the Ginsberg biography and disappeared into the coldwater flats of forties' Manhattan.

Monday 5
Washed out, limp as a rag, exhausted after the weekend. Sat in the YMCA photo booth and took four ugly passport photos: scarlet-eyed, bat's ears, complexion like a shrivelled conker. The results: dazzlingly unpleasant. People show each other their passport photos like dirty secrets. Let me see yours.

~

Saturday evening: leaning against the wall of Comptons with a double vodka, discussing *Edward II* with Stephen, Marc Almond's *Tainted Love* on the sound system. Across the bar, a skinhead lad gives me a dazzling smile. He is quarrelling with his lover, who has his back to me, his hand protectively down the boy's blue jeans. The boy smiles, long lingering looks.

The king could recount Marlowe's play like Scheherazade, ninety minutes of reminiscence and seduction, the executioner as sexy as this skinhead who stretches and pointedly turns his arse in my direction. Edward's cruel phallic death by the red hot poker.

The lover has become aware of my presence. Should Isabel be played by a boy? Piers and Mortimer drift past, black ashes – *My father is deceased*, a crumpled note from the past, scooped up from the floor of the cesspit prison.

For an hour I have been subjected to sexual provocation. Then, while I'm getting a drink the angry boyfriend hustles him out of the pub and I'm left alone with the play.

Tuesday 6
Walked through London with Dagmar Benke from ZDF, the German TV station, to the Sir John Soane museum; and then to the Temple church. She was amazed the lawyers still inhabit the ancient Inns, their names handpainted on the Georgian doorcases.

The church of Clement Danes has a gloomy atmosphere, in spite of Wren's elegant airy architecture. Its rolls of honour to the RAF dead sparked off a long conversation about tradition and the British Establishment.

How in the late sixties as an artist-painter, rather than a film-maker I had met this establishment.

~

We visited Hackett's, a clothes shop in Covent Garden that models itself on a Savile Row tailors, selling more Past than clothes; and the Garrick Club, where we watched elderly men grope their way up the steep-stepped entrance. Howard Brookner told me that in the USA the powerful met as trustees of museums. Art and money lie in bed together.

~

Once, in the interval of a Royal Command Performance of the ballet, Jacob Rothschild gloomily confided in me that capitalism was on its last legs.

~

According to Howard, David Puttnam's assassination at Columbia had been planned after he had unwittingly turned his back on the man who had just given Los Angeles its modern art museum. He refused an invitation rather brusquely, saying he was involved in cinema and had no time for art. Art turned round and bit him.

If you thought film-making had no political aspect, why, before the row over *Jubilee* and *Sebastiane* roared through Parliament, did the arts minister come one morning to the set of *Caravaggio* and later at dinner ask me about the funding of smaller films? The older Establishment has never been shocked by film. Perhaps bored, but never shocked.

Could *The Garden* be blasphemous? There are blasphemy laws in Germany as well as here, said Dagmar. I thought we were the only ones. Someone I knew dropped a quiet word at a dinner into the ear of the censor and *Sebastiane* was passed without a cut. Shakespeare, the *Sonnets, Caravaggio*, Britten's *Requiem*, what more traditional subject matter could a film-maker take on? And yet I'm still seen by some as a menace.

Vincent Canby, who has hated all my films, perhaps none so much as *The Tempest*, slaughtered me again today in the *New York Times*. Perhaps I should be pleased by the column inches: *Derek Jarman has made a movie of epic irrelevance that, when it rises to the occasion, is merely redundant . . . Mr. Jarman, whose films include* Sebastiane *and* Caravaggio, *has a weakness for the kind of baroque imagery that is utterly beside the point.* The last line: *Mr. Jarman decorates a film as much as he directs it.*

Since most of the cinema is an enormous irrelevance, a medium that has crossed the boundaries of intelligence in a very few hands, it does not worry me. No-one except fools expected to find much at the end of this rainbow.

Thursday 8

A wild wind roared through the night, chasing sleep to the edge of dawn. With the tide the storm came at midnight. The stoves roared white hot. If it rained I never heard it. I lay all night tossing and turning, a pit in my stomach. My heart missed a beat at each violent gust.

At three the moon came out, pale in a slate sky. A washed-out ghostly light. The wind dropped for an hour, then came howling back. So the old wooden walls rattled and creaked. I slept for an hour and then woke to find the sun full out in a cloudless sky, which hurt my sleepless eyes.

The storm was brewing as Gerard and I drove here yesterday enveloped in a grey drizzle. I've been away for over ten days, and the house feels damp. It has been raining almost without stop, so the Long Pits are full to the brim and the marsh is a bright clear green.

Gerard drove home in spite of the warnings on the news for people to stay indoors. On our way here we saw a Mini that had come off the road and sunk to its roof in a drainage ditch. Branches off trees, fallen chimney pots and slates marked the passing of the last Great Storm two weeks ago.

Midday

Crystalline sunlight, all the dark humours blown away by the wind. The crocuses open quickly, bright yellow petals spread wide open at noon. The purple and white in the shadows. The snowdrops are out; and before the sun disappears round the house the first daffodil has opened.

Spring comes despite the scorching gales which boil the leaves of daffodils like spinach. Today the sun shines on and on to make amends, turning the sea from a menacing gunmetal to bright azure. As I walk along the shore the sky is filled with countless gulls shimmering angelic white above the dark waves. There is a lightness in the air, the Ness quickens. The sea kale have germinated, the roses are breaking bud.

At five a full moon hangs over the Channel reflected in the sandflats, which glow like mother of pearl.

Friday 9

All night the full moon shone so bright the house cast a shadow across the shingle, contrariwise to that cast by the setting sun. At five I stood at the window looking out to sea.

Waking from the strangest dream. A conversation on a red bus with a naked youth who declared he was the god Dionysus on his way to attend an orgy in his honour. Walking down a desolate twilit street I passed an enormous ruined palace hung with verdigris tiles, the palace of a Ceaucescu: half stupa, half thirties office building. Dead tired I climbed into the house of an old woman and slept. She caught me but was not angry, though she painfully took my address. In the empty street several hundred boys in scouts' uniforms rush past.

Today the sun shines with an unreal intensity, precise as a street corner in a de Chirico, razor-sharp shadows. The crocuses bright as flares in the shingle.

Replanted a row of sea kale in the back garden, my first gardening this year. Then settled down to put the voice-over for the film in order.

In the afternoon I walked to the sea and found the storms had washed away the shingle exposing the sea kale. I gathered several very large specimens and replanted them in the front garden.

The full moon came up deep gold over the sea casting a path of light across the sands which grew in intensity as daylight faded. In this golden path two fishermen dug for bait by the light of their tilly lamps. Then an eclipse bit into the side of the moon, slowly obliterating it; until by nine it had disappeared.

Saturday 10

A cold grey windy day. Compose the poems as the rain blows in. Slowly the puddles form. As the day draws to a close the sun floods the Ness, wet shingle scintillates.

Sunday 11

A gale blue with cold blew up. I rose shivering from my bed and splashed warm water over my face which almost froze on the stubble. Made a bowl of porridge and coffee which was quickly lukewarm.

Finished my breakfast on the sofa, covered by my grandmother's old travelling rug I read Denton Welch's memoirs. Crystalline descriptions and acute observations. I wish writing came naturally to me.

Last night Derek drove me to Hastings for fish and chips in a spartan little takeaway that was the only place open in town. Then we stopped at Jury's Gap to meet six London boys who had taken the house for the weekend; we found them miserably glued to the TV watching Cilla Black's *Blind Date*. Derek said they had been watching the TV when he had called in that morning.

A freezing February in the Romney Marshes is an acquired taste. The fish and chip takeaway was very good: white slices, formica, pale oatmeal tiles. Warm glutinous tea.

Later we went to Blades, the local, and only, gay venue, tucked behind a pub in a side street. The same deafening disco music. Scarlet shadowy room lit by a mirror ball on to which a sodium orange spotlight was fixed, four rotating lights – blue, green, magenta, orange – above a square of red lino, on which some clones danced energetically. Four lesbians were the chic:

Ziggy Stardust haircuts, waistcoats. One wore a businessman's suit and a pullover. They all wore cowboy boots or winkle-pickers. The men were all nondescript: burnt out by alcohol and decibels, with ill-fitting jeans round sagging thighs. For an hour we sat in an alcove watching, till the music overwhelmed us; then we took the road back over the cliffs at Fairlight.

~

What if the present were the world's last night?
Your love stabbed in the setting sun
Dies in the moonlight
Fails to rise
Thrice
Denied by cockcrow
In the dawn's first light

~

At ten a very large fox walks quite nonchalantly across the shingle in front of the house. When he sees me he takes off to the woods by the Long Pits at a brisk trot.

The sun came out. The waves churned a sandy yellow, with white sea horses and purple patches to mark the shadows of passing clouds.

A black storm cloud has rolled in: the wind whistles about the eves, shrieks like a frightened rabbit. The rain blows across the ground in misty eddies and falls from the scurrying clouds in widows' veils, lashing the windows. Sets in even harder. The horizon disappears.

Monday 12

Robin arrived out of the blue – 15 years since he was in London; he's been living in Toronto. He said he had a great deal of film taken in 1972–73 of the studio and Andrew's Miss Worlds – even the opening of Biba's.

He found London very changed: rich, clean, scrubbed – quite a different view from that we all have, of a city suffering from decay and neglect. Though he couldn't believe they hadn't completed the restoration of the tube lines.

~

Finished the Ginsberg biography, which grew as depressing as a chant, om padme hum, sex and drugs and poetry. A laundry list of drugs and boyfriends.

I'm jaundiced today, covered with a 'chicken pox' which itches like a frenzy. I do love *Howl*, but I couldn't help thinking it was all a palaver, America scrutinising its navel, and the myth-making Beats? Quite an ordinary little bunch seriously cultivating slender legends. Another tide of itching overwhelms me.

~

We went to see *Salò* at the Scala in MGM's murdered version. Emerged numbed into the desolate cold of King's Cross. A wave of anger came over me. The pathetic nature of British life: no Pasolini, Genet, or Barthes, no-one here really. Just *Bent* at the National with everyone congratulating themselves. I find the British Theatre tedious, the thespians of Stonewall capitalising on their truly horrid connections with the Establishment. Wept myself to sleep. *Salò*, like the Kincora boys' home.

Tuesday 13

The *Mail*'s 'Gay Jesus Scandal Brews' has brought a hoard of journalists looking for a lead. They're on to Lorraine, my agent, and Kate, the publicist for *War Requiem*. I pour cold water on it all.

The film is looking remarkably good. Watched it, then made the final corrections to the voice-overs.

The horrible itching continues. The American magazine *Outweek* arrives with my photo on the cover. I think I look fairly handsome, a little grumpy perhaps, but not too bad for 47.

There's a letter in *Outweek* that says: *Jarman has been one of the most underestimated artists of the last decade, particularly amongst gays and lesbians.* The situation in the States seems to be on the turn; though, of course, I've had no commercial success there and that puts me in a very weak position. The article is about *War Requiem*, HIV and the difficulties of finding funding as an 'openly gay' director. If you're a straight film-maker like Stephen Frears (*Launderette, Prick Up Your Ears*), it's a different situation. The 'gay' films were given to 'straight' directors because they are seen as safer, more commercial.

Is this a good thing? If gay films are commercial then more gay themed films will be funded – the converse is sadly true.

This itching makes me unhappy with everyone. I'm not feeling persecuted but I have always been in an uncomfortable situation; except for *Caravaggio* I've never had a stable work pattern.

Sandy rang at four. Paul died in his sleep last night.

Friday 16

Voice-overs with Michael Gough in Camden. He liked the poems very much.

The other disciple, he, who Jesus loved

Slept, but his heart was awake in the night.
Hark, my beloved is knocking
Open to me my love
My dove, my perfect one,
For my head is wet with dew
My locks with the drops of the night.

~

Nico said, 'The sky is so high today.' It was a beautiful sunny day as we were walking home from the Sir John Soane museum in Lincolns Inn Fields. Some days the sky is so low it hits you on the head.

Later, watched the middle section of *The Garden*, which took on form and flowed. Ended the day feeling much happier.

~

Lamentable programme yesterday of various Christian sects debating 'the problem'. For tortuous evasion Bishop Montefiore took the Wafer, told us we were handicapped; and then said being handicapped was an honourable condition. The C of E displays that lack of hospitality that was the true sin of Sodom. Various silly, born-again fundamentalists – most of them black – displayed the underbelly of ignorance; but the Bishop wasn't far behind. The programme should have reduced us to laughter at the foolishness of Christendom, but these ill-informed, ill-mannered minds lead us to our deaths; therefore we must fight harder.

Saturday 17

Stephen comes here at eleven and says he overheard Paddy Ashdown on the radio enquiring about the 'melt-down' at Dungeness on January 26. Apparently incidents like this have to be reported and this one wasn't.

We walked across Soho and Mayfair to see the Herb Ritts photographs. I found them much too chic, perfect for a foyer or restaurant. The full frontal cock made it – the only photo without a red sticker. The photos cost £1,000 and more. There must be a lot of interior designers with loose change.

Back here something strange occurred as we left the house. A well-dressed and very nervous young woman buttonholed me and asked me to walk with her. She asked me about the film we took of the shutdown at Dungeness – could we make it available to Greenpeace? She knew a lot about the incident. Apparently the radar was brought down by the storm, narrowly missing some vital ducting – a hit would have been catastrophic.

'I can't be seen talking to you.' Then she suddenly disappeared. She said the possibility of an accident like this happening had been thought negligible. Only a plane crashing into the reactor could cause it. Yet it happened.

Dungeness was a hair's breadth from disaster.

As I write this I'm still disturbed by the meeting, it was like a cloak-and-dagger encounter in a forties' spy film. The earnest manner and obvious sincerity with an element of hysteria. I got the impression she knew a great deal, that the repercussions of this action would be serious for her.

Sunday 18

There is scaffolding around the radar installation on the nuclear plant. The sun shines. Frank Sinatra is singing *What A Guy, What A Fool Am I*. What to do?

The daffodils are out.

~

Is the nuclear industry the rot at the core of democracy, around which shadowy secrets congregate like moths? I told my neighbours and they laughed. What can any of us do? And what information do we have?

Later I walked over to Sylvia's and she confirmed that the radar had come down in the storm.

Monday 19

I counted 77 blooms on the early daffodils I planted two years ago. They are multiplying very slowly. At the water's edge the sea kale is sprouting. The plants have small leaves of two or three inches; they are a deep purple.

The storms have totally altered the coastline. Last summer it was a straight shingle bar; now it's deeply indented with bays and ridges, which have collected piles of flotsam.

Phone call from NYC to say *War Requiem* closed after one week.

Tuesday 20

Annie Lennox rang about the Cole Porter song that she has been asked to perform for charity. I think she has the same worries I have about raising money this way for people who are ill, who should never be dependent on charity. How would either of us feel in different circumstances if we were dependent? I'm all for doing it as long as there is a 'Government Health Warning'.

~

Michael Powell, whose films charmed and surprised us, died last night. *The Late Show* asked me if I would pay a tribute. HB said it might be a good idea, as so many people have recently been enquiring about my health. If they see me on TV it might scotch the rumour that I'm on the way.

Spent the rest of the day making a series of gouaches for the cover of Jon

Savage's book on punk and the Sex Pistols.

~

I must look my best on TV as I am feeling rather fragile. I had one of my fleeting depressions, all the death that surrounds us. Keith Haring, the NY artist, died last week. Paul's funeral, which I will miss, is on Thursday.

Old Mrs. Oiller, my next door neighbour – she called us 'Her boys' – is buried today. So is Michael Powell, who lived into his eighties, though his career was cut short years ago. It doesn't help to keep your spirits up, particularly during these short winter days.

~

Christopher laughed on the phone and said, Well you made your HIV status public! People are continually asking after you *sotto voce*.

~

Walked into the Chinese restaurant in Lisle Street for lunch pretending I was dead, a ghost at a sweet-and-sour banquet.

Being 'dead' I got so lost in myself that I arrived there without any recollection of how I had crossed the roads. Sat opposite a young man with long plaited hair who devoured his food while staring at me. I looked out the window until my meal arrived and in my nervous state found I couldn't control the chopsticks. The whole episode passed by in slow motion, like a bad dream.

Lunch left me exhausted.

I came back here, the phone rang: Derek, are you all right? You sound as if you have flu.

No, no.

The rest of the afternoon was very quiet. I did little, vaguely listened to the traffic.

~

I don't feel sorry for myself, just trapped by circumstances – lying on the bed looking at the white paint on the ceiling as the light fades.

Thursday 22

Boarded the Polish Airline jet with more than a little apprehension as well as excitement. The flying time to Warsaw was two hours. I noticed I was the only passenger with no luggage.

Spent the flight eavesdropping on a conversation about the England we were leaving behind between a Polish woman, an expatriate in her fifties, and a young Finn. It started with the complications of buying a house,

241

which the Finn put down to our long unbroken history, which had created many institutions and patterns of practice that had never been simplified. In Finland you just paid the cash and collected the deeds from the City Hall. The Polish woman said she always felt safe in Great Britain, that the English had a rare sense of the privacy of the individual. They both noted the beauty of the countryside and said the myth of a cold and foggy land was just that. Strangely, the Finn said he had never eaten so well in any country. He praised the Indian, Italian, and Chinese restaurants of Weybridge.

Meanwhile, down below, the great European plain slid past, its neat chequerboard fields bathed in sunlight.

~

Warsaw airport turned out to be about the size of our airport in Lydd. Customs formalities were brief, though the baggage took an intolerable time to appear on the ramshackle conveyor.

Anya was waiting with two young men from the cinema, Wittek and Jurek, in a battered red university van. We rattled into Warsaw, the outskirts of which are the uniform grey that seems to be the hallmark of the 'Evil Empire'. A pall of grey dust covers the cracked façades and broken pavements on which people move like shadows. The first impression is one of empty streets.

Old Warsaw is small and domestic, an oasis in the centre of the grey. People walk here etched in the sunlight. Enigma of a sunny afternoon.

It is a beautiful spring day, but even here the grey dust has invaded – you could trace your finger along the pavement. The shops shrink from announcing their presence – you barely notice them and have to peer hard into the windows to see what they are selling.

Malik, who drives the bus and who has organised this film week, has long hair, hennaed, and blue jeans. He seems very shy as he shows us the cinema of 400 seats, which is also a theatre. I noticed from old posters that Bob Wilson and Sankai Juku have been here.

We sat in the office and had home-made doughnuts and white wine while we waited for the first audience to arrive.

~

There is the feeling of a society that has been short-changed. A quick glance in the bathroom of the hotel revealed no plug. Up until now I thought this was a Western propaganda joke. I knew it would be impolite to ask for one – in fact, to ask for anything, as it would be found, but at huge expense to my hosts.

~

The projection of the film was very good, but sadly the sound system is very quiet; so the music films won't fare too well. However, the audience is so thrilled to be seeing these films the technicalities are unimportant. Kids have come from all over Poland, and the theatre is having to find floors and spare beds for them. The atmosphere is like the old days of the Arts Labs: enthusiasm triumphing over circumstance. The Solidarity newspaper donated my flight, and the films have all been given by the BFI.

After the showing we went to the restaurant of the journalists' union, where we stumbled across a political meeting – which, like every form of protest, had had to use the church. This was their first night in 'public', the change of location very significant. TV crews were out to film.

Elderly and very respectable-looking men and women were queuing for their coats. Jurek said there were a couple of senators amongst them. In Warsaw you can meet a senator in a coat queue. No-one can quite believe what is happening.

The girl next to me at dinner edits the letters page of the Solidarity newspaper. Dinner is spent discussing the future and Mrs. T., whose claim to have started the revolution in the East is almost believed here . . . would it have happened otherwise? I explained that their gain was our loss. But no-one really believed me.

Friday 23
Struggled in the mirror with my allergy, which looks dreadful – I'm covered with itchy red spots. Today they have won every inch of my back and are now rampaging down my arms.

My hotel is an old building and the window has a view of an eighteenth century town house with lead statues of the four winds, each with the wings of a bumble bee. The building is clear Naples yellow; at six this morning, as the sun came up, it was surrounded by a cloud of cawing black crows.

At 10:30 Anya collected me and we walked to the Old City – the brightest spring morning, which picked out the buffs and beiges of the stuccoed buildings. Today they are shining like the Canaletto paintings from which they were restored after the war.

The city is more like a grand country town; it is certainly no metropolis. In this it is quite different from the heavy 19th century grandeur of Budapest, which I visited last year.

Warsaw is composed of buildings on a domestic scale. There is nothing grandiose, nothing built to impress. The old town has the usual tourist shops full of crucifixes and wooden trolls, fake icons, and dreadful kerbside painting that is international.

In the café we had excellent hot coffee and doughnuts; and then we walked for an hour, before sitting on a bench overlooking the river.

At two we visited the tiny studio of the graphic artist Stasys, who made us tea. His work is of sad hollow-eyed puppets, crucified birds, hobgoblins. He has come here from Vilnius in Lithuania. Behind the warmth I could feel sadness and even a dull envy for the freedom with which we come and go.

We went shopping. The shops are not empty, but no-one can afford anything. There is still a complete absence of display. Food is piled in unloved heaps. Anya bought a kilo of sausage, and I noticed the raised eyebrows of the assistant. In the bread queue it was exceptional for someone to buy a whole loaf. Eggs are priced individually. £10 gives you 150,000 zlotys – over a week's wages. The drinks queue was entirely male.

At the cinema we made ourselves sandwiches, and I talked to the audience for *Sebastiane* for over an hour.

I've made a plug for the sink out of a bottle top and I managed to get a towel – last night I gingerly dried myself on the net curtains, hoping no-one was watching from across the street. The lavatory, which does not flush, is clogged with the Communist Party newspaper *Everyone*.

Saturday 24
Another sunny day. An old woman is selling bunches of pussy willow on the corner of the street. The children holding the silvery sprays make such a pretty sight.

~

The café this morning was completely empty. The staff, sitting around, almost jumped out of their skins when we came in. They gave me the impression that the place stands empty for weeks on end. Coffee and cakes cost about 8,000 zlotys for the three of us, about 50p. Wittek's wages are 300,000 a month. In the evening, when we leave the theatre with several hundred others, it is easy to get the only taxi. We don't even run.

After lunch I had an interview with an intense young film student who is writing on Ken Russell and religion. He talks of Buber and French philosophes . . . impossible to imagine *The Devils* in this way? I don't even know how to tell him that many of the decisions were off the wall. Ken and I never discussed religion or the church.

We drove from this to the gay group Lambda's meeting. The organisation was given legal status a couple of weeks ago, which means it no longer has to meet in a clandestine manner, and can probably organise a café. Everything is still owned by the State or the Party.

~

I talked for half an hour before they got down to business, which was interrupted by the arrival of a BBC crew who stayed for three minutes and then left. It's strange how TV programmes sell their work like soap flakes and keep to their tunnel vision. The programme was about Polish youth. They registered no surprise that I was at the meeting, way out in the Warsaw suburbs in this dilapidated student's hall of residence. In their shoes I would have taken a shot for the record.

~

There are no clubs or bars for gay people, and apart from the park, a sauna, and a corner of a hotel bar which no-one can afford, nowhere to meet. They are arranging a big party for March 10th.

The meeting was like early GLF meetings, with one sharp middle-aged queen interrupting: 'You've discussed everything except what's most important. What's going to be in fashion this summer?' This to an audience who can barely afford the clothes on their backs.

The membership crosses the generations. There was an elderly actor who remembered seeing *A Patriot For Me* at the Royal Court in the 1960s.

~

The problem of HIV and AIDS was discussed. The situation here is so desperate, there is literally no information and the subject is treated completely negatively. The doctors won't contemplate treating people. One of the floors of a ministry has been invaded by desperate people who are body positive. There are no syringes and condoms are old-fashioned and not lubricated. At the moment there has been no intervention by the government – perhaps they have so many other problems AIDS is marginalised.

Lambda is hoping to change this, but they are desperately short of funds. The only hope is seen in the West: funding from the World Health Organisation or Dutch gay groups.

~

After the meeting we walked across the park to the theatre and saw the exquisitely produced but infinitely boring work of Kantor. The theatre building was a death trap with huge crowds and one small exit, the claustrophobia overwhelming. Anya nearly fainted. We've been living on coffee and cakes for two days.

Sunday 25
Driven by Slawek and his boyfriend Jurek to the National Gallery to see the Mykosy exhibition.

The building is in a terrible state, looks as if it has been abandoned since it was built in the thirties, its ruined and cracked architecture straight from the drawing board of a Speer. Inside, an exhibition of hundreds of expressionist portraits. Mykosy signed his work with the drugs he was on, plus cocaine plus coffee. One said *Music and Beer*. Others, long-forgotten stimulants.

~

An exhibition of 14th century Gothic sculpture in polychrome wood, the figures larger than life. The most tortured crucifix I have ever seen, like a heap of rotting offal.

~

We had a solid and sensible lunch of turkey in the old town. Then spent the rest of the afternoon at the cinema.

~

Jubilee was a great success: 'It was a tragedy that socialism and freedom were incompatible' drew cheers, and the '50 million copies of *Paranoia Paradise* sold in Moscow' had the cinema in the aisles. At the end I was convinced that, as my doctor, Arnold Linken, had told me, it was the finest British film of the seventies. A great deal more sophisticated than the gauche *Sebastiane*.

For the rest of the day I watched Super 8 films that students brought me and gave a long interview to Slawek on what to do if you discovered you are body positive.

There is so much to do here and so little is needed. They could mount the first 'safer sex' campaign for as little as £8,000.

The beautiful dark-eyed young actor who speaks no English came and stood near me. Must get his name before I leave.

Monday 26

Breakfast in the old town – excellent red currant juice. Then we met the camera crew in the station alongside the Palace of Kultur. This wedding cake was given to Warsaw by Stalin, a gigantic gothick folly with classical porticoes and statuary – graffiti: 'Send Walesa to the Kremlin, Havel to Siberia, and Castro to Hell' sprayed through a stencil.

The station is in terminal decay: broken lights and pavements, graffiti everywhere. One enormous sign read 'Liverpool Shit'. Street hawkers lined the corridors, some with bottles of beer or cigarettes to sell. A group of old musicians playing music, men on crutches, rowdy hooligans.

At one point the tunnels became the plaza of the Markoff Hotel: sparkling clean currency shops, a porter who forbids us to videotape the affluence. It was the other way round in King's Cross: the BR police moved the derelicts away from the camera, said they would damage the corporate image.

We taped the ramshackle vans selling apples and cigarettes. Inside the station, one charming incident: while the cameraman was focusing on a piece of blank white paper for his white balance, two curious gypsy girls watched nonplussed. They thought he was filming it.

~

Across the road at the British Council: painted walls and carpets, desks, files, framed posters, loo paper.

~

Later at the cinema I gave an hour-long interview on camera. Then *Angelic Conversation* was shown. Another interview for a pop programme; and a further interview with a young film student, before a photo session with Wajda who came to see *Caravaggio*. He smiles broadly, is now a senator, says the young people have brought the cinema to life.

~

The handsome drama student is anxious for me to come to a meeting. He is critical of Wajda. We have found a schoolboy French in common; his name is Pytor Subodnik.

He drives me for miles along the darkened roads to a group of tower blocks, where all the electricity has been disconnected. We climb 16 storeys and arrive at midnight. I am dizzy, almost hallucinating. They sit me in a chair and the questions begin again: film, Poland, Germany and unification, politics. They are all 'political', but none belong to a political party.

The conversation ends with HIV, which I bring up. It creates an almost embarrassed silence; smiles evaporate. At two in the morning in the candle light, with a violent storm beating against the windows, they look like lost children. Suddenly the lights go on, the tension is broken.

Meetings like this, with an exchange of ideas, have quite disappeared in London. Music there is so loud no-one can hear a conversation any longer.

Later, in the taxi, it is blasting out. The taxi driver says he is the only disco in Warsaw. My friends agree, there is nowhere to go at night for them. At 2:00 the streets are quite dead.

At a corner of a deserted street a drunken old man exposes himself while his muffled old wife looks on with resignation.

Tuesday 27

Nine o'clock start to videotape in the National Museum.

The elderly curator who has worked here for forty-five years is thrilled at my interest in the sculpture. He talks of the English medieval alabasters – they have one here – and is incredulous that we should wish to tape the exhibition, which is obviously his darling. He finds a book on Polish Gothic art and hands it to me with a bow.

~

The weather has changed – Metek says there have been more storms in the West. Meanwhile I sit in front of the university on a garden bench and give a long interview about HIV and the emotional effects of finding you're anti-body positive. By the time we finish I am shivering with cold.

Outside the university gates is a hive of activity: stalls selling long-banned books; a young man marching down the street with a drum in front of a smashed and filthy car covered with graffiti announcing it as the Communist Party.

In the university union there is a meeting of Plas and Lambda, and we discuss the plight of those with HIV in Poland. At a four hour debate in Parliament on AIDS, homosexuality is mentioned four times. It is not acknowledged here. 80% of those infected are IV drug users. The gay situation is hidden, excluded from statistics.

~

Catholicism/condoms: these charming people are trying to find their way in the new dispensation, to find words and to form plans. The idea of taking action is still quite new. How? Against whom? And where? With no funds, Plas is hoping to open a hospice.

When the meeting is over it is back to the theatre for a long question and answer session.

Wednesday 28
Up at five to catch the plane.

Collapse with a headache at the flat, and sleep fitfully through the day. HB does not come home from the edit until two in the morning.

At ten Dickie Salmon arrives and we have a meal in the Greek restaurant. Isaac Julien has mounted a happening around the reception of *Looking For Langston* in the States. Langston's family took exception to the film.

MARCH

Thursday 1

Peter and HB are nearly at the end of a rough cut. Two more days.

Much of it is wonderful, but what a relief when it is over. We have to re-film two sequences that went down in the dreadful rushes; this has brought up all the arguments about what some felt was the incompetence of the team who worked on the film. Behind the smiles everyone is shouting at each other.

Ploughed through a mountain of mail and was asleep by nine.

Friday 2

On the train to Ashford. The wind is from the east – a cold sunny day. Sad to leave HB behind in the edit suite.

I had a morning rushing around buying food – then left behind half the things I meant to bring. Hauled everything to the station. On the train read the *Independent* without much relish. And my letters. A sweet one from Michael Powell's widow thanking me for my appearance on *The Late Show*. Also another letter from Aunt Moyra with more childhood information:

> One thing I think I should point out. When Betts (my mother) *was young she was strictly brought up according to the code of the times. She was never allowed to be alone with a boyfriend until he had been vetted by mother and father. Consequently the field was very narrow, and your father was virtually her first and only boyfriend. I was fortunate to escape that way of life, as things changed drastically after the war.*
>
> *Your dad really was a strange man. Yes you were impossible with food, he used to try and force feed you, and meal times became a battle.*
>
> *I wonder how much you remember of Italy. Betts and I used you as an interpreter. When you passed the Colosseum the first time you remarked on the 'bomb damage'.*

At Ashford I was picked up by the Indian taxi driver, who made me very worried by his insistence on talking about radioactivity. He said nothing would persuade him to live at Dungeness, life was precious. As we approached the reactor the taxi slowed down, crawling at a snail's pace towards Prospect Cottage.

The house was very cold. I lit the fires, then walked in the garden. All the daffodils have been shrivelled by the wind. The sea kale are a little further on and the elder has broken bud for a second time.

The garden feels under siege this winter. In my absence the gales have freeze-dried everything. In spite of the rain the plants look parched.

A lark sang very briefly, then the sun disappeared.

I sat and made telephone calls to put the various AIDS organisations in touch with Lambda and Plas. The dark closed in. In bed before nine, slept fitfully.

Saturday 3

Another sunny cold day. Walked along the seashore after breakfast.

A second inspection of the garden this morning showed nothing has moved in the last ten days. The rosemary cuttings on the windowsill are covered in flowers. In the front bed hyacinth and grape hyacinth are in flower.

Most of the wild flowers are doing well: the yellow horned poppy, scabious and oxeye daisy are all flourishing. The burdock has germinated and the tansy and achillea are showing new leaf. Wormwood and foxglove have survived the cold, and many poppies. The iris are putting out new leaves, so are the lavender.

Toby arrived in his little red car at three. We walked with Derek along the beach, and then drove to the nursery. We bought nothing – the weather is too changeable and the shock of being transplanted to Dungeness too extreme. Wait another month.

Sunday 4

The cold wind blows across the Ness.

Feel better this morning. After a feverish night the mattress is soaked through. Yesterday I felt nauseous all day – a reaction to the hectic days in Poland. I know I'm not *ill*, but I'm very depressed. I longed for this weekend to be warm, but found myself shivering – with an anorak on and all the fires blazing. A dull ache in the stomach has made eating unpleasant.

Tuesday 13

For ten days I've been in a feverish sweat, wet T-shirts all over the floor. I faithfully swallowed my antibiotics at two in the morning, but my temperature stayed at 102° for five days, then dropped a degree each day. Until this morning, when I woke dripping wet, 98.4° and 1½ stone lighter.

The razor bumps over the bones of my face. Even the bones themselves have shrunk. My hands seem half their normal size. My raw stomach aches and aches.

~

After 3 hours at St. Mary's: blood, and X-rays. I'm none the wiser. An immense lethargy, though I've dressed myself – cannot continue lying in bed, every position quickly gathers its aches. After ten days in this twilight I feel I have lost control.

A request for me to speak on AIDS and civil liberties put me in a blue funk. I rang to say I couldn't make it as we were filming. I could hear the cold disbelief; these organisations are really pushy. I asked not to be amongst the speakers – I'm not qualified like Simon [Watney] or the others. But there I am, announced. The letter made me very angry. Like the virus, the organisations involved with it can take you over.

A phone call from a photographer. I said I wouldn't be photographed looking the way I do. My face is covered with a shaving rash.

The illness is a severe blow. Is it HIV-related or just a bloody infection?

Whatever, at 102° it seems you're fighting for your life. Half of me says I've had enough, the other, illness is so unpleasant I'll beat it.

Gave up worrying, drowned in my sweat.

Wednesday 14

A second sleepless night. With a pile of a dozen T-shirts wringing wet at my bedside, I was up before six to have a bath and make a cup of tea. Stomach red raw, and very weak. I sat in the kitchen sipping the peppermint brew for over an hour trying to let HB have some sleep. He curled up in a silent ball.

This morning I don't seem to have a fever: two below normal. If only the fucking thing would stabilise. A. – in the same boat – arrived and spent an hour here last night. He is suffering from lethargy and is overwhelmed by total detachment from everything and everyone.

Is the severity of this due to the HIV? I've got all the classic symptoms: night sweats and weight loss. Or is it just a virulent bug picked up in Poland? The hospital, it seems, would have me think the latter.

I gave a 'gardening can' of blood and had X-rays. My chest's OK, I don't have TB. Torches shone in the eyes. Liver slightly enlarged. Yet part of me says, after ten days let's get it over.

Decided on action. I can't sit here and feel sorry for myself, nor 'get up'. Strike a balance, so I don't exhaust myself.

Walked to the British Museum, I barely managed to climb the main staircase to see the exhibition of fakes.

Some fakes are so obvious. The Van Megren painting looks like twenties' decorative work, with horrible subaquatic colouring. You can't imagine anyone being taken in. Others are the most beautiful objects; the crystal skull from South America. And, oh heavens, my little twelfth century pearl reliquary from Scotland is there, the most precious object in the museum. But it is so exquisite, being 'fake' cannot diminish it.

Thursday 15
Slept little last night. At dawn five cold damp T-shirts in a pile, my temperature back to normal. All my joints ache, particularly my hip joint, and the small of the back. Sitting up or lying down is very uncomfortable.

I sit here wondering how to pass the day – hard to find the concentration necessary for reading. In the end I resolved it by falling asleep until one.

Friday 16
Woke with a temperature, which faded away in the morning. All my joints aching most terribly. Weaker than ever. I must put up a fight – otherwise I'm going to melt away in the night.

I can tell that everyone is worried now. It's obviously going to take more than a week for me to pull together and many more weeks for me to put some weight back on.

A large bunch of roses from Lynn fills the corner of the room.

Gerard arrives. A large bluebottle flies around the room, black and menacing. He kills it.

I find it too painful to lie down, so sit in front of the fire till one. When I have to get back into bed I lie absolutely still till the pain subsides, then sweat the night away.

Saturday 17
The doctor said to come into St. Mary's if anything got worse.

I'm off the antibiotics now, feel on a knife edge. Up at 6:30 to bath and shave; then make mint tea. Can't face solids.

It's exactly two weeks since I started to feel ill. The slightest pressure, mental or physical, is like a steam roller bearing down. HB turning in bed hurts. The worst is the disorientation: I haven't been able to read, or muster the concentration to skim through the papers.

James brought a copy of El Europeo with great photos of Dungeness. Happy last summer. The pot plants that I nurtured for the garden will be dying on the windowsill. I would love to go down for a day but daren't chance it.

Sylvia, my neighbour in Dungeness, rang to say they have formed an anti-poll tax group. The £80 rates for the railway carriages, no facilities at all, are now £380. I can afford this, but what about my neighbours? Most of them are already hard-pressed. It's a total mess. It would take a rat as blind as Mrs. T. to dream it up. I vow to see her out come what may.

~

Midday, my temperature is still normal. I'm not quite certain what to do – get up or stay lying here. Still can't focus on anything, my concentration the length of a newspaper article.

Lynn's roses have opened in this hot room, have a delicious, delicate scent. There are twenty-four.

Monday 19
Very sleepless night, temp still at 100°. I went to St. Mary's at ten.

~

The taxi ride to the hospital an agony, each bump and jolt on the road and the traffic lights an eternity. The doctor takes me into his small consulting room – prods, taps, and shines bright lights into my eyes. I feel weak and helpless. He says he is putting me into hospital; immense feeling of relief. But meantime I have to give more blood and walk to the radiology department for a stomach X-ray. The girl who does it is amused – it's only a week since I had my chest X-rayed.

Shivering with cold I got back to the clinic, one of the nurses walked me over to the Victoria Ward.

~

Hospital is like a liner – lots to see. People walking around with drips like Dodgems. Opposite, an entire Greek family has taken up residence round a sick man; in another corner a young Canadian reads a book on the liturgy and is visited by an ebullient priest.

~

From the moment I got into bed nurses introduced themselves: Gerald, Brian. Then endless questionnaires: next of kin, age, address. Then more blood, particularly nasty arterial blood. This hurts. More tapping, reflexes, lights in eyes.

The day passes. The whole thing happens again. Curtains are pulled round for privacy, pee in bottle. Feel pampered – a relief after the last 14 days struggling at the flat.

The clock on the wall is haywire. Confused, I waited till it struck 10:00 for HB to arrive; it was only seven. HB brought me flowers and an elegant dressing gown.

Supper I nibbled. Then, with a couple of paracetamol, some antibiotics and a lethal emerald green sleeper the shape of a rugby ball, I settled down to a terrible sweat. The bed was soaked right through. At midnight, quite unexpectedly, I found myself bundled into a wheelchair and rushed through the empty corridors to a radiography department, where I was given another X-ray. I lay awake into the small hours, until a nurse arrived with another green rugby ball.

Tuesday

My temperature was very high this morning, so I downed paracetamol and sweated it out for an hour, then piled into a bath.

Everyone working here is kind and efficient. I haven't sorted out who does what, but the nurses wear loose green overalls which look comfortable, none of that Victorian starch and polish. The ward is quiet, everyone talks *sotto voce*; even the TV is kept to a whisper.

The Greek family have an armchair this morning. It is extraordinary how close they all are.

My drug is metroindozol or some such name – that's a good stab at it.

The open ward brings constant surprises: rattle, rattle, rattle – the Canadian runs up and down with his drip trolley as if he is in a supermarket. Everywhere there are helping hands. The doctor says, 'You have not had an AIDS diagnosis, have you?' I say No. I wonder if they will decide this nasty little bug has taken advantage of a damaged immune system.

~

There are curtains round our beds which are drawn and then opened again: like looking through lines of washing, a glimpse here or there. It's ten now and I'm feeling relaxed.

~

When I told the doctor I had not been in hospital before it was not quite true. At the end of a summer term at the age of eleven I came down with good old-fashioned yellow jaundice. After two weeks the summer holidays began and I was put on to an old steam express to York with a lady from the St. John's Ambulance. During the journey I came up with huge heat spots which she desperately dabbed with calomine, getting more and more worried. Summer was spent in York General Hospital, on a strict anti-fat diet. My grandfather came from New Zealand, a delightful elegant old man who looked like Leonard Woolf. I missed most of his visit.

~

A nursing sister comes over, says she is called Dorothy. Is she some sort of religious?

The newspaper man does his rounds – I buy an *Independent*. Then a lady pushing a large wheeled bookcase with novels. What next? Cleaners in emerald green swab down the floors.

I worry about my garden; all the rosemary cuttings I so carefully nurtured will have died. Gerard says he'll go down to Prospect and take the old hospital bed we used in the film – I can't sleep on the floor any longer.

My sister Gaye phones.

The emerald green cleaners have put up a sign with a man in a triangle falling over: it says 'slippery surface'. The kind-looking Canadian is wearing a red and white rugby sweater. The poor Greek man, who coughs so dreadfully, is a jaundiced yellow. He makes me feel unfairly well.

Others in the ward are on drips for diabetes, and one man is strapped to a large oxygen container – a clinical figure from Bosch.

The nurse brings over pepper and salt pots – lunch is on the way. I regret choosing steak and kidney from the menu, for when it came I had great difficulty in stopping myself from vomiting.

After lunch Christopher Hobbs arrived and we talked a little about the film. Then an elderly man came by selling postage stamps.

~

After Christopher has left a nurse comes over and we prepare for a meltdown. I worry that Tilda or other friends might arrive and find a sweating heap.

Sweat.

Jeannie, my doctor, arrives and takes more blood. I'm breathing slightly fast and there is an infection in my chest.

6:40, the man comes round with the *Evening Standard*: Late paper! Late paper! Supper has come and gone, I ate little. Jeannie has left me with a needle in my arm as they may drip antibiotics straight into me tomorrow.

The nurses continue to throw up their hands when they read my temperature. They work in Centigrade so I haven't a clue how high my temperature is. I'm pegging 40°. Gerard has sat here for a couple of hours. Read the *Independent*. It's quiet, there is not a lot to say. He asks me if I'm worried. Not really, just hope I don't find myself blind or debilitated. I'd rather just fade away as Paul did.

Tilda came and sprayed me with her Bluebell perfume.

Wednesday

Sleepless night, lay awake watching the comings and goings in the hushed ward. This morning I completed lung functions, blowing into a machine. It was the other side of the hospital, so I had a long and bumpy ride in a wheelchair.

HB very sad last night – I think I'm going to be here a lot longer than I expected.

Sweet Nene from the Philippines noticed I hadn't got an *Independent* and said she would get me one.

My sister arrived looking wonderful, tanned. She had been visiting her eldest boy – Sam – in Switzerland, where he's learning French washing up in a skiing hotel.

I dozed away after she left, and was then brought up short by new pains. The diarrhoea has started again. I worked out a simple method of stopping it splashing all over the place – by filling the loo with toilet paper. Why haven't I thought of this before?

~

Connie Giannarris came and held my hand. He has a most warm presence, it was unimaginably comforting. My temperature went on up.

Then I had the most unpleasant anal tests with air, and samples taken. I couldn't help whimpering.

~

Paracetamol is the only thing to bring down the temperature.

I sweated away till HB and Peter Cartwright arrived with the film. I don't know if it was my roaring temperature but halfway through I wanted to shut my eyes: all of Simon's second thoughts for the music are less interesting – he's replaced the beautiful and simple piano music that ends the film with a medley. The music is so beautiful I wish he'd leave it alone.

~

Lorraine Hamilton, Sally Potter, and Tilda arrived with masses of beautiful flowers, the most exquisitely scented miniature rose plant. We were all very jolly. Then as the lights went I started another sweat which left me stumbling through the night to the bathroom. Later I sat with the nurses in their lounge, chatting about the light and skies of Scotland.

I dozed – woke sopping wet, had all my bandages adjusted. Shaved. My temperature was normal.

~

I hardly ate anything yesterday, the sight of food makes me nauseous. They still have not tracked down the bug. I float on this kindly support system.

I hope I'm behaving myself – what use to let the dark waves of depression take over?

Mr. Gorbachev has adopted the Sinatra Doctrine. Mine is Doris Day,

Que Será Será, which we hummed through the fifties.

Thursday

I talked for an hour to a lady who is training to be a counsellor about the impact the virus had on me emotionally, about pain and death. As I write this down I cannot remember what I said. The temperature acts like a tape erasure.

~

I'm amazed how I've shrunk. I haven't turned into a little old man; but as I have a bath my bones grind against the enamel, creak ominously. Shaving now is like traversing an unfamiliar terrain, each turn and corner topsy turvy. I still splosh handfuls of hot water at my face to soften the hairs. It is a ritual. I count, for some reason, to 68. I used to say to myself each splosh for a year of life.

~

My mind keeps floating back to Dungeness – how I would love to be putting the seed in the garden. It shouldn't be too late if I get it in by April.

~   *Potter*

Tilda says my conker trees are thriving up at Kimmerhame. My friends gathered here last night brought much joy. To see Sally was wonderful, she has a beautiful sense – or should I say sensibility? Having just finished the Lamb biography – Lytten, Ottoline, Virginia, Stanley – the whole gang spent so much time disliking one another. I hope our time isn't written up that way. Though I have my villains, I don't wish them ill.

~

I dreamt last night of organising a great public concert, Beethoven's Ninth, Jerusalem, etc., to celebrate Margaret Thatcher's downfall. Announcements full page in every paper. A night of joy – what a scandal the eighties have been. I know my choice is fairly conservative, but we could throw in a hymn or two to turn the screw.

My concert would be oversubscribed, and we could use the proceeds to set up a monument, an obelisk telling future generations every shady thing that has happened – the spies, Belgrano, Westland, on and on. For a freer society, not this trampled one. Lay flowers to wipe away the memory of so much mean greed.

~

Jeannie came in, said, 'You look quite low.' Not really, I'm just allowing myself the luxury of feeling dreadful. I'm going to perk up later.

The rose Lorraine brought has a blissful scent. My temperature chart looks like a child's drawing of the jaws of a shark. The sun came out for a second – warmth on the back of my neck.

~

Sally brought me a little book of cigarette cards from Wills: of all the country flowers – most precious.

Spent a blissful evening with HB who helped me through my sweat, and then bathed me.

All the touching brought strength, so late at night I felt totally at peace. He made me scrambled eggs but they were so rich I couldn't swallow them – like that second piece of cake you know you shouldn't have.

HB, love.

~

Earlier Tony Pinching, my doctor, gave me great confidence. He has a clarity of speech which puts me at ease. He told me they would do lung tests – the bowel tests are back tomorrow; that I had developed thrush in my throat because of the antibiotics. I'm in such good hands here. Try to make all this an adventure.

Swimming with sweat – *I Know Where I'm Going*. A landscape trickling rills, splash drip, perhaps more a dark cavern, stalagmites and stalactites, drip drip drip. The sheets are changed again.

Friday

I'm feeling much clearer this morning, planting the garden in my mind, sowing fennel and calendula. The sweat-down has brought my temperature back to 36°. I potter about slowly.

Somehow the low temperature has brought the weakness home.

I told HB last night about my grandmother. After my grandfather died – it had been a long illness – she moved out of her home, Manor Cottage, which she could no longer afford, into a dull thirties flat block on the main road alongside the Metropolitan railway line in Northwood. You had to climb five flights of greenish composite stairs which stank of Jeyes' fluid, continuously mopped by 'Mary of the stairs'; who I remember as a dark silence.

Inside, Moselle's flat had three small rooms, a kitchen and a bathroom, the hall mysteriously dark with Grandfather's black marble clock in the shape of a temple, ticking away.

My grandmother was small and rather plump, wore twin sets in pale blue with a string of pearls. She had lovely fuzzy grey hair.

During those war years Mrs. Peachy came in to help – small, slight, her hair done in a bun.

Peachy and Gran formed a duo: Peachy dusted and broke the little jade pigs, the ivory tiger, the three wise monkeys on the mantelpiece – arguing all the time. Gran stuck them together with Secotine, which looked like toffee. Peachy and Gran, dusting and breaking, throwing the peach satin table cloth over the dining table that stood in the hall, polishing the silver cruet with its sapphire glass.

Dry between your toes, Decky, or they'll fall off.

Gran looked after me when I fell ill for the first time, with an inflamed ear drum – hot milk with a tablespoonful of brandy to put me to sleep. The doctor came, etherised me, and drained the ear.

I sat on the balcony and watched the trains pass, observed by a large ceramic frog. Peachy had a feather duster – another disaster: the jade pig had its leg shortened so it wobbled.

Many years later Peachy visited us with her son, who had become a wealthy man in Australia. Ninety years old she brought her Decky a vine. We sat in the garden for a glorious afternoon while she reminisced, and talked about how much she missed Moselle. 'Oh Miss Betty' – she and my mother were off down memory lane.

~

Lunch came. Deeply hungry but so food shy. I ate more than I have since I came here. This night HB saved me – mopped my brow, bathed me with such tenderness, and we wept a little. Late in the night he left me in peace.

~

Fascinating conversation with the doctor about my chest. She asked me if I'd had any chest problems as a child. I didn't think so; but as the conversation continued I remembered my asthma, which became so bad one summer Gran took me to Eastbourne for the fresh air for ten days, a holiday spent without my parents. And then there were the bouts of hayfever that ended with a lengthy course of injections when I was fifteen.

When the nurses came to change my sheets I suggested they took all the flowers away from the windowsill – Gran never allowed flowers near the sick, said they ate up the oxygen.

They had just made the bed and were removing the first vase when it caught and pulled another over, soaking the bed – we all collapsed in hysterical laughter.

Maybe this is an allergy – all the flowers have gone.

Jon came and we spent a pleasant half-hour.

MODERN NATURE

Saturday

I've called my bug General Jaruzelski. The general gave me four bouts of the shits like explosions (Russian tanks). Then, since Citizen Antibiotic had gone on holiday, I did my sweats; but the temperature rose instead of falling. I panicked a little and asked if I could see Dr. Jeannie. She put me on a saline drip.

At 10:00 at night, Kim, Hilary, and Dr. Jeannie, working with precision, wired me up. Cool water flowed up my arm. By 2:00 my temperature was normal, cool. The General retreated to my gut.

I do not sleep at night, just doze and dream of *Edward II*.

~

This morning I awoke clear-headed. Have we succeeded? I was unplugged, took a bath, and shaved at snail's pace and with the precision of a soldier. My sister Gaye came bearing live yoghourt. HB brought me devil's pyjamas, Tilda the blue of the sky. I'm only half devil this morning as I have a white T-shirt on above the Prussian blue and carmine jimjams.

HB lay at my bedside till midnight, gave me a regimental bath.

Sunday

Clocks go back, but time here flows. Coping with these temperatures I'm becoming something of a juggler, morning and night. I bring it down with three aspirins, and as the sweat splashes and trickles I pretend I'm in Fairlight, in a beautiful bluebell wood on the cliffside beyond Winchelsea, dancing splashing streams under huge old trees, moss and a myriad of wild flowers.

~

During this week I have explored my body and have become acquainted with it for the first time in my life. I have learnt to relax every muscle so that nothing is stressful.

Today I can say I am in control of the General, although he still keeps pushing up to 39°+. I'm eating little, but I *am* eating; and my sister's live yoghourt has settled my stomach.

All in all I'm in good shape. The immense love of all my friends and their good tips keep me smiling.

Tina, who changed my bandages this morning, comes from Folkestone and knows Dungeness well.

Monday

Dream journey. At noon I was taken off for a bronchoscopy. Sat bolt upright on a bed; an anaesthetic liquid, pink and tasting of stale beer, was in-
haled into each nostril and down the throat. The numbing effect was instantaneous. Then I was given a series of small injections, valium and a
sleeper, not to put me out but to relax me. The probe was put through my
nose – everyone had made such a fuss I was expecting the worst. In fact it
was just a strange tickle in a place you would not expect.

There was a second eyepiece so I was able to watch the whole event. How
amazing to be able look into one's own lungs, twisting and turning through
the passages; all the time more numbing fluid was squirted down, so bubbles gurgled past. Then the doctor said, If you look now you will see your
heart beating. And there it was pumping away. I wish it had gone on longer.

A comatose afternoon. I really don't like mind-bending drugs, so it was a
great relief when the valium wore off in the evening.

HB came and we had a warm sweet time. Spirits up.

Tuesday

The ward is run with panache, friendly, completely informal. If you decide
you don't want to do something no-one puts any pressure on you. All
smiles, laughs and intimacies.

I'm very weak, write at a snail's pace. Every perception heightened. I
notice the bubbles in the water as I wash my hair, they are hallucinatory.
Food also – cornflakes, yoghourt; and some blueberries, which I ate individually they were so delicious.

People come and go rapidly. They still haven't found out the cause of all
this, the tests have come back negative so far. The antibiotic has slowly
brought my temperature down: I'm now peaking at 38° rather than 40°.

I organise two sweats a day with aspirin on an empty stomach. The last
two brought me down to 36°. The bed is awash but I've decided to enjoy
them rather than fear them. It's like deciding to enjoy the rain rather than
scurrying into a shelter.

Wednesday

After a hard sweat in the small hours and a bath my temperature is back to
normal. Today is the day of the ultrasound scan – so no food or drink.
There is a sign above my bed, NIL BY MOUTH.

I'm like a harlequin, HB has bought me so many pairs of bright coloured
pyjamas. Today I'm dark blue-green. Yesterday pale pink and blue stripes;
he says there are more on the way.

I managed to read the paper through from beginning to end. Continue to settle.

NIL BY MOUTH. Starved morning.

Lynn arrived happy and smiling, glad to be in London. She's here with her children for a week, brought me some beautiful hyacinths.

The ultrasound scanner is passed over your body after a liberal sloshing of KY jelly, so the probe slips about and lo and behold a picture appears of your spleen and liver. The doctor seemed very engrossed in his work, so I did not talk to him.

Back in the ward, I lay propped with pillows as my temperature climbed. Now 39°, I boiled up for my evening delirium. At 8:00 we began the sweat-down with the three aspirin. HB held my hand. Then we had our bath, most relaxing; so that at 11:00, when he left, I felt human again.

The doctors laugh when I say this illness is psychosomatic, but I'm certain the letter from Moyra was the trigger for all this. She revealed Dad's extremely violent behaviour: force-feeding me at four – screaming, shouting, thumping me, and even once throwing me out of the window, with Mum protesting ashen-faced: 'That's enough Lance.' Now I see why I spent so much time with Gran. Anything to break the pattern.

I've had a dodgy stomach all my life: it's been tested, nothing wrong there. Working so hard in Poland and back here the breakdown occurs. This time it's worse – is it an abscess?

The wound opened by Moyra's letter: I see the past more clearly. Before all of this had been suppressed, no memory at all. I told this story to Ewan, the young Scots doctor. He said it is a probability.

Thursday

Richard Salmon visited. We had a long and very pleasant chat, which cheered me up. He brought me a bundle of magazines and left with a smile. I sat quietly and waited for my temperature to climb. By seven it was 39°+.

Tony Pinching came and brought great news, though no solutions yet. He said the illness was not HIV related – the ultrasound scans are still being interpreted.

HB here, lovely evening, sweats, baths, and cuddles.

Friday

My day was made by an unexpected visit from Terence Davies. He told very funny stories for twenty minutes, said raising money for his new film was like kicking a football in treacle.

My temperature soared. Matthew and Andy came; then my sweatdown started, which was so violent when it had finished I had to have help walking. Hands shaking in a palsy, shaving increasingly difficult. I can't calculate where the razor is going to land.

MARCH

~

Today is the anniversary of my parents' wedding. How should I recall them? The relief I felt when they were gone, buried, and could no longer pry? That they remained like an echo in the silence of my privacy, though long dead? I could write of them with sympathy, forget to tell you that my heart danced on their last breath. The past retains its privacy, it is always misrepresented, no eyes can see past the grave. What I write of them now is a self-portrait.

~

The bungalow in which he had the stroke that killed him was called Merryfield – the second home of that name. My mother sewed the net curtains; behind them was no history. My father took my mother's ashes from the crematorium and hid them. Did the carpets and chairs come from mail order? The pictures from the gift shop? The pistols, sextants, barometers – all seemed to have escaped use. The tables and chairs seemed unrelated, random; the garden unplanted.

The door chimes echoed across the shipping forecast; Dogger, Heligoland, cold grey waves. My father came to the door tanned, athletic, in shorts and running vest, nearly eighty, In a year his mortal dust would cross the world in a registered envelope to his childhood home.

As I packed up his house I half expected to find my mother's ashes in his bedroom, but if they were there I missed them and put them out with the huge pile of rubbish for the refuse man. Maybe he had scattered them. My father's house had many secrets.

~

My father flew his Wellington bomber straight as a die through the war, never avoiding the flak. He terrified his crews – my father often terrorised those nearest him. He climbed mountains, boxed and sailed for the RAF; late in life he exhausted young seamen whom he examined for the Master Mariner's Certificate. World-weary he taught astro-navigation at the City Poly. Bowler hatted, he clutched a tightly furled umbrella which was never opened – even in a thunderstorm.

As a young man, in 1928, he had sailed from his home in New Zealand, two hundred gold sovereigns in a money belt to seek a new life in the Old World. On the night he arrived London was shrouded in fog; he slept at Toc. H in Kennington.

For the next ten years he lived the life of a young RAF officer; he had his own plane, fast cars; he disliked Lawrence of Arabia; befriended Syrie Maugham, designed for her; played the piano; took excellent photographs and film – in the Middle East he used this talent to record inaccessible ancient ruins for the Archaeological Society; in Kenya he kept a leopard.

In the sad postwar married quarters daubed with fading camouflage on windy, desolate airfields – more desolate and alien than any council estate – the glamour faded. My mother whom he married in 1940 'in high hopes', their photo on many national newspapers 'this windy March day', laughed through it all.

At four he threw me through a window and the arguments grew terrible. They remained like that throughout my childhood.

Conversation died. Into the vacuum came the TV and the weather forecast which was watched in a dread silence. Each free moment he sailed his firefly on the Welsh Harp. The colder the day the happier he seemed.

We travelled before this: 1946, in Rome; '47, Cambridge; '48, Abingdon; '49, Long Hamborough; '50–51, Kidlington; '52, Yorkshire; '53, Somerset; '54, Pakistan, Karachi. Inventories, broken crockery, no possessions except the stamp album that travelled easily.

As my mother and I sailed through the Suez Canal – was it the last boat? We knew we would not see him at our journey's end because he was watching H-bombs explode in Nevada. The silence set in from this moment. We communicated only to find the other's whereabouts.

~

In 1960 I left school for King's College in the Strand, and then after graduating with a degree in History, Art History and English Literature I took the Diploma in Fine Art at the Slade. I visited home less frequently; my mother was diagnosed with cancer and the first operation was successful, but for the next eighteen years she became increasingly invalided until her death in 1978.

My father watched over her, counting the apples for his daily apple pie. We returned home to be recorded in increasingly regimented photos – at attention, hair carefully combed.

He mowed the lawn in straight lines, cursing any tree or plant that destroyed the grid of his prison. Afterwards he drove me back to London at 45mph – no slower, no faster. He cursed any motorist who broke the rhythm. On the motorway he was a snail, in Regent Street a hog.

He drove and sailed to win, his moustache, which covered a small scar, gave him a fearsome look. He never spoke of the past – it was closed off from us.

In 1978 he moved to Lymington in Hampshire. There he lived alone in an ugly red brick bungalow called Merryfield for the next eight years, until his death. I visited him there only once. His first words on meeting me at the station were 'When are you going back?' He allowed me only briefly in the house, then brewed me a cup of tea which we drank on the lawn before going to the local for lunch.

'Good afternoon, Air Commodore, how are you keeping?' My father glanced at the menu through his monocle, watched me eating, then put me back on the train to London.

The next time I saw him he said proudly, 'Derek has never asked me for anything.'

On the night he was to die my sister and I were packing up his home when the telephone rang unexpectedly calling us to his bedside. He had been in Southampton General for several months after the stroke that paralysed him but left him smiling for the first time I could remember. Was it the relief of one who had never allowed anyone near him? Suddenly dependent for his every need?

The hushed reception at the nursing home, the dash up the stairs to see him, unconscious, should I speak to him? No it was far too late, and the slightest emotion would have been a melodrama. There had been no language for the emotions in this suburb and now it was too late to invent one.

Downstairs we organised the funeral arrangements with a woman at the desk who could hardly disguise her distaste at the speed with which this was done, and the way my sister and I had left the deathbed to others.

~

On my twenty-first birthday my father presented the account, my school report and bills, the cost of an education to make me 'an Englishman'. I had been brought up in the very tradition that had ridiculed its colonials. Accent? My father lost his with his youth in the fight to save the Old Country – the first bombing mission of the war – DFC with bar.

My father, though, believed his inferiority so he raced to win and win again. The hundreds of silver and pewter trophies brought no satisfaction, were put into the dark cupboard under the stairs. And then there was the attic – why not take what had been taken from one? My father 'collected' antiques and sold them at Phillips – at profit; but unlike yours my father's collecting was clandestine. No money changed hands, he stole, and stole from his friends and relatives. Anything that glittered or was loved.

My mother's engagement ring.

My sister's wedding presents.

His grandchildren's toys.

Merryfield was a mayhem, its net curtains hid great disorder: bottles of whisky; chocolates; toilet paper; all supermarket-high spilled from cupboards and drawers, enough to make you laugh and cry, and it was for this that I came to love my father.

The never-ending boredom of Northwood was the only certainty of my adolescence. In this suburb of a great city there was not the echo of one shout from the angry young men. Only the spluttering lawn mowers, the sound of sprinklers on a summer's evening.

The sun had set on the vain imperial ambition that had built these homes around the Château de Madrid – now NATO's nuclear HQ where my father's friends tinkered with the Button and watched the oblivion digits.

Sore ankles from an adventure, ice skating to Strauss in Wembley was the furthest we strayed; held in check by a lack of knowledge that was not dispelled by the 'O' and 'A' levels we acquired late in August. *Bilko* and *Lucy* on TV, *The Dambusters* at the Esoldo – the soma for which his generation had died.

~

My mother loved flowers, but had no interest in gardening; her favourites were lily of the valley – which she carried in her wedding bouquet; and the herb pennyroyal – after which she nearly named her one home, deciding instead on Merryfield after the airfield in Somerset which she remembered as a happier place and time.

Merryfield was built in an old orchard. I planted pennyroyal under the trees and it spread through the lawn. My mother carpeted her open plan house from wall to wall and covered the sofas with cabbage rose chintz that the neighbours admired and envied. She dusted the shiny French polish of the reproduction furniture ceaselessly.

During my mother's lifetime the house was uncomfortably empty. There were no books – they were too heavy to pack – though my mother belonged to the Boots lending library. There were two paintings: an oil of an ice-blue empty sea, and a corner of the Palace of the Knights of Malta in Salita del Grillo – both brought back from Rome. We had no gramophone, and no television until well after all our friends, I hardly remembered a radio. At Christmas we went to a few pantomimes, saw *High Hazel* in Oxford, and several musicals: *Salad Days* and *Hernandos' Hideaway* were favourites.

My mother's friends talked little. Hen parties, then husband's jobs, marriage, no death – no-one died in Northwood, though the cemetery stretched over the hill. The hair salon, the perm, and clothes – my mother made hers on a Singer, she was always in vogue, and would wear the mink coat/stole with the tails of the little beasts hanging off, looking uneasy. My mother was always friendly and welcoming – a spare place could always be found at lunch – two, three. We quarrelled over washing up. My mother said, 'It is a pity you and your sister haven't inherited our good looks. She was practical and untouched by the racialism and snobbism of fifties surburbia. She had been born in Calcutta. She would tell you she had everything she had ever wished for and I believed her. She kept up appearances in all the years of her cancer – never a shadow crossed her face – ever-smiling Betty.

Now sometimes it occurs to me that the smile and charm was the disaster of her time and class – putting on a good face – then it seemed heroic.

To me my mother's marriage was happy, I never remember my parents quarrelling, my arguments with my father the only shadow, but perhaps they broke the monotony of the packing and unpacking, the inventories, the occasional 'do' in mess kit and evening dress. Most of the time my sister and I were at boarding school.

Northwood was without drama, pickled in its well-heeled selfishness. My mother was full of life, but for the life of me I don't know how she survived this world. As a young girl she had spent time at Harrow art school, worked for the couturier Norman Hartnell – against my grandparents' wishes. She met my father – her first boyfriend – at a dance in RAF Northholt. Marriage, children, the war. After that she cooked and washed, washed and cooked, and watched my father go to work, until she fell ill.

My mother was much loved by all who met her, acquired a serenity and wisdom she would say was the gift of her pills. Her condition never shocked her. She smiled on her deathbed.

Saturday

To my surprise I slept the night and my temperature was 37°; so I was let off the morning sweatdown. Anything to break the monotony.

They still haven't found the source of my infection but I'm having further tests on Monday. The nurses, Gerald and Shaun, have treated me with such gentleness.

This afternoon Neil Tennant, Lynn Hanke, Mike and Jane O'Pray all arrived at once. We had a wild half an hour with Neil at his best. He 'performed' Grace Jones in the process of public auto-destruction. Since she was a total fabrication and didn't really exist it seemed quite logical. He's off to Germany to record, gave me a beautiful Simeon Solomon book. Lynn sadly goes back to America.

My temperature rose and Gerard arrived at 7:30 to hold my hand.

~

As I lay here I heard someone singing a deep, quiet, comforting song, it came and went like a will o' the wisp. I called the nurse and asked her who was singing, 'Mildred the cleaning lady.' So, drenched with sweat, I opened the curtains a fraction to hear better. When she passed by I called out to her and she came in; I said 'Your song is wonderful' and she smiled. She said the spiritual was called *Spirit of the Living God*; she placed her hands on me and very quietly, with a voice of great beauty, sung to me. It was the most moving moment, I couldn't hold back the tears. She smiled, blessed me and carried on with her round.

Calls from HB, he's walled up in Charing Cross Road by the poll tax march, which is a mayhem. Two friends had sought refuge in the flat. Hours later, when he arrived, he described the chaos: every shop window on the road had been smashed and looted, all the rubbish bins set on fire. The most extraordinary sight was the music shop, where a constant stream of guitars were handed out like a giant caterpillar which wove along the road.

APRIL

Sunday 1

I was woken by the newspaper man. HB never materialised – I thought he was definitely coming this morning. Mind in delirium.

I asked Geraldine if she would phone to see if he had been pulled over last night. The police would give no information. Now worried I lay in the bed and talked to him very quietly for five minutes. Where are you? I love you dearly, and suddenly the phone rang, he had heard.

At 3:30 Lynn Hanke, my sweet American friend, who was showing her five and six year old children the bright lights of Leicester Square, became aware of the riot. She grabbed a taxi and it was immediately surrounded by a gang who attempted to turn it over. Riot police rushed in, they turned away to deal with some other rioters. Immediately the gang closed in again, but they managed to escape. What a way to spend the last day of a holiday.

The looting in Charing Cross Road was remarkably organised – none of the book shops, including my friend Ian Shipley's, had their windows stoved in. The car showrooms were not so fortunate; neither were Foyle's – because of Christina's right-wing views – music shops, jewellers' and banks.

~

Very tired and weak.

Monday

The move to a new ward took up the whole day. Every single item, fridges, lockers, bed, all the paraphernalia, hauled up in an already crowded lift – all this made me forget the unhappiness I felt when I heard my scan was not till Tuesday. I'm in a bright airy room with a view south over London, to the Albert Hall. The sudden privacy is a relief.

~

Chaos on the film front. James tells me nothing, invites people to shoot the missing sequences without any communication.

The day swallowed by the move, I'm swallowed by my temperature. So many of the patients look desperately ill and sad, the helplessness and despair in their faces. One young man choking himself to death in the lift and there was nothing I could do to help, if only just to hold his shaking hand. No-one invades the other's privacy, so communication is a 'Good morning Bill, feeling better?' – not much more; perhaps a short conversation.

I fell asleep, was woken by the nurse, I didn't recognise Peter Logan, one of my dearest friends – called him Keith. We were at the Slade together. He said he was worried – I looked so ill asleep.

We gossiped of things past – the visits cheer me up. At 7:30 Gerard came and held my hand as I went into my sweat. HB arrived and they bathed me; a competition developed – who was the best at toes? They decided I had all I deserved: two handsome men towelling me down. No Roman Emperor had it so good.

Tuesday

Scan day. Last night I slept in a bath of sweat – the sheets had to be changed three times. The result: this morning I'm tottering, almost unable to walk, grasping at the furniture to get about the room.

~

Extraordinary turnabout. My temperature has remained below normal all day. I lay in a trance, and images flowed through my mind: leopards, waves, stars. I thought I could get in touch with my mother, so I talked to her. It must have to go a long way, I haven't met up yet. I remembered her very beautiful face in all the stages of her life, always smiling Betty.

Andrew Logan brought me his sculpture 'Guru', a shell in shining gold and blue glass; sitting at the base, a little Mickey Mouse made from a piece of cactus he found. It made the day – next to the bed with the light illuminating it.

Wednesday

I am out of sync. I had a terrible shock this morning when I discovered that I had muddled the days so much that I missed my scan. Worst day of my illness. Very depressed I awoke with a temperature 1° below normal and freezing shivers for nearly three hours (this happened today . . . no, I think yesterday . . . no, it's today).

My temperature shot up to 40°, so I was burning hot, couldn't eat; and when Jeannie came in she gave me such a shock that I spilt my orange juice all over myself, my hand was shaking so much. She told me to calm down, said everything was under control.

When HB arrived in the evening he brought me out of my depression. I'm so confused by what has happened that I've forgotten whether it was today or yesterday. But in fact it was today.

I'm suffering from a confusion in time. When people arrive, I'm focused and can talk quite coherently. I'm not stumbling over words, although I've forgotten a few names.

~

At 2 o'clock Richard Salmon and Christopher Hobbs arrived. Richard talked to me about cataloguing my paintings; I told him to get in touch with my lawyer so that a codicil can be put in my will which gives him sole right to deal with them.

Christopher shot the Deposition with HB and Johnny on the coldest day of the year. They were very good about it – he covered them up whenever he could. He had made a storyboard, which he stuck to. Everything was shot on a tripod. He had a polaroid, which looked very beautiful. He was very excited as this was the first time he had been behind the camera. He said he was longing to see the results.

Richard went to the shops and bought me six bottles of Evian water – I'm drinking gallons of it, I'm always thirsty.

They left and a doctor arrived and gave me a thorough run down. He said 'We are narrowing the field, we'll see what the scan shows tomorrow. We saw two strange bugs in an early sample. They might be a form of TB. I think we're going to treat you without waiting for results because the cultures take up to eight weeks to develop, it's very slow.'

Tilda arrived in the middle of a funny Spike Jones show from the fifties. We sat and watched it. She says that Khrushchev and Chekhov, the two conker trees, are looking stickier than ever.

Thursday

I was woken up very early and taken to CTS: a large white plastic arch through which you slowly travel as the whole of your stomach is imaged. A voice says 'Breath in', 'Breath out', 'Stop breathing', 'Breath normally'.

A fire alarm went off as the scan came to an end, and I was rushed up some stairs and on to the street, where someone brought me a chair. We sat for ten minutes in beautiful sunlight. It was a false alarm.

At about 3:30 Virginia Bottomley, the junior health minister, made a visit. I told her how I had been here for three weeks and that the CT scan had originally been set for April 18, but because I was very ill they had managed to do it within 8 days, still a long time. This hospital is starved of funds. She said that in dealing with a huge organisation like the NHS there were bound to be grey areas. She assured me the government had put billions into the health service, that they were rebuilding hospitals on the outskirts of London and demolishing the older, central London hospitals.

I feel terrible. The drugs they have given me for the CTS stopped me up.

To bring my temperature down I took some aspirin, but it didn't work.

At eight Tony Pinching came on his weekly round. He said, 'You have TB of the stomach which has probably been with you for years.' It was the very best news. Relieved that I am starting treatment tomorrow. I am very ill. I took more aspirins. At 10:15 HB arrived and bathed me. I am so exhausted. I am dictating, HB is writing it down.

Friday

I woke this morning feeling relaxed. I could hardly wait for the first pills to bomb the TB, imagining comic-strip warfare – Zap, Biff, Crash, Splat.

My doctor arrived and set me up for my liver biopsy. He gave me a local anaesthetic and then plunged two fine probes into my liver. Everyone had said that this was going to hurt, but I hardly felt anything.

After it was over I had to lie on my side motionless for four hours. By the time I turned over I was a frozen statue. I had to lie on my back for two hours and then the pills arrived. Imagine the joy after all these weeks. Down they went and immediately I started to feel better; it was great to know the TB had been targeted. I'm certain my temperature didn't rise because of the pills. It's 37.7° – no horrible sweats tonight.

At 7pm a lady arrived and put a tube down my nose into my stomach. The chief reaction was one of tickling. She said I was the best patient she had ever had. Now I'm waiting for the X-ray people, who are going to see if it's in the right place.

~

Jeff, Steven, and Terence Davies arrived – we had a lively old time. Terence said that Mr. Greenaway had said there were only two auteurs in England and he was one of them. Why, wondered Terence, does everyone in the film world treat everything like competition.

After they left Richard Heslop arrived and described the riot. Richard, without fear, climbed the scaffolding on Grand Buildings until someone shouted, 'We've set it on fire.' There, a young boy of fifteen threw an enormous lump of concrete on to the police below. It was a miracle that no-one was killed. The most poignant moment was the man who dresses as Charlie Chaplin weeping in front of a burning car. 'Why are you doing this?' he said. 'Please stop.'

Saturday

Temperature 36°! Slept! Pills come! Swallow like lightning. The food flowing down the drip tube looks like coffee. Feel happy. TB, madness, old-fashioned, lady of the camellias. Must go to the opera. The bugs are zapped. Stomach has disappeared.

Writing nearly legible – still can't read yet. Print floats about. I can't remember what's gone before. I've became a TV addict – it's so disconnected I'm on the same wavelength.

Jean Marc Prouveur, who I lived with many years ago and who I haven't seen for years, came through the door; for a moment I didn't recognise him. Reminisced for three hours. Amazing, after all these years so much to talk about. We exchanged addresses and are going to meet as soon as this is in order.

Can't eat, have to swallow each mouthful with water to bring the whole enterprise to an end before the first gag. I'm about 9 stone – I was much too fat at 11 stone 5.

The doctors are worried about my weight, say I can't leave looking like a skeleton.

I will be here another three weeks. This makes me happy, I've grown used to all this pampering and long night chats with nurses, everyone telling each other their deepest secrets.

Grand National: lost myself in the race.

Spencer Leigh arrived and we sat and talked for most of the afternoon. Spencer has just returned from NYC, says it's more expensive. He spent his time at the latest movies, brought me some of Mark McCormack's badges: 'May Peace Prevail On Earth'.

I've missed the beginning of spring. Used to the shadows, my eyes cannot adjust to light. I have planned the garden in detail, won't be out too late to plant the summer seeds – I've started the change to the wild plants that grow in Dungeness: cabbages, fennel, valerian, daisy.

Sunday

Liam and Seamus visited. I described the frightful journey to Gibraltar when I was 15.

My father announced that I could go on holiday to Gibraltar if I put on an RAF uniform and became the batman to some air-marshal (he died only a week ago).

I put on my cadet uniform and we boarded the Dakota at Bovington – I was set at the controls of the plane and told to aim South. We crossed Europe. When we got to the Rock my Father put me in barracks with the eighteen year olds doing National Service – who were extremely curious about this fifteen year old. It was terrifying.

In the evening he returned and took me to meet a Group Captain Reville, who had a ridiculous RAF moustache. We drove to dinner in Spain – ham and dry white sherry. The unspeakable Reville talked endlessly of matadors and bulls.

The Dakota flew back to England leaving me behind for six frightening days. Shy as a mouse I experienced terrible displacement and fear.

~

HB arrived last night and showed me the new rushes. I was quite amazed by them. HB and Peter had said they were terrible, but was wrong. The footage at Dungeness of him and Johnny were some of the most beautiful of the whole film, though sadly out of focus.

~

I went to sleep, my temperature still normal. Very happy.

Sunday

Awoke early, at 5:30. Feeling tense. Tina came and unplugged me from my food and water drips, which was quite a palaver. I was able to have my first shave, and a bath. Tina said the TB was quite a long haul and I might expect my temperature to go up again. I have ten weeks of pills ahead of me. You can't imagine the amount I swallowed this morning – must have been nearly twenty. When breakfast arrived I said I'd already had it!

In the afternoon Tilda arrived and spent an hour giving my feet a reflex massage. I hardly noticed she was doing it. HB came, looking tired; long cuddle up and half the dose of sleeping pills. At 12:30 woke after a small sweat. Poor sopping yellow jimjams. I hardly slept the rest of the night. Lay dozing.

Monday

Much better this morning, though the pills make me sick. The doctor said, 'Let's take you off some of these poisons.'

My sister came. Unplugged, shaved and bathed. I've put on at least three pounds – they've upped the dose of the drip to 90. Ate lunch quite heartily. I can't read the Jackson Pollock book because it rests too heavy on the chest.

~

Tilda here for massage with Jo. Slept soundly, feet came alive, too alive, ouch!

Tuesday

Peeing and water consumption back to near normal. The pills make me nauseous. I have to swallow them at 7:30.

Watch the early news, breakfast. Unhook from my feeding machine (which goes through my nose) to shave and have a bath. Stronger today, appetite coming back. I can concentrate on reading.

Picked up the Pollock book, then wrote 20 notes on hospital paper in reply to the last three weeks' mail. Jean Marc arrived looking handsome and relaxed. He's off to Italy tomorrow. It's really wonderful to make contact again after all these years. I asked him how old he was, 33. Much smiling.

Lunch: soup, salad, and roll mops, semolina pudding and fruit juice. Back to the TV and Pollock.

All seem happy with my progress – it's only now I realise what a delirium I have been in for the last five weeks, no sense of time. This diary gives the wrong impression, it's much too focused. I'm emerging from a strange dream.

Today time seems to have some measure of form. Late in the afternoon Nico and Tilda arrived – Nico with the most enormous bowl of fruit and a smoked salmon. The drip-feed is out and I'm feeling hungry again. Food has been the true nightmare of these weeks. Today I managed to get some down.

My pee is bright yellow from the drugs and I hop on to the commode in bursts. Still have persistent diarrhoea. Linda the aromatherapist came and massaged me with oil of vervain. I slept during the session – the first time I have had a massage. Relaxed I climbed back into bed. Lights out, reconnected to my feeding through the nose. I attempted to masturbate – absolutely no come!

Rather restless night with fleeting fevers, though my temperature is still quite normal.

Wednesday

Pills at six, watch early TV. Bowel trouble in the early morning, up five times. At 8:00, breakfast; then detached from my drip-feed through the nose – it's like being tethered. And another day begins.

The morning speeds by, the doctor arrives: you can leave on Monday if you wish. Plans, plans, so many plans: everything is going to change – clear the flat, send papers to the National Film Archive. Give paintings to AIDS charities, rearrange Prospect's filled bookshelves. Clear Phoenix House entirely – get rid of everything, no more clutter, start painting, get *Edward II* underway. Plant the garden.

I'm going to be on these pills ten months. The infection is in the liver and the lymph nodes; then I'll be on the anti-TB for the rest of my life. They are happy here with my recovery. I am eating! Dropped a thousand black peppercorns over the floor – the pepper pot lid was loose. The days still seem to hallucinate – maybe it's the drugs. My weight's up, I'm now 9'10 from 9'4 in a week. The doctor says to put on another stone. Everything is to change – I'm to spend the next three months quietly getting everyone else to do the work, like a pasha.

12:30. Peed standing up – the first time since I came here!

Nibbling fruit.

3:30. Got myself unhooked, no more tubes. Yolanda Sonnabend came with perfect garden flowers. Made myself sick on Nico's smoked salmon, ate and ate. Stomach settling.

Thursday

Eyes tested. One of the drugs I'm taking can make you go blind. Everything OK. I'm on the drug for another three weeks. Beware, first the world turns monochrome – it's reversible, thank heavens.

Walked out in the street. The eye drops turned the view psychedelic. People staring, workmen joking, my dream state. In sun I hardly see.

Back, bath.

Food still a slight problem.

I had a very restless night, plans drifting.

Ken came, magazines.

The Jackson Pollock book is a feast, but too heavy for a hospital bed. It makes my arms ache.

Andrew brings garlic, hey ho bugs away. Then Spring and Robert arrive.

I'm out on Monday. Slept much better, though my feet are paralysed with pain from Tilda's massage, and I have very inflamed patches. HB here late in the evening. I was dog tired.

Friday

Up at six, made my own breakfast; dressed in trousers and sweater I walked in the rain and cold to find a newspaper.

Thin as a rake, tottering along the street, I must have looked a sight.

~

Blinded by weeks of TV – even investigative programmes skate over the surface. Dull and endlessly repetitive news and adverts.

Still have a terrible stomach, burning and boiling away. Everything else is in order today. I can eat, though the food is torture.

Dickie's coming to take me for a drive. My eyes are shining; but the bed sores are real sore, itchy and inflamed.

Easter.

Planning the home revolution.

~

Prospect Cottage is the last of a long line of 'escape houses' I started building as a child at the end of the garden: grass houses of fragrant mowings that slowly turned brown and sour; sandcastles; a turf hut, hardly big enough to turn around in; another of scrap metal and twigs, marooned on ice-flooded fields – stomping across brittle ice.

Ice flowers left out overnight in glasses, chrysanthemums suspended in frozen water – pink with cold.

~

Long wet afternoons with my cacti, building crystal gardens with a chemistry set, and floating paper fish in the bath which I then stuck all over the bathroom wall.

Long afternoons in Watford, returning from the junk shop, with a stamp, a book, or a small drawing. There the ancient Punch-like proprietress would flutter about with quiet gentility, myopic and frosted white as a sheet.

Back on the bus past the gasworks and the old waterworks with their fading camouflage in the sunset.

I lost the stamp album, gave the cacti away.

Ice skating in Wembley and weekend drives, with my father in a bad mood. Salad days. Evenings wandering in the garden, making large charcoal drawings of the blossoms, or a painting of Armageddon like a Romanesque tympanum, full of writhing figures.

No sex thoughts – vague girlfriends. Oh the boredom of it all. Only the flowers, the gentians and the blessed sempervivums.

~

Holidays at Seaview, worse sorrow. The swimming was OK but the rest – sitting around with strange suntanned yachtspersons, tedious visits to Blackgang Chine, where I once saw a viper. RAF Vampires low over the house – a pilot turned his plane over and crashed into the sea.

Shooting rabbits by car headlights late at night on the runways.

Shooting crows with an airgun – I regret this terribly. Brought down two.

Tonsils out at RAF Halton in a ward of limbless casualties from Korea.

~

In Pakistan the garden turned *fauve*, purples and scarlets of bougainvillaea; large butterflies, scarlet and black swallowtails. I collected butterflies, until one night an army of ants swallowed them together with a stuffed peacock the bearer brought from the North. The last wing disappeared across the floor. Late at night watching the turtles throwing up plumes of spray as they lumbered through the rollers. No pets – my father hated dogs; though I had a tortoise, which soon died.

I painted, but could not read. Shy, reclusive, with a few close pals, very close, no sex.

Fifties' cinema shows, the TV Coronation, Skylon, open plan, pastel, Atomic gadgets in the kitchen.

Dad watched the bomb in Nevada. We sat at home watching *I Love*

Lucy. Dick Barton, Beyond Our Ken – bona eek.

~

Back at that flat I cleared the paintings with Richard.

Saturday

Childhood flowers, dew-bowed peonies, dark red, along the paths at Curry Malet. The ivy stencil veins of the crocus purple and white, stamens yellow for painting. The buddleia covered with tortoiseshell butterflies, peacock and humming-bird hawks. Purple mulberry – should you eat it? Scarlet geraniums, jasmine, scent of the night stock, *Aloe variegata*, the camellia – exotic in February; wisteria on old stone walls, wallflowers – wild and draught-defying – balsam poplars brown purple; celandine with yellow brimstone flashing across the lawn.

Dried chincherinchees sent across the world to bloom at Christmas. Güta, the Christmas tree ablaze with candles. Petunias, stock, lupins in school gardens – mysterious spires. Privet and lime. Moth-hunting in the bathroom deep in the night: ermine and emerald. Drinkers; mysterious hawk moths; the multicoloured lackey; puss moth caterpillars on the cliffside with forked devil's tails; goat moths thick as your finger; all the wild meadows now long vanished.

Syringa in the vases. A cream white rose climbing through the old apples. Gathering worts in Holford. The great monastic poplars by the stream.

At Kilve: fossils grey on the muddy reefs of the beach. The wind, the great yew; bulrushes in the moat; tall Lombardy poplars.

Cowparsley peashooters, ivy ammunition, smell of cowparsley. Stolen carrots and radish. Cress in the bathroom. Eating the ripening corn in a den carved in the fields. Clove-scented white ragged pinks along the borders. Shy aquilegia, wild in the woods. Walking on air high above in the trees.

My cacti gardens. Beans for salting: scarlet, french and broad. Never a cauliflower. Spinach, radish and Tom Thumb lettuce.

~

All this I remember at 12:30 after a night sweat.

~

Richard told me a trapped bee had flown up and down his window. In the morning it was curled up nearly dead on the sill. He put some water near it. It did not move. Then a large glob of honey. Its long proboscis unfurled and in ten minutes the honey disappeared. The bee grew glossy, bright black, its eyes twinkled; and suddenly it took off like an arrow into the sunlight.

~

Back home to my garden.

Thursday 12

Cold easterly winds blew in a violent thunderstorm last night; in the morning the mists cleared, bringing a bright but overcast afternoon which turned cold again in the evening.

The terrible January gales have left a trail of damage: the broom is all dead; over beyond the power station the sea thrifts are a withered brown; there are no foxgloves. But the old wartime bunker is adrift on a sea of bluebells that look startling. The concrete has disintegrated but the flowers live on, a memorial to those patient Home Guardsmen straining their eyes towards France, fifty years past.

I took cuttings from a clump of purple iris that was once the centre of a rose bed.

What a joy this sunlight brings. The flowers in bloom are primrose, speedwell, groundsel, buckthorn, daisy, gorse, wild pear, heartsease. About fifty little plants, white and yellow in an isolated clump: ragwort, sea sandwort, periwinkle – the large variety that has invaded the sallow woods, elusive pale blue stars; early forget-me-not, so small that you could easily pass it by.

Common dog violet, henbit dead nettle, narrow leaved vetch, dove's foot cranesbill.

The little pink flowers glow all over the bank – blinks, spotted medick (this on soil brought in to build a road for the fishing boats), whitlow grass, alexanders – again one isolated clump of about ten plants along the verges – dead nettle and bluebell.

Easter Saturday

The long Easter weekend stretches ahead. God, I'm bored by the TV . . . I've lost myself in the Jackson Pollock book, which details every twist and turn. Nothing to do. Richard rings, he's in the same state.

Richard is lovesick: the whole weekend turns around this unrequited love.

I'm happy. My pills have made me light-headed, and I hum my Doris Day motto, *Que Será Será*. I've lost all sense of time, float detached through the afternoon.

We drove to Plaistow, where Gerard keeps the keys for Phoenix House. Richard's old Bristol smells of leather and polished wood, glides through the grey deserted streets of the East End. We spot architectural gems of the sixties isolated in a sea of post-modern 'classicism'. Rufus sits with Lily, his Cornish Rex, who looks as if she has jumped out of a bath in a fright. We have tea, go for another drive, then back to Phoenix House.

The flat is empty, HB is in Newcastle. The spaghetti pesto at Bruna's, usually so tired, tastes like manna: after weeks off my food I'm suddenly hungry again. Dark-eyed Oliver, who played in Julian's film of Pasolini, stops me. I'm weaving all over the street. The steroids.

~

I take the first steps to disentangle myself from ten years in which every nook and cranny of the flat has been stacked with film books and paintings. We find paintings amongst the clothes, wedged behind the bed, piled behind jams and coffee in the kitchen. By seven the paintings that I was given or bought are stacked ready to leave – everything.

Richard was surprised at the quality of the hundred or so canvases and lithographs. At six we drove back to St. Mary's.

The sun is out. We take a long diversion to look at buildings and gardens and arrive at seven. I make plans to meet Richard in the morning and tuck my aching body into bed. My feet are bent double with pain, my skin frets against the protruding bones. I decide to discharge myself in the morning, not wait until Monday.

Easter Sunday

Sunday morning, HB is reading the lesson, *Matthew* 23, in Burnhope, while I sit here surrounded by black plastic bags filled with (his) clothes for Oxfam. Under a chair thick with dust I find my six pairs of brown leather shoes that I bought second hand to last me to the grave. HB has long been antagonistic to my dusty shoes, but as I tidy I find his collection far outstrips mine: there are families of Doc Martens, and aerodynamic Travel Fox that he loves so much.

I sort through the chest under the old gothick electric fire which shorts and sparks, and catalogue my papers for the film archive, and the hundreds of Super 8's from the seventies for James. Maybe we could make a film from all this rubble, *Glitterbug*. Jon is the only one who sees how clever this title is, *Glitterbest, Glitterati, Glitterbugger*. Back at the hospital I discharge myself, return home for another sleepless night waiting for the dawn in a light sweat.

Easter Monday

Dungeness
For ten minutes I follow a large bumble bee along the track that divides the wood behind the house as it hums from flower to flower.

~

The garden is replanted with help from the kids next door, who shouldered the heaviest digging.
The days are full of sunshine, I'm as brown as a berry.

~

The Ness is sweet with the song of larks. I put Vaughan Williams' *Lark Ascending* on the new CD player and sit in front of the house, barely following the pen across this clear white notepad. I pause and a fly lands and crawls across my skeletal hand.
A small copper butterfly is exploring the wallflowers, and I find the first dolly bell in bloom – white and frilly as a Victorian bridesmaid.

Tears
The TB unleashed floods of tears. I cried through the Rachmaninov *Piano Concerto* this afternoon, wept for the sad state of things. Sylvia has had to give her two precious goats away as she cannot pay the poll tax. They cost dear. Now she takes off each day to a part-time job.
Following my star to this Eden, I cried throughout Tuesday for the sky and the sea. I cried late at night with HB for my films. No-one will ever know the thousand little decisions that make or break my little movies. So late at night. I weep for the garden so lonely in the shingle desert. Dear Jean [Cocteau], am I the only one who, besides you, has funded a film on his name?
Joris Ivens' perfect film of the wind? So few escape to tread this path. Hedges of money, fixed stars.

Sunday 22
The smallest wren is pottering about the stones, I barely see it. There are two of them! Stepping across the silver curry plant. Hundreds of ladybirds are purposefully crawling across my plants. This year the aphids have been done to death by the late frosts.

~

Out by the Long Pits: the barrows trimmed by the rabbits to a mossy velvet are scattered with the innumerable stars of blue forget-me-nots.

~

The garden is the centre of surprise. Today a lizard dives into the lavender, while a large grass snake, basking by my rubbish tip, makes off in a series of sleek S's.

~

Alasdair Little's

Alasdair Little's is James's favourite restaurant. The waiters all know him. Michael is an old acquaintance of mine. The food is excellent, and the clientele rich and suited media of the better sort, hard as nails under the casual success. If you want to see the ugly disguised as acceptable, come to Soho. The days of Muriel Belcher, 'the French', eccentricity and creativity, have long gone. The restaurants are now so expensive no-one can afford them without an expense account. Remember Madame Mora-a-dozen-seats? Pink pig in the window, her daughters preparing the vegetables and the best fruit flans? A student could eat there.

That's all gone. This is not an exercise in nostalgia, it is fact. The old shops close. Vinorio's has pulled down its shutters. The creeping 'gentrification' of bollards, pedestrian precincts; York stone paving covers the old pot holes.

My pills and the euphoria of escaping from the confines of hospital have caused me to create a scene. Michael asks me how I am.

'Fine,' I say, but then launch into the state of the NHS. Where, as my weight drops below 9 stone and I sweat it out, a scan takes three weeks; and Virginia Bottomley, junior health minister, sits sweetly at the foot of the bed saying everything is improving – quite impervious to the serious advice she is being given by everyone who works here. How can such charm have such deaf ears?

I shout this across the restaurant – the diners freeze, counting on their medical insurance: Have they put enough aside for the London Clinic?

As I weaved my way home very unsteadily I felt glad that I had made this scene. The pills loosen you up – no-one raised a voice against me.

~

It's icy cold here, the wind has veered off north. Reading Horace Walpole's delightful letters, vivacious and full of high spirits:

> I keep good fires and seem to feel warm weather while I look through the window, for the way to ensure Summer in England is to have it framed and glazed in a comfortable room.

The greenhouse effect has abandoned us to cold winds and drizzle.

Friday 27

A tea time drunk weaving his way down Old Compton Street in the blinding sun stops me, and with a smile says, 'Son, I want to give you two shillings.' I was quite taken aback, as my hand was already in my pocket fumbling for change. He gave me the two shillings, I thanked him and he said 'Good day'. 'It is,' I said. 'All sunlight.'

MAY

Saturday 5
HB popped out of Jon's car like a Jack-in-the-box and, green eyes sparkling, threw stones at everything in sight. Then he slapped bergamot oil all over himself and lay in the sun to tan, and every creeping, crawling, and flying insect made a beeline for him.

Sunday 6
A week has passed without a cloud in the sky. At dawn the sea kale, a froth of white flowers, is covered with small copper butterflies drunk on nectar. They freeze as my shadow falls across them. More flowers have bloomed; though the broom was cut back in the violent January gales, so the Ness is a shadowy grey. There are very few flowers, and the golden blaze we had last year will not be repeated.

Sea campion covers the shingle with its tiny white flowers fluttering in the breeze – and woody nightshade, marguerites, plantain, bird's foot trefoil, star of Bethlehem, creeping buttercup, scarlet pimpernel, may, cinquefoil, hound's tongue, and yellow rocket.

At midday the breeze gets up: a black and red burnet moth is blown past; the cabbage whites cling to the purple iris. The sun is burning bright; it sets to the cuckoo, slowly, behind the woods at the Long Pits.

The ivy-leaved toadflax by the lifeboat station clings for dear life to the tar and rubble dumped from the roadworks. Jack-go-to-bed-at-noon, the goatsbeard, is out by the kerbside. Though everything is tinder dry, most plants seem to struggle on.

I water the front garden.

Tuesday 8
I'm knitting together, except for the terrible itching brought about by the steroids. Nothing I have tried makes much difference. Derek B. has brought both myrrh and, last night, frankincense to put in almond oil; but apart from smelling like an old church I'm afraid it hasn't done the trick. When he came with the frankincense yesterday he said, 'Gold next.'

~

Everyone has returned to London. The bank holiday cars have disappeared. There is one lone fisherman on the shore, he hasn't caught anything. A silence broken only by Sylvia's cockerel – who crowed the holiday makers away. Mist drifts over the towers of the nuclear power station like a steam kettle. I miss HB – who danced about threatening to cover himself with tattoos of lizards, which he spent time hunting in the garden.

Evening
David and Andy lit a bonfire on the sands to complete the filming of *The Wanderer*; later we all came back here and watched the rough cut of *The Garden*.

Wednesday 9
Howard's friend Donny rang early and worried from America; he'd heard about my TB.

The sun almost disappeared in the clouds. Welcome the cooler weather. I walked along the Ness and brought back an armful of metal and driftwood to add to the garden. The fishermen had brought up a large and ancient anchor in their nets, which they brought to me for the garden. It's becoming an attraction. Sylvia came over to admire the irises and I gave her a rosemary cutting.

Thursday 10
It rained in the night, bringing colour back to the landscape. I walked to the Long Pits. The first of the yellow flag irises are out, as are bristly oxtongue, welted thistle and, over by the power station, curly dock. The sorrel has turned the ground a misty red.

Christopher tucks into brains, which he buys in Soho, though they have long been banned. He knows nothing of mad cow disease. Vision of him with a spongiform brain, crashing legless around his drawing room, pulverising antique cabinets and Roman glass, historic titbits overturned and trampled into the Persian carpets; where he expires like the wicked witch, mad as a hatter, in a little pool of frothy cells.

He sends messages, thinks I'm dotty, but day by day more people are giving up gorging themselves on the roast beef of old England. Though last Sunday at the pub in Lydd Neil Tennant and Jon Savage ate it with gusto. No angel, I stuck to pork.

The scent of May
The scent of the sea kale is rich and honeyed. At dawn when I'm watering the garden the scent is caught by the breeze. The seeds I planted three years ago, which struggled through a first summer, have grown into plants five

feet in diameter, – a mass of white blossom, like the May bushes that border the lanes of the marsh. Driving here last Tuesday in the evening sunlight: empty roads, drifts of white flowers, a bouquet for the coming summer.

Friday 11

Ne'er cast a clout till May be out. A northeasterly has set in.

I feel better today, I've been poorly all week. My liver aches, all my nerve endings are inflamed by the pills, which heat me like a furnace and turn my pee barley sugar orange. My hair is growing topsy like Lily's – the Cornish Rex. It has turned silky and grows at silly angles. I itch and itch, under my chin and down the sides of my legs. I've swallowed the five pink pills and the two blue ones the colour of the pottery they used to sell in Corfe when I was a child.

Stephen McBride stops by on the old delivery bike; he'll buy me a newspaper and return for tea. I've lit the fire and ventured a few feet from the front door. Heat and cold hurt. A hot bath burns, an orgasm overwhelms with pain.

Last night I tried to read Shelley – he escapes me; can't concentrate, though I've read Trelawney and Biaggi the last few days. Fall back on a history of herbals that cost a fortune at John Adrian's bookshop in Cecil Court. Though since he has taken over a hundred books, many of them now priced in his shop at over £100, £120 didn't seem too much. No money changed hands.

The easterly roars around Prospect Cottage, *Pomp and Circumstance* playing loud. The Royal Ballet rings to say it's reviving *Jazz Calendar* at a Gala in October.

Another long chat with Annie Lennox over the Cole Porter song, I've never met her but I feel we can talk like old friends, we are meeting on Monday.

~

Stormed out of a video showing of *The Garden* for the investors: James put on an editing copy to save money! It was missing whole sections, the tape had destroyed itself through being constantly stopped for sound.

Lorraine rings to say the radio wants to do an 'in-depth' psychological interview. OK.

We sit here working on *Edward II*.

Painting finished this afternoon. Prometheus. Liverish.

~

The sea blue-black gunmetal, white horses. The sharp easterly has blown the clouds away. I sit at the back of the house well sheltered.

~

Alasdair rings to say Spud Jones has a cancer. Philip phones to say his friend Peter is dead.

Saturday 19
I'm not feeling too well. Spent the day asleep on the sofa. The wind blew terribly, it brings on depression. Didn't the Sirocco drive the unwary mad? The sun shines in mockery: it is very cold. But the view from the window at seven is more beautiful than ever, white horses. The sea indigo, almost black, and the white cliffs glinting far in the distance across the bay.

Sunday 20
There is one foxglove out behind the house, and along the lakes, just three. Last year there were thousands.

Alasdair phones to say Spud has had his cancer removed. Hardly a day passes without illness invading. I find it disturbing. My own predicament does not help.

~

All my new pictures are signed with thermometers. Derek B. sent round a CD of a dreadful Puccini opera called *Sour Angelica*, a perfect short for Ken Russell, with wasp-stung virgins and a mother superior who is an amateur gynaecologist.

~

Stephen had a night of Littlestone sex. He pulled a boy from the pool table in The Jolly Fisherman and lured him back to *El Rey* for a midnight barbecue. He won't be doing it again.

Tuesday 22
I'm not feeling at all well. My concentration is shattered. The police sirens set my teeth on edge and give me a dull headache. When I hear these sirens in New York I feel someone is rescued from the hands of a mugger; here I feel the police are out to beat someone up.

~

The beautiful old Soho fishmonger's has become the seediest peepshow.

~

Vinorio's, the Italian delicatessen, is now a hideously lit TV sandwich bar, tuna coloured.

Wednesday 23

Driven to Dungeness by Donald, with Juliette, the researcher for the psychological programme. By the afternoon I was so drained of energy just walking down the corridor made me dizzy, and a hacking cough leaves me breathlessly hanging on to a chair by the table.

Very disturbed night with a fever, my hair sopping wet and cold.

The wind got up in the night.

Thursday 24

The sun shines but the wind continues to blow cold. Walked with Stephen over to the sallow woods.

There we sat for an hour and watched two hawks the like of which I've never seen – black and white like magpies, chattering to each other with a high pitched mewing laughter. They crossed each other's paths flying loop-the-loop in crazy patterns, so fast if you blinked you lost them; like otters they twisted and turned and skimmed along the ground. Watching them, I forgot my sluggish steps, my halt and wheezing progress. They raised my spirits. They need a Manley Hopkins to celebrate their abandoned flight. Maybe they were hobbies, I'm not certain; but of all the birds I've seen they were the most thrilling.

~

Takashi said the film had him crying, particularly during the landscape at the end. The terrible damage inflicted on the two boys transfers: they become sky and sea.

I can feel it. Looking at the Ness through sick eyes I notice the burnt-out broom, the foxgloves that have disappeared, the stunted poppies in the bright dry sunlight. Even the sallows, burnt black by the gales, rattle like dead bones. While, high above, the black and white hawks still loop-the-loop without a care.

A photographer

Clive, a photographer, stopped to photo the garden, and stayed the morning. We took some photos with me looking into the lens, the first photos this year. It was very cold. I've not enough flesh to keep the chill from catching me by the neck, and the cold, like the sun, burns my irritated skin.

The sea has turned jade green with a myriad white sea horses.

~

HB phoned to find out how I was. He said hobbies were very rare.

~

The prettiest kid walked by late in the evening, staggering under the weight of a package wrapped around with a cloth. We watched him progress along the empty road, eventually I dared Stephen to offer to lift his parcel on the bike.

When Stephen returned a minute or two later, he said he'd given the kid the shock of his life – he was carrying an old engine which he had obviously stolen. When Stephen asked if he could help he dived off the road, throwing the cloth over his loot and stammered he was OK. We both dreamt of him.

~

I pickled some fresh garlic bulbs. Standing on the dresser they make the kitchen look very professional.

~

I sit down like a constipated dowager. My balls hurt when they hit the sofa, so I perch on the edge of the chair.

~

The hop trefoil and Nottingham catchfly are in flower. The catchfly enjoys the drought, but the poppies, which are also in flower, are small and stunted. Other plants in flower are: restharrow, toadflax, camomile, white and red clover, common stork's-bill, woody nightshade, mouse-eared hawkweed, cinquefoil, the scarlet pimpernel and dodder.

Saturday 26
Julian drove down here with three students from Oxford who interviewed me for *The Word*. I coughed and spluttered my words, not all of them too gentle. Later we ate at Demetrios'.

~

A day in which my eyes scarcely opened. The wind dropped. I was up at 11:00 and spent the morning bumping into the furniture to the sound of Frescobaldi. Then at three collapsed into bed for another three hours. I didn't shave. Stephen sung in the background, he has a very charming voice. It's 7:30, the sun shines so brightly you can't face west. The sea is aquamarine blue and the porcelain sky is tinged with pink.

Conversation throughout the day has revolved around the greenhouse effect and HIV. Both Stephen and I know of couples who had full sex till both were body positive. Who should have been responsible for whom? It's a terrible thing to have done, but the onus is always on those who have been brave enough to get tested. Are they always the guilty ones?

Sunday 27

Night sweat, hair sopping wet and freezing in the small hours. I have no strength at all. I tried to dig up a dead plant and collapsed. I can just walk to the end of the garden.

~

The garden is looking bright and cheerful. The Californian poppies shimmer in the sunlight – deep blue sage, pinks. The cabbages and the lupins are all out. Stephen is stripped to the waist in the sunlight. I'm freezing in a winter pullover and anorak.

~

Rang Alasdair, who is at sixes and sevens.

~

I'm as breathless as an octogenarian.

~

A red admiral new minted, fluttering against the kitchen window.

~

At five Derek B. drove me back to London. It took me ten minutes to walk from St. Giles's church to my front door. I would not have been able to walk from the station. Phones ring, doorbells.

Almroth Wright ward

I keep on seeing a glass falling in slow motion, to smash in a thousand pieces. It's so terribly slow. It takes days. Will it be a loop or clip?

~

Joris Ivens walking breathless into the desert to find the wind. Asthmatic. My childhood asthma takes me to the seaside, Bexhill, with Grandma Moselle. Breathless in the hotel.

Now I cannot move. If I do I'm overwhelmed with coughing, my breath stops up, panic. Pneumonia plays its own pipes that wheeze and grumble. Simon Watney says it's an 'after tremor'. What more do I need? Pneumonia and TB. Will I stand up to this?

The shadowy black bats of breathlessness swarm through the evening, roost in my lungs. The oxygen whistles up my nose like water gurgling at the dentist's. There is nothing quite as frightening as losing your breath in an attack of coughing. Clasped by the velvet wings of the bats, I throw the sheets back. At the end of the film Joris found the wind in the desert. Septrin drips into my arm, blood taken from the arteries stings like a bee. Pneumo-cystis – till they learnt you died from this. I would mercifully pass from asphyxia to unconsciousness.

'You'll take time to recover.' TB below, pneumonia above, the line of pills has grown again. Chemical wedding. The slightest move threatens blackout. I lie facing the ceiling. I cannot turn left or right. Sleep as if I've been laid out.

Thank God you don't attend your own funeral. I wonder if I'll end up with tacky white marble – or a slab of black Purbeck, like the old tombs in Romney church, with fine freehand lettering. Nurses rush by. They are short staffed. The oxygen bubbles away. In the night it roars like a river in full flood. The doctor worries that the sun will disappear before the weekend. I say not to worry: before his time's up he might wish he could switch it off.

JUNE

Tuesday 5
A great big HB sits at the end of my bed, tickling my feet, eating nuts and fruits. A huge vase of pink peonies delicately scents the room.

~

Mike O'Pray has received a commission from Colin McCabe at the BFI to write a book on my films.

Castle of the sleeping princesses
At the junction of Green Lane and Rickmansworth Road 'aunts' Phil and Vi lived in the house in which they were born, ruled beyond the grave by a tyrannical mother. The childhood rumour had her rejoicing at the news that her daughters' suitors had sunk without trace in the *Titanic*.

Phil's hair turned to grey, her sister's white with a yellowish tinge. Small and birdlike, they talked in unison, or antiphonally, as they slaved hour after hour polishing the enormous gloomy pile, that they had been chained to for all their time.

Though aunts Vi and Phil were charming, they were also austere in habit, and sharp of tongue. I dreaded staying. Their high Victorian morality was reflected in the mirror polish of the mahogany dining room, which was never used – in fact three quarters of the place lay empty; except for the little parlour by the front door and the kitchen – big as a semi-detached, slate flagged, and unchanged since the 1880s. Four incoherent storeys of red brick ending in an attic pervaded by a sinister gloom.

Polish, polish, polish, top to bottom. No light penetrated. The stained glass doors gave the front hall the gloomy atmosphere of a church – a church dedicated to 'Mother', the slaver.

Phil and Vi were as fragile as butterflies, but beware: they had steely, practical hearts. Life was a struggle. Then suddenly a wicked, almost vulgar laughter at a risqué joke. They kept a 'Bohemian' artist in the stables: Gaby was a man straight out of *The Horse's Mouth*, wayward as Hancock, unshaven, always drunk and loudmouthed.

The garden of the house reflected the strange flawed geometry of the place: a corner site that resembled a squashed thrupenny bit surrounded by tall dark woodland trees. Nothing flowered there – but if it did its position seemed quite arbitrary. Only the honeysuckle filled the air with its heady perfume.

Marooned here for days on end during the holidays, my parents in Pakistan, I mooned around hoping to be invited by Gaby for something stronger. Phil and Vi would scold him and his gin bottle then accept a drink from their pet troll.

Phil and Vi defied time. Like old soldiers they faded away: their hair grew whiter, their conversation dottier, more absent minded. At twenty they had looked fifty, and at sixty, ninety.

The house has gone, but one of them lives on at 100.

~

Can you imagine missing the sound mix of a film? I'm doing that lying here at St. Mary's. I missed the edit, and I'm going to miss the Japan opening; the doctors say it is too much of a risk.

~

HB sits here each afternoon typing, bouncing about, tickling my feet, flashing his green eyes, flexing his new muscles so his lizard tattoo crawls about. He kept me laughing for three hours. Without him I wouldn't have got this far, he's so naughty.

~

All my aunts were small but the smallest was Aunt Gwen, who sat in bed and ate chocolates for an entire decade. There she was looked after by my cousin Beverley. Her garden was a ramshackle affair, the pride and centre an asparagus bed. Gwen hopping about, sparrow-like.

Wednesday 6
After 7 days I walked to the bathroom and back. I'm on my feet again.

Thursday 7
Dressed and walked to the shops late in the afternoon. I'm re-discovering breathing. HB held my hand.

Saturday 9
Stephen rang to tell me the rain had brought out the flowers at Prospect Cottage. I'm up, and off the oxygen, though still breathless. I spend the mornings working on the script for *Edward II*. It's becoming increasingly Jacobean, sexy, and violent. We have brought the classical references to life:

Apollo, a Roman triumph, Prometheus. I think we can take it further.
I make plans for my convalescence. I don't want to die yet.

Monday 11
I'm allowed home tomorrow after two weeks flat on my back. I'll see the summer flowers at Dungeness, the poppies and tree lupin. I'm very weak, my physical self has taken a battering. I'd like to recover, I've never been in bad health. Can I win against the odds?

Tuesday 12
I left hospital. Red letter day.

Thursday 14
I can walk across Soho without feeling faint. Bought a painting at Birch and Conran of the battle of Anzio, then had my hair cut.

Friday 15
All day being interviewed by the Japanese in Richard's studio.

Saturday 16
Julian, HB, Stephen, and myself drove to Dungeness. Not a breath of wind, brilliant sunshine, and a swarm of red admirals chasing each other in the evening light.

Sunday 17
Quiet blissful day, the sun up and a slight breeze. Walked to the Long Pits. Back home my garden is ablaze with poppies, all the work of last year come to perfection: scarlet poppies, dark red poppies, field poppies, white and purple opium poppies. My garden is as bright as a fairground with Californian poppies, which have seeded themselves like natives.

~

I counted these flowers on my walk: broom, gorse, bird's foot trefoil, hop trefoil, yellow rattle, toadflax, bristly oxtongue, good King Henry, plantain, houndstongue, ragged robin, willow herb, musk mallow, agrimony, alkanet, lesser convolvulus, sea campion, scarlet pimpernel, sea pea, valerian, woodsage, stonecrop, dog rose, elder, cinquefoil, ragwort, thistle, yellow horned poppy, catchfly.

~

I worked here all afternoon. Surreptitious watering (there is a hosepipe ban). Sylvia came with fresh eggs from her chickens.

Another walk along the road and down to the sea. Here was restharrow, dead nettle, scabious, yarrow, bedstraw, red and white clover, grass and tufted vetchling, black mustard and camomile. Brought back iron and wood and built new sculptures.

Monday 18
Clouds mask the sun, up early. Stephen arrives and cooks bacon and eggs for breakfast. I start up the illegal hose. There are huge white caterpillars with yellow and black spots demolishing the mullein.

The poppies are blown away by midday, and the sun disappears behind a ridge of cloud. A breeze has got up, but it is hot and close. Stephen has weeded the stone circles in the front of the house. The pale yellow curry plants are in bloom, set off by the lavender.

It is silent and deserted here, just myself and the swallows.

After an enormous lunch I picked up Thoreau's *Walden* as the rain blew in. Distant rattle of gunfire at the Lydd ranges.

Tuesday 19
Cloudy day with sunny moments. The rain has put green in the landscape, the moss is damp and spongy underfoot. Four magpies in the front garden never stop still.

~

Gerard drove me pillion on his bike up to Dungeness A where we picked samphire, St. Peter's herb, and came home to pickle it. It looks very exotic in the Kilner jars next to pickled garlic.

The wind blows as warm as shirtsleeves, a quiet day. Thoreau, a penny for your thoughts. Where do you think that comes from? The penny post.

Liam arrived in his old yellow Deux Cheveaux. The sun came back at five. We drove to the nursery and bought a fig tree.

~

Elgar's *Enigma Variations*. Poor Elgar – music stolen for *Land of Hope and Glory*, words he detested. The *Enigma* puts muscle into my weeding. Stephen and the kids next door were roped into gathering white pebbles for the front garden. At the day's end we lit the windlights. The sun came and lingered golden until the shadows turned the shingle a ghostly white.

~

The bathroom is painted Granny's pink.

My father once welcomed Queen Mary to RAF Kidlington. The talk of the whole station was the specially installed pink lavatory, a tourist attraction until it was dismantled. I like the pink bathroom – it makes pallid cheeks rosy; it's obvious (odious) to perfection.

Wednesday 20

My bookmark is a photo of two handsome naked men hauling a rope. Posed in a NY studio, this photo is by Donald Herbert, taken in 1938.

I primed over 20 small canvases early in the morning. The garden has flowered red, yellow and blue: poppies, hawksbit and bugloss. A medieval tapestry. Crickets chirp and hop around the house.

Toby, Tilda, and Julian arrive; we eat fish and chips at The George – in the bar, as the dining room is occupied by the local antiquities circle. Picked samphire along the nuclear power station. Delicious local strawberries for tea.

By five the rain set in and my visitors were back on the road to London. I worked through my mail, dread letters full of scripts and thoughts of scripts. One I consigned straight to the bin: 'The life of Stradella can be read in the original Italian in manuscript, item 200000 BM library, nothing else is published, you should make a film of him.' This, and sweet violence in SE London, drug addiction in Bath – all suitably drear. And a sunny day outside.

Thursday 21

Liam drove me back to London this morning in the little yellow Deux Chevaux. It took us nearly 3 hours to get to St. Mary's. The traffic in the West London streets was appalling. The doctor tapped at my chest, suggested AZT – which he thought on balance was worth trying. I feel dizzy when I stand, and he prescribed more of the cortisone.

I'm sitting in the radiography department waiting for a chest X-ray. There was a small nagging dread as we drove past Paddington station on my return to the hospital: I wonder if I will die here, of all places on earth – next to these seedy souvenir shops.

The charm and good humour of the doctors and nursing staff does not quite dispel the sadness of overheard conversations.

How are you?

Doing quite well thanks, the night sweats have not been so bad this week.

We are all cheerful, but at moments I feel far from happy. The doctor agreed that I should cancel all my work. I'm ticking over at about 70% of my capacity and the X-ray shows a lot of fuzzy white marks. I'm not quite better, am I?

Friday 22 – Prospect Cottage

Julian drove me down here late in the evening. HB left for Newcastle.

I gave the interview for the Japanese programme at Richard's. South Edwardes Square is so calming, the rooms dissolve depression. Tilda drove me home, dropping Richard at Sotheby's. He's after a fine drawing for the *Duino Elegies* made by Keith Vaughan – 'Who, if I cried, would hear me?'

Saturday 23

My depression overwhelming – so bad I ache, though I have no temperature. By lunch time the wind and sun started to disperse the sadness. Dearest Alasdair on the phone for nearly an hour, he's in the same state, says the world is a foreign country. He goes through the motions with friends, whose fears and preoccupations he can no longer share. We are refugees here.

I cancelled the little film with Annie Lennox. This has created much sadness – I didn't know how to ring her and tell her. Her answerphone was on when I got up the courage to dial, thank heavens. I hate failing people. I had always dreamt of working with her, was a fan from the first. How silly all this is, of course I can make the film; but I'm so dizzy I doubt I would do it well – it's too close to home for me to see straight.

Richard tried to console me, he said that charity and publicity – witness G&G – were very problematic bedpartners. 'Surely' said Julian, 'these gifts should be private.' I said I believed in charity but the PR necessary to raise these millions had muddied the waters. Annie agreed with this, but what are we to do? Trapped. Every time we say goodbye.

The Garden

Tilda said she experienced *The Garden* quite differently from *The Last Of England*. It was as if she was 'trapped' in my dream. She found the film intensely personal. The preoccupations of *The Last Of England* were shared – here was something different. I feel the same way, can't really talk about the film. It's like talking about yourself!

~

The cornflowers have seeded themselves – I found another plant in a corner of the garden. The poppies dancing in the wind – Julian said it was illegal to grow them in California.

The garden has been burnt by the winds of the last few days, the sculptures uprooted, the flowers snapped off. The fennel lies almost parallel to the ground.

~

Overwhelmed by pain in my stomach and back I took to my bed in the afternoon.

~

I am conscious, as I write this diary, of the limitations and loyalties that it has imposed – as I have always been aware that it would be published. How much can it tell of our dilemma?

Great unhappiness has been caused by the discovery that X's friend, twenty years his junior, has caught the virus from him, would it have been, could it have been, any other way? They did not practice 'safer' sex, but safer sex might not have protected them. Not one of my friends on enquiry can touch their hearts – all had stories of condoms tearing.

Many, the majority, I told him, hide behind the fact that they have not been tested, claim immunity from the foreign dilemma, what can they know of what they have given and received? – Is beside himself with guilt and unhappiness: 'It was my responsibility.' Such a terrible time of tears, bring back the days of laughter.

Sunday 24

Stephen arrived for breakfast, after a 'low life' adventure that started at The Seahorse, and ended with him sleeping between a dope fiend and a child molester in Greatstone. I got up full of aches and pains, so much so I could not bend to wash and had to get a chair in.

~

A perfect summer's day. Sunshine, slight breeze. The Ness ablaze with flowers.

~

Amongst the visitors to the garden today were Beth Chatto and Christopher Lloyd. They were taking notes and photos. I realised quite quickly that I was in the hands of experts. Beth knew the Latin names of every plant, and when she told me who she was I nearly fell off the Ness. I must ring Lorraine, who is a great fan.

~

A large toad, asleep in the shirley poppy by the front door, winked at me as I walked by. I tried humming to it, without much success. I don't know quite what I expected it to do, get up and dance?

Monday 25

Another painful night. Woke at dawn with a large bluebottle buzzing in the net curtains. Grabbed the *Independent* and swatted it.

At seven I put the Mozart arias sung by Lucia Popp on the CD. Her voice so insistent it started to hurt. Jettisoned the Mozart for Poulenc – there was a programme about him last night. They referred oh so briefly to his 'life-long companion'. I had no idea he was homosexual; you would have had to be a detective to pick up on it.

Stephen and I carried on filling in the ivory parterre. Grey cloudless day. Later I curled up with my aches and read John D'Emilio's *History of the Homosexual Minority in the United States*.

~

Saw my first meadow brown and a new-minted painted lady late in the afternoon.

~

My doctor rang from St. Mary's about five. I described my symptoms and he insisted I came to see him tomorrow. I quickly packed, said goodbye to Stephen and took the train to London.

~

A violent attack of muscular pain as I lay down to sleep. HB rushed out and returned with aspirin, which to my great relief stopped the convulsions. Slept very well in his arms.

Tuesday 26

The doctor tapped around my chest – my 'lung functions' have climbed to 52 from 30; he suggested I came in on Monday for a bronchoscopy, and Friday for blood tests. Sat reading Larry Kramer's book while I waited.

~

At four I caught the train to Dungeness.

Wednesday 27

Very close, warm, and overcast. Stephen put on Liza Minnelli full-blast and washed the kitchen floor. Later, we picked white stones for the garden.

Liza was ousted by Poulenc. I tidied up the studio.

My aches are going, but my energy level has dropped. HB sent a card which said 'I love you', which made me very happy – poor thing, having to deal with my aches and pains.

The silence today is a blessing. The sun set in a chalk-white sky, with the blackest clouds blowing in from the west.

Thursday 28
Liam arrived at nine with his photos of the garden. We walked out to the seashore to pick white pebbles.

The centre of the garden is nearly complete.

A bright, breezy day.

Saturday 30 Gay Pride
March from the Temple at two.

Much preparation, and muscle-flexing. I sat quietly all morning reading Rousseau's *Confessions*, conserving energy, besieged by Fred Perry shirts and a red hot iron.

The march was larger but more subdued than last year. Perhaps the weather, which threatened rain, played its part. It was a long hard walk from Charing Cross to the Oval, bright with pink balloons and deafened by shrill whistles which gradually lapsed into silence as the marchers grew tired.

We passed a 'Margaret Thatcher' and a group of drag queens mincing around in the pink hybrid tea roses of a nice garden, worried South Londoners peeping from behind net curtains. The park was so crowded no-one could see the stalls, and everyone was stumbling over each other. Old friends disappeared. We sat with Julian and Harry until time swept us apart, and we took the tube home.

The march, as usual, had a wonderful atmosphere, the only march that achieves its objectives, of solidarity and good humour. Even Christopher enjoyed himself. Later we went to Nicholas de Jongh's play at the Royal Court, a courageous attempt to deal with the HIV epidemic. And then later to Julian's 29th birthday celebration at Richard Salmon's studio. By this time I was very tired and collapsed in his enormous sofa.

JULY

Monday 2

Bronchoscopy at St. Mary's. The doctor seemed satisfied I was on the mend. Sailed through the rest of the day very tired and drugged.

The Garden film was shown at Andy's preview cinema. I think people liked it.

Later we caught the train to Ashford and a taxi to Dungeness.

Tuesday 3

Took a taxi into New Romney and bought a week's food. My walk to the Long Pits brought no new flowers, but these were all still in bloom: sorrel, woodsage, hawkweed, poppy, yellow horned poppy, valerian – this is fading fast, sea campion, ragwort – covered with orange and black cinnabar caterpillars, bugloss – the most spectacular flower of the Ness, cinquefoil, sedum, bacon-and-eggs, meliot, thistle, scarlet pimpernel, willowherb, marsh mallow, toadflax, agrimony, dog rose, curled dock, Nottingham catchfly.

Stephen cooked an excellent supper of pork chops in apple and onion. I spent the evening scattering poppy seed around the garden.

Wednesday 4

Cold drizzle belting in from the east. Retired into the studio with gold leaf and a large pot of Venetian red. Primed and gilded canvases all morning. Shostakovich and Schnitke on the CD.

Last night a walk at sundown along the beach: opium poppy, scabious, sea pea, white clover, restharrow, wild carrot, woody nightshade, evening primrose, mustard, mayweed, camomile, mallow, alkanet, daisy, larkspur, wild pansy, snapdragon, sowthistle, tufted vetch, hare's-foot, herb Robert, hop trefoil, sun spurge – all in flower.

The wind blows over the lavender and santolina which wave about like sea anemones on a coral reef, yellow and purple. The cornflowers are the most perfect blue, more iridescent than the bugloss or sage. On the kerbside red clover and dead nettle.

Breathless in the wind, picked white stones.

Thursday 5

The gale blew through the night into the dawn. Disturbed sleep, with the house creaking and groaning. Whenever the wind gets up fears of another hurricane lurk. The wind roars across the grasses, over the pale grey sea tumbling with billows. The lovage, six feet tall by the front door, has survived the battering; the wheelbarrow has tipped over, and rain spatters across the windows blurring the view.

The garden is dying in the wind; little enough will be left for the filming in ten days. The poppies have shed the last of their petals. Though behind the wind there lurks a breathless excitement. I pick up the hoe and clear the weeds. At eleven, in the studio, I paint two memento mori, and finish a necklace of stones. Not all is lost. Add dead nettle and convolvulus to the list of plants flowering.

Peter arrived in his van at one; we drove to Rye. Then we finished the white stone oblong in front of the house.

Friday 6

Self-heal grows along the path to the sea.

Saturday 7

Took cuttings from the gorse. At 10:30 Alan Beck arrived for Stephen and they left for the E.F. Benson celebration in Rye. I stayed behind and read the biography of Augustine. Then made corrections to the script of *Edward II*. I found a copy of Queen Isabella's account book in Rye, read this late into the afternoon before everyone returned with home-made cakes from the Benson Society stall.

Another very cold and windy day with a sea mist clinging to the nuclear power station, which had an ominous fit of hiccoughs at three.

Monday 9

St. Mary's for T cell count, and the question of AZT. They want me to take it.

HB typed and finished the Edward script, and I sat on the bed correcting proofs.

Tuesday 10

At eleven in the morning I walked to Working Title and delivered the first draft of *Edward II*. Met Deborah in the entrance, all rush as usual. Sarah was not in – the days we whiled away long gone. I stood in the entrance three paces from the door, and handed over the goods. No-one suggested a cup of tea, or glass of water.

Going down in the lift I reflected on Colin McCabe's remark at lunch that there was a definite pattern in the short lives of English film companies: the sudden success with a small film slowly eroded by the pressures of finance. Sarah did say at one point that although they had funds it would be difficult to push them my way with a project like *Edward*.

Friday 13
Drove to Dungeness with Derek B. – everything went wrong. The old white Citroën developed a fault, which reduced Derek to a desperate silence. The traffic was appalling – at the end of the A20, stuck for nearly an hour in the heat, he put on a tape of *Mapp and Lucia* by E.F. Benson, which turned a bad dream into a nightmare.

Any thoughts of shopping for food for the weekend were dashed, but Derek stopped: at the shop in Headcorn and bought six bottles, large ones, of wine; at a service station to get cat food for Baby, who prowled about on the back seat and, whenever we stopped, bolted out of the window; and at a house in Lydd-on-Sea that sold the local fish. Back at Prospect Cottage, Baby bolted one last time, and disappeared into one of my henges.

Saturday 14
A very bad migraine in the night.

Sunday 15
I have partially lost my sight. I couldn't read the Sunday newspapers. This left me disorientated. I kept forgetting and would pick up a book to read. Phoned HB, who came down to look after me, leaving his work in London. Great relief when he arrived, no panic. Phoned the doctors and made an appointment on Tuesday.

Monday 16
Sleepless night, it was very hot and close. HB kept awake by the creaks and groans of the wooden house cooling in the dark.

The crew arrived at ten to make the documentary of the garden. A very happy day. At 7:00 we left and drove to London. Met my dear friend Peter Docherty on the Charing Cross Road; he came to dinner with HB and myself. He hoped *The Garden* would cause a stir – be viewed under plain wraps. We could all attend the première wearing plain brown envelopes! John Maybury was in the Presto and came over, he's just made a video for Marc Almond with a group of well-hung boys.

Tuesday 17

Caught up with my writing waiting for my appointment at the clinic. My fuzzy eyes more out of focus. Today it's as if I am drunk.

Monday 23 11:05

All 'jugsy' as Mildred said, I was taken into hospital on Thursday for an emergency brain scan, which picked up the toxoplasmosis that had destroyed my sight in the previous days. With relief I returned to my friends at the Almroth Wright. The heat, my disorientation – I did not recognise HB sitting on the chair until he spoke – and the constant nagging migraine laid me out. Within minutes Jeannie had linked me up to a sulphadiazine drip.

~

Who makes up the names of drugs? Fansidar, Triludan, and one called Dom Perignon – near as dammit, why not Petal or Fleur for a bit of fancy?

~

I've lain here itching with drugs for several days now, no books, or TV; though my sweet next door neighbour came in with a compact disc player which was unbearably clear. Jeannie asked 'What do you think about all day?' I could not reply. My mind drifts forwards and backwards.

How many assaults will my body stand? At what point will life cease to be bearable? I worry for HB, who keeps my spirits soaring. When he is there, I could cope with blindness.

Am I unhappy? The answer is definitely not, although I wouldn't have believed it if I had dreamt up this scenario. Scuttling across the road like a rat on my way here, I took my life in my hands and arrived on the far pavement safe. Like taking a first high-dive.

No books to read, no newspapers. So, what did I think about during the long hours?

I watched the clock.

On the first day its face was a fuzzy halo, the digits telescoped and disappeared.

On the second day I could see the red second hand move in a jumble of black.

On the third day I paused, looked and looked again and read the time.

On the fourth day I could read the numbers round the dial – people appeared out of the gloom, some younger, others older; their outlines filled in like pieces of a fancy jigsaw.

Beware of very hot water reads the sign above the basin. The number 13 in the corridor slowly came into focus. It's 11:25, I have written three pages.

JULY

My writing is illegible. It is remarkably easy to lose your sight: a bad head-ache on a Friday evening and the words slide off the pages. Within a few days they disappear altogether.

In the waiting room of the West London Eye Hospital I was barely aware of the drip sticking in my arm watched by curious children. I read the flashing dot in the machines and longed to get back into my bed.

~

When someone dies here a hush descends. I imagine the same atmosphere in a prison on the day someone's death sentence comes up. I hear a patient say 'Who's next for the cooler?'

This afternoon was a nightmare – two distraught young sisters of the dying boy, hysterical in the corridors: 'Nurse, doctor, help, help.' The sound of running feet as the staff rushed to the death bed. Unable to move or help I lay here, paralysed – it would be such a small slip and the toxo's, furry little one-celled beasts, could push me into terminal spasms.

'Nurse, doctor, he's having a fit.'

'David is dying,' says sister quietly as she passes. Helplessness, even among the helpers, who I know are more upset than they appear, losing a patient. I do hope there is no hysteria on my death bed, at least spare me that.

Later the vicar came in and we chatted. Life's like that. Oh dear, and on with it.

I feel I should be able to record more than I have or more deeply and find I cannot . . .

~

Mildred comes in and sleeps for a moment on a chair. The heat is intense. My drip clicks off the litres of sulphadiazine. Will my jugsy sight return? Make the hazy furniture solid, turn these will o' the wisps back to human beings?

~

Two eyes look better than one, in a smiling face. HB keeps me smiling, tells me about a bonfire in which an elderly lady burns a coat made of the skins of seven leopards; of Diana Dors' mink bikini. This furry conversation starts as I stroke his short hair. Mink sheets.

We laugh the evening away, HB says one of his friends, camp William, spotted a bishop in a gay bar, walked over boldly and sat on his lap introducing himself as 'Daughter of Satan'. It's silly stories like this that keep the minutes ticking by. I love my right foot tickled in the middle, just above the ball. In my jugsy state HB twizzles away and types.

My face itches under the eyebrows and chin. My eyes are circled with irritation. I wear my canary yellow pyjamas and my barber's pole espadrilles. My hair grows longer. So does HB's. He looks most handsome with a little more on top, greased and parted. Today he is wearing blue, flexes his muscles.

~

Last week at Prospect Cottage I made excellent blackcurrant jam, slightly tart. How does Dungeness fare under these flaming skies?

~

On the second day I had enough sight to shave and cut myself bloody in the mirror. Another patient, Eduardo, comes in, stamping the virus to death in a war dance as he talks of the death of our neighbour.

~

I noticed the film was out of sync. No-one else did, till Nigel the sound editor confirmed it at a second screening.

~

Jeannie says my symptoms are unusual as normally you would expect one eye to go. They've never seen two eyes affected in the same way.

~

My symptoms are a first. I will be written up in the *BMJ*.

~

This hospital is run with true hospitality. Thank heavens chance brought me here.

~

Here goes, Schokolade mit . . . something or the other . . . my eyes have improved since this morning, I can just read the lettering on the chocolate bar. Though there are strange gaps, black holes into which information disappears.

Tuesday 24

Tossed and turned on a wave of itching through the night. This drug exhausts me. Outside the sun shines. Along the corridor the cleaners come with their humming polishers. Ed comes in, says he's just received the news he has the virus. This is exhausting. My face burns dry with inflammation, my jugsy eyes come slowly into focus. Over the roof the sky is blue. He smiles and says, 'What to do?'

Next door a second death is expected. We sit like clay pigeons, shuttled nearer to death like the bubbles travelling along the drip. The migraine circles. I see the blue sky veiled with shadows. I pass the long hours of the day waiting for HB to arrive.

The nurse said today that this must be a frightening experience. It isn't, just aggravating – so silly to lose your eyes. I can write clearly and in straight lines across the gloomy page. How many aftershocks must I endure till my body, broken, desiccated and drained of colour, fails to respond. I live in a permanent hangover, after years of good health. A little green light flashes in the drip, the cool poison runs into my arm.

Lorraine rings. The Japanese journalists want to bring in a camera! Boss-eyed and unshaven. Terminal shots for *Marie Claire*. No go.

The itching eyes swim about.

Despair is a cardinal sin, says Augustine of Hippo. He did more damage than most.

St. Derek of Dungeness, a hermit in the wilderness of illness.

I guess my temperature now. Don't tell me, I'll tell you: 37.4° on the decimal.

Julian suggested I get friends to read to me. I can't imagine friends of mine settling down with the biography of Augustine, stumbling through the intricacies of his war on Pelagianism as the Empire cracked up.

~

Blind as a bat he took to finding his way with sonar, flitting this way and that across the empty page, the starchy whiteness of a page of St. Mary's foolscap. Silent as the salt lakes, dazzling, blinding white to the horizon.

~

Waves of icy sulphadiazine breaking on the farther shores after we have crossed over in a blizzard of pills, a rainbow-coloured confetti of serpent poisons, sharp-toothed as the adder. Words, no longer strung out on the lines of narrative, escape and hang round corners waiting to jump out of the dictionary, restore primal disorder. The emerald apple sits on my bedside table, its perfection disordered in my mind's eye, a pulsing sea anemone in the depth of field, visionary green on the comb-raked wood grain. Apple of my eye.

Someone else says losing your sight must be frightening. Not so, as long as you have a safe harbour in the sea of shadows. Just inconvenient. If you woke on a dark day, had only the mind's eye with which to see your way, would you turn back?

My drip ticks away a long afternoon. The sulphadiazine battles with the cysts to bring me second sight. By tea time the migraine takes over. They play the 'theme tune' from *Death In Venice* as I enter the brain scan.

Monday 30

A waiting room with a hundred dazed people who looked as if they had grown old here.

Vision tests. Sent to the ophthalmic hospital: the nurse here sharply unhelpful: 'St. Mary's have done this once too often.' I didn't give up, smiled, said, 'I have an appointment. My eyes are being written up for the *BMJ*.' She reluctantly tore open the envelope and said, 'First floor.'

I waited for my turn in this sad room as the day ticked away, feeling confused. Ed was in the lift saying, 'I'm here again'. Yesterday, while I was having tea with friends, my neighbour had a cardiac arrest. Sister came in to say they had won through. In the corridor a sweet young man frets over his friend who has just been admitted: 'He's my life.'

My eyes are back, I can read. Though the grey shadows circle at the periphery, and the drugs make me dizzy and disorientated. Fiona says I could be out by Saturday. I'm stronger, have put my weight back on; but feel like an invalid. I can't believe I'll ever be well again. The drugs have brought on a rash. I'll be on them for life, and how long will that be?

The lilies Lynn sent me have lasted eight days.

~

A woman leads a blind child slowly down the stairs.

In the vision field you gaze for an eternity at small bright lights and press a buzzer each time lights flash on and off. It is confusing and my eyes, heavy with antihistamine, fall asleep. An eye for an eye. I return to the waiting room. A child turns over the pages of a book, 'Mummy, what's this? What's this?' – like Hell in *Huis Clos*. We wait and wait for the surgeon. The pills sap blood, strength running away in an hourglass. The young man, 17 or 18, is standing in the doorway of my room, dazed. He had taken an overdose. A nurse sits outside his room all day long, reading.

AUGUST

Wednesday 1

Day after day I lie here trapped by the sulphadiazine drip. Outside the sun blazes through the ozone haze. At six it has circled the building and falls through my window. I read the paper, cross-eyed, page by page, scratching my rash. The kid who has lost his mind wanders through the ward, and comes to stare at me, motionless in the doorway. I pull down the blind to hide the sun.

~

Richard came. We had a long discussion about AZT and DDI. The general opinion is that AZT at a low dosage might stabilise me. I wish I had brought a video and recorded these last weeks here. 90 degrees in the shade and my eyes fuzz the newsprint. I've started to watch TV again, an hour a night. I switched it off when the appalling TV Dante appeared this evening with its silly pundits whose explanations were more obscure than the poem. Trite video wallpaper.

~

Turning the Stone

'If everyone put their egos in a drawer life would be bliss' said Peter as Nene wheeled in the lunch.

Turning the Stone

What the eye doesn't see the mind doesn't grieve for. Peter said when he 'came out' he was told he would not work again at English National Opera. Openness in all the professions, even the arts, is frowned on, still.

~

This afternoon I recounted the symptoms of my latest illness to a group of medical students. Almroth Wright, who this ward is named after, campaigned to remove moral censure from medicine. In the eye hospital my nurse, who was wearing bright trousers, was criticised: 'Do the nursing staff at St. Mary's dress like that?' I came to her rescue: 'When your sight is like mine it's a help.'

The eye hospital used to cover the chairs of AIDS patients with polythene. My feeling is that those who work there are unhappy – high principles manifest in frustration.

~

The day of our death is sealed up. I do not wish to die . . . yet. I would love to see my garden through several summers.

~

Noddy has been rewritten, purged of racism and sexism. Perhaps the sodomites should be written out of Dante's *Inferno*. I'll offer myself as the ghost writer.

~

I view the world through drunken eyes.

Friday 3
I have so many pills to take away. It will need a clear head to swallow them in the right order – on top of this everyone feels I should take the AZT, so in a couple of weeks I'll be adding *that* to the list. The temperature is in the 90s – at 10:30 I wait for HB to help me home. The horizon has closed in.

~

Peter here with Lionel Bart; we all had dinner in the Presto.

Tuesday 7
Full dusty orange moon glimmers over the sea, climbs over the house.

A midnight hedgehog rustles through the flower bed. I switch the light on in the kitchen and the spiders scatter. Over beyond the Long Pits bush fires flare. A house burns down at Lydd.

Thursday 9
Peter drives us to Hastings in his van. I buy a pale blue T-shirt and shorts. The sun shone down on semi-naked boys in bright green and pink acid pants. Old ladies in sailor hats passed us in the fish and chipper. I had a cola float. Souvenir shops, a cornucopia of kitsch, shells and plastic Madonnas, jumbled with the postcards. Everything a little too expensive.

Friday 10

My strength is coming back. Beachcombed all day, and finished the grey stone circle – waterfall. In the late evening the moon came up dull orange on the axis of my dolmens. The searing weather has scorched the garden all shades of brown: bone-bleached sea kale, ochre curry plants, and santolina; black seed pods of the tree lupin.

Saturday 11

HB here with his Geordie friend Martin John – we walked to the Long Pits. There are hardly any wild flowers left. The teasels and knapweed, which were plentiful when I came here, are now almost gone. Large dragonflies rustled across the open spaces in the wood.

Late in the evening the boys lit a bonfire on the beach, and chased hedge-hogs under the moon.

Sunday 12

The Sunday papers full of the oil crisis in the gulf. HB cooks his own meals and washes mountains of dirty plates. I paint the back of the house. Tar varnish stings the eyes. HB dresses in blue overalls and looks like a hillbilly on the roof; he puts honey in the mallow flowers for the bees. Stephen and Martin cook a vegetable goulash in the kitchen. The sun shines. Later a half moon comes up bright in a starlit sky.

Monday 13

A red admiral landed on my overalls and shut its wings; I did not move for several minutes while it rested. Trimmed the lavender and santolina in the front bed – every flower has a small copper butterfly feeding on the nectar. I counted seven on the mint.

Tuesday 14

Collected stones for the garden along the beach. Cut back the curry plants. Dark clouds and suffocating heat. The slightest spatter of rain. High on a ladder Brian is painting his house black.

Mrs. Richardson, who was born in this house four years after it was built, came to look at the garden. She was pleased that Prospect Cottage is loved.

Wednesday 15

A red letter day. There is drizzle in the wind. Sleepless night with my itching allergy. Anthony Clare interview on the radio seemed clear and honest, though it was much more difficult to speak than to write my thoughts on HIV and family.

Thursday 16

Home to London. Gray and Jo drove me. It had been raining all day, Romney Marsh was as yellow as the Sierras. Low flying swallows swooping everywhere caused Gray to brake.

Arrived to find a letter from the New York Film Festival turning *The Garden* down. This is strange as they've taken all the films since *Caravaggio*. Jon said, 'It's obvious they're frightened.'

Lynn said later that the New York Film Festival was going through financial difficulties and, with Jesse Helms and the 'born agains' knocking at the door, had to keep a 'clean' image.

Still, it makes me sad. I had so wished to take the film to New York this autumn. Long hot days, the bookshops, wandering aimlessly in the Village, perfect breakfasts in any diner.

Another phone call confirmed that *The Garden* had been pushed aside for the fund-raising cocktail party. I've been the subject of this insidious censorship all my life: What gets funded, what doesn't, what is shown, when and how – it all seems quite ludicrous. Laugh it off, but feel a little sad. Nothing can be proved.

Friday 17

Sunlit cool autumnal day. Writing this diary on my way to St. Mary's in a taxi that cruises down Oxford Street alongside a lovely lad on a bike.

Today London is a joy. I took alcohol last night for the first time in months. Slight but delicious lethargy.

There's a poster in the clinic: *Sponsored Bicycle Ride for The London Lighthouse*. Large sums from Cole Porter, Gilbert and George, Ian McKellen. But sitting here I am wondering what would happen if we were completely dependent on charity. Thank god this is not the 19th century.

~

Made my decision to take AZT in a low dose – DDI is on trial, mostly with people who have shown extreme reaction to AZT. The side effects I can expect are headaches, nausea and muscle wasting. I write this quite nonchalantly in the X-ray department at St. Mary's; but it has been a difficult decision – with help from many friends.

Now I have another pill to swallow twice daily – 500mg, the lower dosage, is what I have decided to take. The decision is completely my own – I don't have to take it if I don't want to. But all the advice points that way.

X-rays take an age. I hate this waiting room. Old men and children stranded in wheelchairs, glum patience of everyone. Silence broken by the warble of the phone. A sign says *Come Early, Save Time*. An Arab woman in an apricot habit fringed with white lace, a gentleman with beard and turban, two bronzed elderly men who talk of canaries share my bench.

My X-ray has disappeared into the machinery. I smile at a charming porter who wheeled me round the hospital in March. Another blue poster says *SOS for the National Health*.

My X-ray is clear and my lung functions have improved. The Wharfeside Clinic is an island – Albinoni on the tape player, friendliness, everyone helpful. Conversation and smiling faces. I take my prescriptions to the pharmacy: AZT, Ritafer, Pyroxidine, Methamine, Folinic Acid, Triludan, Sulphadiazine, Carbamazepine.

SEPTEMBER

Monday 3

This illness snatched me into its demon Disney World, where chairs and tables dance and fight and the room swirls about. Excruciating pain. Surely someone else is ill in bed with catheters and drips.

I returned to London from Edinburgh frozen with pain on the express, with people fighting over mislabelled seats and children screaming their way south.

My appendix was chopped out on Saturday, when they were sure it could not be cured or calmed by antibiotics. I struggled out of the twilight with a metal zip from top to bottom of my stomach. My traumatised guts, spilled out on the operating table – so much offal – were now back in a stomach taut as a balloon. I could not move, but lay for several days staring ahead like a tin soldier, knocked for six.

The night's dreams, aided and abetted by morphine derivatives, grew increasingly menacing. Demons lurked in the room.

Ten days later I pick up a pen, my appetite lost for recording and writing. It's six months since I became ill. I've lost a stone and a half and the razor bumps across my face again.